EUROPE
1500 – 1848

By René Albrecht-Carrié

EUROPE

1500-1848

By René Albrecht-Carrié
PROFESSOR OF HISTORY
BARNARD COLLEGE, COLUMBIA UNIVERSITY

A HELIX BOOK

ROWMAN & ALLENHELD
Totowa, New Jersey

ACKNOWLEDGMENTS

In addition to the original maps prepared especially for this Outline, several others have been reproduced, by permission, from other sources. The publisher and author gratefully acknowledge this courtesy.

The maps appearing on pages 2, 17, 56, 100, 147, 168, 170, 250, and 266 have been reproduced from *A History of the Modern World* by R. R. Palmer, by permission of Alfred A. Knopf, Inc. Copyright 1950 by Alfred A. Knopf, Inc.

The map appearing on page 127 has been reproduced from *A History of Europe from the Reformation to the Present Day* by Ferdinand Schevill, by permission of Harcourt Brace and Company. Copyright 1951 by Harcourt Brace and Company.

The map appearing on page 162 has been reproduced from *A Political and Cultural History of Modern Europe,* Volume I, by Carlton J. H. Hayes, by permission of The Macmillan Company. Copyright 1932 by Carlton J. H. Hayes.

Preface

The purpose of an outline is to facilitate the study of a subject. Most history texts inevitably tend to be voluminous, and the wealth of detail which they are likely to contain, while important and even in some respects essential, has the effect of burdening the student's memory and blurring the outlines of the total picture that is formed from reading them.

An outline is not a substitute for a text. Its function is to simplify and clarify by emphasizing the essentials, arranged in such a way as to bring out the "outline" of a skeleton.

To this end, short sections with headings set in different type and numbering are designed to call attention to the underlying structure of the outline. Details not indispensable to this purpose have been eliminated, save on occasion when they may serve to sharpen or illustrate a point.

The result of such treatment is not, however, a mere accumulation of fact. Such a collection, even when reduced to essentials, would merely defeat its purpose of aiding memory. Despite the task of simplification, therefore, the outline has been so written as to tell a story which, when read by itself, presents an organized picture of the whole course of the history that it covers.

The retention of factual information by memory is indispensable. But it is only a first step and a beginning which, if one should stop at that stage, would be of little interest and value. Such a subject as history especially would have little justification unless pursued to the point of understanding. This understanding tends to be at first in the light of contemporary experience, which is perhaps the reason why there is no finality in history and why history is rewritten by each successive generation.

This is both inevitable and proper, but an effort should be made in addition to place oneself as much as possible outside the context of immediate and limited experience into the different framework of other times and places. This caution applies especially to the American student of European history, since Europe presents within itself such great diversity in both time and locality, and it applies with even greater force to the earlier period covered in this first part of the outline, more remote in time and when the rate of change is slower.

But the process of understanding cannot be divorced from that of interpretation. It is indeed the intention of the present outline to convey certain major themes that run through the entire period and over the whole of Europe. Having mastered a sufficient body of fact and formed a coherent picture of their relationship and significance, the student should then proceed to develop his own critical views. This is the purpose of the reading lists which have been appended to each chapter of the outline. The student can easily select from these lists a book dealing with the particular period, country, or aspect of development about which he wishes to enlarge his knowledge.

When it comes to remembering information and in preparing for his examinations the student will find it most profitable to adopt a set procedure and to adhere to it. He should first carefully read his text and whatever collateral reading is assigned in the course, all the while making notes as he proceeds with his reading. Turning then to this outline, he will notice that a certain body of material is common to it and to his text and notes. This points to the more important material. But certain divergences, especially of interpretation, may also appear. These should be noted and used as a stimulant to independent thinking on the student's part. There is indeed a body of factual knowledge on which agreement exists, but one cannot go far in history without meeting conflicting views of episodes and personalities. This is at once the asset and the shortcoming of history when compared with more precise fields of knowledge.

Next, the student should prepare an outline of this outline by copying out the topics in bold type in the chapter or chapters he is studying. This is recommended because most of us have visual memories; putting things down in writing helps store them in the mind. Moreover, that skeleton outline, owing to its brevity, will be easy to remember. Having learned that outline thoroughly, the student should be able to recall the more detailed treatment of the present fuller outline, and from that most of the subject matter in the text.

From the textbook to the outline, from this outline to the student's own outline; the whole rounded out with some additional reading, is the best procedure for obtaining the knowledge and understanding which history has for its purpose.

R. A-C.

About the Author

1. Present Position: Professor Emeritus of History in Barnard College and School of International Affairs, Columbia University.

2. Publications: *Italy at the Paris Peace Conference* (Columbia University Press, 1938); *Italy from Napoleon to Mussolini* (Columbia University Press, 1950); *A Diplomatic History of Europe Since the Congress of Vienna* (Harper, 1958); *France, Europe and the Two World Wars* (Harper, 1961); *Europe Since 1815* (Harper, 1962); *One Europe* (Doubleday, 1965); *The Concert of Europe* (Harper & Row, 1968); *Britain and France* (Doubleday, 1970). Has written articles and reviews dealing with history, international affairs, and issues of contemporary interest for *American Historical Review, Journal of Modern History, Journal of Central European Affairs, South Atlantic Quarterly, Political Science Quarterly, The American Scientist, The Scientific Monthly, The Annals, Orbis,* etc.

About the Book

1. Material has been systematically arranged with varying sizes of type and numbers or letters to emphasize the organization of the outline.

2. In addition to giving the essential factual infomation, the arrangement of chapters and the division of the whole into three parts is designed to give a more connected and coherent picture of the entire story.

3. An average of some ten books per chapter has been selected among the most useful, dependable, and (when possible) recent books. But in order to avoid repetitions, these references have been grouped together before each major Part of the outline.

CONTENTS

CHAPTER   PAGE

PREFACE V

PART I: THE EMERGENCE OF MODERN EUROPE (TO 1660)

1 INTRODUCTION: EUROPE IN 1500 3
The Land and the Peoples. The Institutions.
The Map of Europe about 1500.

2 THE RENAISSANCE 21
The Renaissance in Italy. Literary Aspects of the
Renaissance. The Beginnings of Modern Science.
From Renaissance to Age of Reason.

3 THE AGE OF DISCOVERY AND THE COMMERCIAL
REVOLUTION 39
The Foreign Trade of Europe. Exploration and
Discovery. The Commercial Revolution.

4 THE REFORMATION 50
Western Christianity in 1500. The Protestant
Revolt. The Balance Sheet.

5 THE SPANISH CENTURY 70
The Age of Charles V. The Reign of Philip II.
Eastern Europe in the Sixteenth Century.

6 SPAIN, FRANCE AND THE EMPIRE 87
The Reconstruction of France. The Disintegra-
tion of Germany. The Franco-Spanish Struggle.

7 THE ENGLISH REVOLUTIONS (TO 1660) 106
The English Constitution. The Prelude to Revolution: James I (1603-1625). The Revolution.

PART II: THE STATE SYSTEM OF EUROPE AND THE EMANCIPATION OF EUROPEAN THOUGHT

8 THE AGE OF LOUIS XIV 120
The France of Louis XIV. The Foreign Policy
of Louis XIV. The Glorious Revolution in
England.

CHAPTER   PAGE

9   THE TRANSFORMATION OF AUSTRIA AND THE RISE OF
    PRUSSIA 141
        The Situation Before 1740. The Austro-Prussian
        Conflict.

10 REARRANGEMENTS IN EASTERN EUROPE 156
        The Emergence of Russia. Russia Enters the
        European Stage.

11 COMPETITION FOR EMPIRE 173
        The Situation up to 1689. The Anglo-French
        Conflict. Continued Growth of Britain and the
        Empire after 1763.

12 THE ENLIGHTENMENT 186
        The Age of Reason. The Age of the Enlight-
        enment. The American Revolution.

            PART III: THE ERA OF THE FRENCH
            REVOLUTION AND THE NAPOLEONIC EPISODE

13 THE FRENCH REVOLUTION 202
        Background and Causes of the Revolution. The
        First Phase of the Revolution: the Constitutional
        Monarchy. The Second Phase: the Democratic
        Revolution. The Revolution Tamed. The Di-
        rectory.

14 NAPOLEONIC EUROPE 236
        The Consulate. The Empire. The Failure of the
        Napoleonic System. The End of the Napoleonic
        Episode.

                    PART IV: EPILOGUE

15 THE STRUGGLE BETWEEN LIBERALISM AND REACTION   267
        Europe in 1815. The Restoration, 1815-1830.
        The Eastern Question. Liberal Successes and
        Failures. Europe in Midcentury. The Intellec-
        tual Climate of the Period.

    INDEX 293

MAPS

PAGE

Topographic Map of Europe 2

The Hapsburg Supremacy, 1526-1648 17

State Religions in Europe about 1560 56

Europe in 1648 100

The Expansion of France During the XVII and XVIII
    Centuries 127

Europe After the Treaty of Utrecht 133

The Growth of Prussia, 1614-1795 147

Expansion of European Russia in the Eighteenth Century   162

The Partitions of Poland, 1772-1795 168

Power Changes in Central and Eastern Europe, 1660-1795   170

European Overseas Empires About 1700 178

Europe at the Height of Napoleon's Power 250

Europe, 1815-1859 266

EUROPE
1500 – 1848

PART I

The Emergence of Modern
Europe (to 1660)

Topographic Map of Europe

CHAPTER 1

Introduction: Europe in 1500

"MODERN" EUROPE

The use of the word "modern" in association with a period of history cannot help have an element of the artificial and the arbitrary. There were no medievalists in the Middle Ages: any age must, in its own eyes, be modern.

But just as our own time has witnessed a great change in the prevailing political, economic, social, and intellectual climate since the outbreak of the First World War—a change which, to be sure, we may not yet assess in adequate perspective—so likewise it has become accepted practice to consider the sixteenth century, an era of marked transition, the beginning of the "modern" period in the development of Europe.

Allowing for the fact of pedagogical convenience, and for the incomparably slower pace of change in 1500 than in 1900, allowing also that change is always gradual and that its rate and kind vary with time and place, a case may be made, especially with the advantage of hindsight and perspective, for placing at this time the division between the medieval and the modern periods. The case will appear stronger if one thinks of discovery or reformation, sharply defined in time, than if one stresses the more elusive categories of economic transformation or change in the field of ideas and the climate of thought.

But we may put all these aspects of change together and say that it was at this time that there began to take place the transformation which was destined to make Europe the center and master of the planet, using these terms in a broad sense that will include crude military conquest as well as the more peaceful, but not less significant and effective, penetration that follows the origination of new ways and ideas. Science and technology are essentially new phenomena, European in their inception.

There can be little question in any case that the sixteenth century was an era of great transition and change, the manifestations of which will be surveyed and summarized in this outline.

I.   THE LAND AND THE PEOPLES

A.   Physical Europe

The accidents of geography, the diverse features of the land, while they do not account for all, have ever been fundamental factors in shaping the course of nations and of cultures. Europe in its totality, especially that part of it west of modern Russia, is little more than a peninsular appendage of the Asiatic land mass.

1. The Great European Plain. The bulk of Russia is plain, which the low barrier of the Urals hardly divides from the endless spaces of Asiatic Siberia. This plain, narrowing down in the west between the Baltic Sea and the Carpathian Mountains, extends along the North Sea and the Channel down to the Pyrenees. The absence of any clear natural boundaries in the region where the Polish people dwell goes a long way toward explaining the vicissitudes of the Polish state.

2. The Mountains. The southern part of Europe by contrast, the lands bordering on the Mediterranean, is characterized by the presence of much mountainous territory. The whole of the Iberian peninsula is cut by mountain ranges and separated by the Pyrenees from the rest of the continent. The Italian peninsula, along which the Apennines unfold, likewise is clearly marked off from the rest by the wide circle of the Alps around its northern end. This range of mountains extends through the heart of Europe. From the mountainous section of central France it stretches eastward through modern

Switzerland and Austria, extending into southern Germany, and connecting, around the head of the Adriatic, with the various massifs that cover most of the Balkan peninsula. An eastern spur, the Carpathians, engirds the Hungarian plain through which the Danube flows.

At the northern extremity of Europe, the Scandinavian peninsula presents a clearly defined contour. Its western side is a long range of mountains closely hugging the coast.

3. Coastline and Climate. Perhaps the most significant aspect of the physical map of Europe is the length of its coastline. Its highly indented shores and the large peninsulas which have been enumerated, Scandinavian, Iberian, Italian, and Balkan, present numerous harbors and have the consequence that no inland point is very distant from the sea.

This fact is of importance because of its effect on climate as well as on communications. Especially in the west, the combination of proximity to the ocean and of the Gulf Stream gives Europe a temperate climate in unusually high northern latitudes. Bordeaux in France lies on the same parallel as Montreal in Canada and the British Isles correspond to Labrador.

4. The Rivers. Until the application of steam to transportation, waterways had been the easier and preferred avenues of communication. There are no very long or great rivers in Europe outside of Russia, by comparison at least with such streams as the Nile or the Mississippi, but the European rivers have had outstanding economic and historic importance. The Rhine and the Danube between them form a northwest-southeast line dividing the continent in two from the Netherlands to the Black Sea. The French rivers fan out from the center toward the various maritime borders of the country; together with the Rhine, they furnish an Atlantic-Mediterranean connection without passing through the Straits of Gibraltar. The Rhine again, the German rivers, and the Vistula form a roughly parallel network flowing north or northwest into the northern seas. Except for the Rhone, the Mediterranean rivers are either too short or their water supply too unreliable. The Russian rivers provide access to the heart of the country from Baltic, Black, and Caspian seas.

B.   The Peoples of Europe

Repeatedly, Europe felt the impact of masses of humanity stemming from Asia. Within Europe itself, the Germanic barbarians had broken through the Rhine-Danube border and overrun much of the Roman world. By the time our story opens, the large migrations of peoples had given way to stability out of which has crystallized the modern ethnic map of Europe. Not until the nineteenth and our own centuries have we witnessed serious attempts to alter the ethnic composition of the land.

Racially, all Europe is an inextricable mixture, though different types prevail in various regions. There would be little point and less profit in trying to disentangle the racial components of Europe, even assuming that the word "race" could be adequately defined; but of ethnic and cultural differences we can speak.

1. Ethnic Divisions. By the sixteenth century, the "nations" of Europe are identifiable, and while it would be a mistake to read the modern concept of nationality and of nationalism into a sixteenth-century Europe, nevertheless, in view of the fact that for some centuries one of the major factors in the history of Europe has been the tendency to organize itself politically along "national" lines, it is useful to cast a glance at the ethnic map of Europe. It will be easiest described in terms of present or recent political units.

The overwhelming bulk of Europeans belong to one of three large ethnic groups: Latin, Teutonic, and Slavic. Much of the history of Europe could be written in terms of the broad conflict between Teuton and Slav or between Latinity and Germandom.

The Latin group occupies the southwest, corresponding generally to the present units of Portugal, Spain, France, Italy, and part of Belgium. Much of Roumania in the east constitutes a Latin island.

The Teutonic or Germanic group covers the area of the 1938 German Reich, Denmark, and the Scandinavian peninsula, Holland, and part of Belgium. It predominates in England, parts of Scotland and Ireland. Most of Ireland, much of Scotland, Wales, and Cornwall have preserved a predominantly Celtic character, as has French Brittany.

The Slavs account for the rest: Russians, Poles, Ukrainians, Czechs, and Slovaks, and the Balkan peoples other than Roumanian and Greek.

2. Ethnography and Language. There are some minor groups, remnants of earlier settlers like the Celts and the Greeks, or of later invasions: Magyars or Hungarians, Finns and Estonians on the Baltic, Turks in the Balkans.[1] Some things should be pointed out about this list. When we speak of Celtic remnants, for instance, we obviously do not know what proportion of the original Celts have disappeared by absorption in Saxon Britain or Romanized Gaul. Likewise, modern Roumanian and Magyar have undoubtedly large admixtures of Slavic "blood." It therefore appears that we are largely dealing with a cultural factor where language plays an overwhelming role.

Language can indeed be largely equated with nationality, but there are some significant exceptions. The Swiss are either Germanic or Latin, and they speak either German, French, or Italian. But there is undoubtedly a Swiss nation. Alsace, Germanic in speech, became absorbed into French nationality.

Finally, the ethnic lines of demarcation are much clearer in western than in eastern Europe. If we draw lines from Riga toward Trieste on one side and toward Odessa on the other, the region between these lines and the sea in the south is that in which ethnic groups or nationalities are most completely intermingled and consequently most difficult to unscramble.

II. THE INSTITUTIONS

A. The Unity of Europe

The variety of the peoples of Europe is what has made that continent so rich in cultural diversity. Much of the story of "modern" Europe could be told in terms of the increasingly successful assertion of this diversity, culminating in the nineteenth-century phenomenon of political self-determina-

---

[1] Albanians and Basques may also be added for the sake of completeness, and also Jews scattered throughout Europe, but most numerous in the east (Poland, Ottoman Empire).

tion. But the novelty of this trend must be understood and stressed.

It is well to realize that the fumbling twentieth-century efforts toward the realization of *One World* represent gropings for an ideal that was once reality. Old Rome did for a substantial period of time encompass the unity of western civilized mankind. From the Euphrates to Hadrian's Wall, and from the Sahara to the Rhine-Danube *limes* a single political power ruled. With time, the suitable combination of internal decay and external pressures destroyed this unity. From one point of view, the thousand-year story of the Middle Ages is the record of the disintegration that followed the fall of Rome and of the slow and painful process of rebuilding on a new and different basis.

B. The Church

Through this millennium the memory of old Rome did not die, but rather left as legacy the myth that the unity of mankind was a proper and normal state. To a degree and in a sense that unity even persisted. In the dark and evil days that followed the demise of Rome, what there remained of culture and of organized society was preserved in the main through the agency of the Church. When Rome fell it had already become Christian and the Church was the chief heir of the Roman tradition. The Barbarians after a time also accepted the allegiance of the Church of Rome.

1. Extent and Division of Christian Europe. This Church was catholic and universal, but the emergence of the prophet Mohammed in the seventh century was soon followed by the Arab conquest and the Islamization—hence the removal from Christianity—of the southern Mediterranean lands and most of Asia Minor; henceforth Christianity was purely European.[2]

Within Europe itself, a schism occurred in the eleventh century, roughly along the older line of cleavage between

---

[2] Spain had been conquered by the Arabs in the eighth century, but gradually freed herself from their rule. In 1492 the Moors were finally expelled from their last foothold in Granada, and Spain, allowing for the strong imprint of Arab culture and of Islam, may be counted European and Christian.

Hellenic and Latin cultures, that split Christianity in two: Roman, and Eastern or Byzantine (Greek Orthodox). Conversion of the peoples residing beyond the former Roman *limes* extended the line of cleavage northward: Russia received its Christianity from Byzantium, Poland and the Baltic lands from Rome. As our story begins, the Church of Rome still claimed the allegiance of Europe westward of Muscovy and north of the Balkans.

2. *Evolution and Structure of the Church.* The vicissitudes of this Church had been varied and numerous from the time of its foundation. It was now a powerful institution organized along lines modeled on the structure of imperial Rome. At its head was a Pope, topping a pyramid where bishops and common priests constituted the most important successive layers of authority.[3]

The function of this Church was primarily spiritual: in simplest form, to insure the safe earthly passage of human souls and guide them to salvation in the eternity of after death. The discharging of this mission was the essential task of the clergy, endowed by divine dispensation with a sacred character that other men did not enjoy. For the performance of this duty an elaborate system of sacraments and ritual had been developed and a no less elaborate theology had been evolved to guide the faithful. St. Thomas Aquinas had given this theology its best and crowning shape. These beliefs were accepted in common by European mankind—with the qualifications indicated earlier.

C. The Holy Roman Empire

But if the Church looked after nonterrestrial matters, mankind on earth must also be organized and governed in its purely worldly relations. Here also the Roman ideal of the political unity of mankind persisted, but the reality was in this case removed from the theory and ideal in a way that the Church was not.

1. *Evolution and Weakness of the Empire.* Charlemagne

---

[3] The Conciliar movement, which aimed at vesting authority in the more representative Council of the Church, had definitely lost out to the monarchical and authoritarian tendency that Papal supremacy represented.

in the year 800 had the imperial crown set upon his head while in Rome. The gesture was symbolic, but in actual fact the territory that he ruled did not go far beyond the Pyrenees in one direction and the Elbe in the other, to which Italy may be added. Also, even within this territory, the unity that he had created did not long survive him. The Frankish state, unlike the Roman, tended to be regarded as "real estate," property to be inherited and divided by the ruler's sons. The imperial dignity was revived again in the tenth century, but it was now that curious creation that its name expressed, the Holy Roman Empire of the German Nation.

What this meant in practice was that the imperial control was largely confined to Germanic and Italian territory.[4] On its western border, the French monarchy, finally consolidating its holdings in the fifteenth century, had already embarked on the process of pushing to the north and east the area under its rule. The southern half of Italy had also escaped from imperial control by 1500, and in the east the struggle went on in the borderlands where German and Slav came together.

At the beginning of the sixteenth century the Holy Roman Empire was an important state, but also, by later standards, a peculiar political institution. The imperial dignity had by this time, to all intents and purposes, become the appanage of the House of Habsburg. But the fact is important that the position was attained by election, while the hereditary had long superseded the elective principle among other rulers. There was an inevitable struggle between the centralizing tendency represented by the imperial crown and the decentralizing pull of the princes within the Empire. The end of the fifteenth century had witnessed an attempt at constitutional reform in the imperial structure. We shall trace, in the first part of our period ending with the Treaty of Westphalia, the vicissitudes of this struggle ending in the victory of the centrifugal force.

2. The Struggle Between Empire and Church. But there was another aspect of the Empire to which the word "Holy"

---

[4] The eastern sections of later France, beyond the Rhone in the south, Burgundy, Lorraine, and Flanders, were part of the Empire. In the east, the Empire also included Bohemia and the western part of Hungary.

in its name gives the key. By contrast with old Rome where the emperor had also been Pontifex, the new imperial office was divested of religious function, special prerogative of the Papacy. In theory, there were two coordinate and distinct powers, charged, respectively, with material and spiritual functions and destined to cooperate in the exercise of these functions.

The distinction could not be maintained in practice: the Church had much material wealth and power; nor could it exercise its functions without penetrating the daily and material lives of men. It could not help impinge upon the sphere that the temporal power regarded as its own.

The issue of the proper relation between Church and State has not been settled to our day, despite the modern secularization of the latter. During the Middle Ages the story of their relations is long and intricate. On the general plea of the higher status of the spiritual the Pope put forward at one time a claim to superiority and even to the right to depose temporal rulers. The zenith of the churchly power was reached at the beginning of the thirteenth century during the pontificate of Innocent III. This status declined rapidly thereafter; less than a century later a Pope could be arrested by the envoys of Philip the Fair of France. But the interconnection between spiritual and temporal power was particularly intimate and correspondingly troublesome in the case of the Holy Roman Empire.

3. *Feudalism and National Monarchies.* The collapse of the institutions that had held society and the state together in Roman times had resulted in nearly universal anarchy. For a long time brute force and military power reigned supreme. When some sort of new order began to emerge, it was found that the element of personal relationship and allegiance introduced by the Barbarians was one of the basic factors in the new society. This was feudalism, when knight, count, or duke was bound in allegiance primarily to another man rather than to a law prevailing over a specified territorial extent.[5]

---

[5] Medievalists debate at length and with learning the precise origins and components, Roman and Germanic, of feudalism. The emphasis on the personal, instead of the territorial, character of law need alone be stressed here.

In the nobility or military class each man was at once lord and vassal.

Throughout this chaos, the principle of kingship, however weak at times the office, managed to survive. By the opening of our story, and especially during the fourteenth and fifteenth centuries and in the western parts of Europe, the king was in process of emerging in a position of higher status and, most important, of stronger power. By the beginning of the sixteenth century the bases had been laid for the formation of those *national* monarchies that were to dominate the scene for some centuries to come. The power of the nobles was still great, but in the countries bordering the Atlantic the king was definitely in the ascendant.

The change was gradual. Although the monarchical institution had long been vested with an aura of sacredness, the king was far from being the absolute divine right ruler that he was to become in most of Europe. The contractual factor was strong in the whole network of feudal relationships, in which the monarchy was included.

D.   The Structure of Society

1. The Nobility. The structure of the state and of society at the close of the Middle Ages may, to the modern eye, seem a picture of chaos owing to the multitude, intricacy, and confusion of existing relationships. This state of affairs was the result of natural growth. In a time when all were insecure, the value of protection that armed force alone could provide would inevitably be paramount. Explicitly or tacitly, the military class had emerged into a recognized position of primacy. In simplest form, the fighting man would furnish protection to the peasant, who would in turn supply the former with the means of livelihood.

Thus the nobility or military caste, adding to the primitive function of defense the tasks—duty or privilege—of administration and the dispensation of justice, emerged into a privileged class. Contributing the tax of blood, it was exempted from meaner forms of taxation. The nobility, perpetuating itself by the inheritance of birth or by the consecration of higher power such as that vested in kingship, constituted the second estate.

2. *The Clergy or First Estate.* The first estate was made up of the clergy. The function of this class, stamped with the seal of divine investment, in a society that universally acknowledged the necessity of a priestly caste, endowed it too with privilege. In theory at least, the clergy were celibate, hence not able to perpetuate themselves save by recruitment from other classes of society. The upper layer of the clergy, bishops and abbots, was normally recruited from, hence generally allied with, the nobility. But the parish priests were apt to be not very different from the peasantry whose spiritual needs they tended and in whose midst they lived.

Keeper of what there had remained of literacy and culture, especially at the point of darkest decline, the clergy had come to play a large role in the administration of the state. But an important fact is that, however much honored in the breach in practice, the doctrine of the fundamental equality of souls and of the essential dignity of man was one which the Christian Church could not disown and still survive. The word "democracy" is an anachronism in the vocabulary of medieval and early modern Europe; yet what there was of it in those ages may be said to have been in the keeping of the Christian Church.

a. Monasticism. The clergy may also be divided according to a different classification. The secular clergy, that living in the world (*saeculo*), performed, or was supposed to perform, the basic function of spiritual guidance. But there were in addition large numbers who had withdrawn from this world and lived usually in communities under some such rule as that of St. Benedict.

Religious orders were numerous. They were likely to arise at times when the Church had fallen to a particularly low estate, when some saintly individual felt strongly the impulse toward personal salvation or that to purify the larger institution. These orders were an important and often a powerful element in the Church. In time they too fell upon evil days, grew wealthy and corrupt; medieval literature is rich in ribald comments on the monk. But a continuous process of renewal took place. St. Francis and St. Dominic had followed on St. Benedict, and the Church as a whole had managed to maintain its hold and to survive—sometimes

suppressing with success by force—a succession of heresies
and schisms that had threatened its unity.

3. The Third Estate

a. THE PEASANTRY. The overwhelming mass of the population belonged to the third estate, and of this the far greater
part lived on the land. In the sixteenth century, as well as
long before and after, European society was essentially
agricultural.

Such a society tends to be static and conservative in its
ways. Change there had been indeed through the centuries,
but outside of such concrete calamities as the Black Death
that destroyed a substantial part of the population in a short
span of years, the pace of it was such that the prevailing
picture in men's minds was one of immobility. The peasant
was quite likely to spend his span of life within the narrow
compass of the parish of his birth. He was illiterate, toil was
his lot, his ways were his father's ways and they would also
be his sons'.

b. TOWNS AND TRADE. It is well to remember that Rome's
civilization had been an urban one and that at the low point
of medieval decline society had become reduced to a collection
of largely self-sufficient manors whose contacts and relations
with the outside world were virtually nonexistent because unnecessary. But for some five centuries prior to the sixteenth,
though uneven in time and place, a process of recovery and
reconstruction had steadily been under way. Towns and
trade, related and interacting manifestations of this recovery,
began to reappear and grow.

More will be said about them later, but at this point it will
suffice to mention that townspeople, bourgeois, traders, and
artisans, though few in proportionate terms of number, had
become an important element in society. This importance was
far in excess of their relative numbers, for it is from this class
that the main impulse to further change would come. Already
for some time, princes had found it useful to draw upon
this class for counsel and administration. Some of its members
had acquired considerable wealth, and through wealth, influence and power, even if not the formal sanction of privilege
attached to noble birth.

Generally in Europe, society was divided into these three classes or estates. Within each there were considerable differences,[6] but the fact must be stressed by contrast with the modern egalitarian concept that the contrary one of class distinction had legal sanction.

Such in brief was the Europe of which the further story will presently be outlined. It will be useful, before proceeding, to cast a glance at the political map of this Europe as it was at the opening of our story. Much of history is contained in the record of shifting lines of demarcation between political units.

III.   THE MAP OF EUROPE ABOUT 1500

If one should look at the political map of Europe at intervals over the past few centuries, the fact stands out at once of relative stability in the west by contrast with the center and east.

A.   The Western or Atlantic Countries

Along the Atlantic, the main political units of our day have already achieved recognizable shape. In the Iberian peninsula, we have Portugal and Spain. The latter has just been formed out of the marital union of Ferdinand of Aragon and Isabella of Castile, while the Moors, in 1492, have lost their last European foothold in Granada. With the Spanish kingdom goes Sardinia and the Kingdom of the Two Sicilies, appanages of the Aragonese house.

France, under the Valois, approximates her later form. She has reached the Alps in the south, but a substantial slice of territory along the east and the northeast is still lacking for her completion.

In the British Isles, a separate state exists in Scotland, while the House of Tudor rules over England proper, Wales, and Ireland. In the north, the Scandinavian countries from Denmark to Finland and Iceland are joined under the Danish king in the union of Calmar dating from 1397.

With the necessary qualification in the Scandinavian case and in Scotland, these are the "national" monarchies where

---

[6] The status of the peasantry, for instance, presented marked variations. Serfdom had virtually disappeared in the west but was and long continued to be prevalent in eastern Europe.

a strong monarch, destined to grow stronger, has already
emerged.

B. Central Europe

The map of Central Europe, the modern Low Countries,
Germany, Austria, and Italy bears no resemblance in 1500
to its more recent shape. The Holy Roman Empire consists
of Germanic states, the Low Countries, Burgundy, later
Switzerland, and northern Italy.

1. The Emperor. The Emperor, as mentioned, was elected
by seven electors, but in all there were more than three
hundred discrete pieces in the Empire, ranging from the territory of a sizable state to that of a single city. The Emperor
was normally a Habsburg, at this time Maximilian I (1493-
1519). The Habsburgs held considerable territory in their
own dynastic right. The crowns of both Bohemia and
Hungary were also to become theirs early in the century.
Moreover, in 1477 Maximilian had married Mary, heiress of
Burgundy, which at that time meant Franche Comté and the
Low Countries.

2. The Italian States. Italy at this time was a mere geographic expression. The north was still, though loosely,
connected with the Empire, and the southern third of the
peninsula went with Spain. Next to it, occupying the middle
third, the States of the Church had gradually developed. The
theory was that the unhampered exercise of the Pope's
spiritual function required him not to be a resident of any
other state but his own.

Most significant in the case of Italy was the existence of
city-states, relatively small territories where in the long and
confused struggle among medieval municipalities some had
emerged to a position of greater importance. Florence was
one such, still battling with her rival Pisa. Venice was the
most powerful of the Italian city-states; her power, reminiscent
of later Britain's, was founded on maritime trade and naval
strength.[7] Genoa resembled Venice, though she was no

---

[7] The oligarchical government of the Venetian Republic offers the interesting illustration of a long period of orderly management of the state.
Florence gave greater scope to freedom and to factions. In general, this
was the age of petty despots in the Italian states.

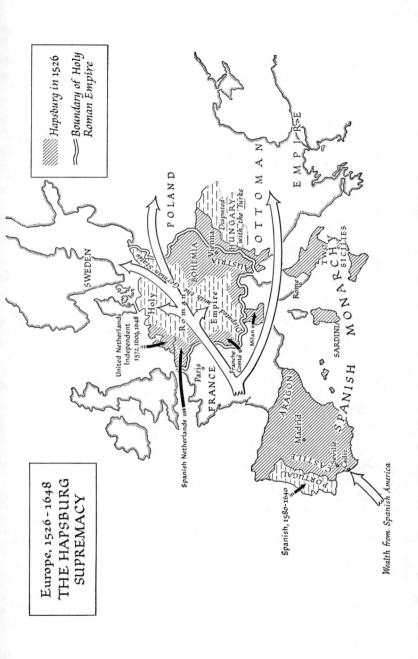

Europe, 1526–1648
THE HAPSBURG
SUPREMACY

Hapsburg in 1526
Boundary of Holy
Roman Empire

SWEDEN

POLAND

OTTOMAN EMPIRE

Holy Roman Empire within the German States

BOHEMIA

AUSTRIA

Vienna

HUNGARY—
with the Turks

Disputed

United Netherland
Independent
1572, 1609, 1648

Spanish Netherlands

Paris

FRANCE

Franche Comté

Milan

Rome

TWO SICILIES

SARDINIA

SPANISH MONARCHY

ARAGON

CASTILE

Madrid

PORTUGAL

Seville

Cadiz

Spanish, 1580–1640

Wealth from Spanish America

longer the threatening rival that she had been. The Duchy of Milan occupied the middle region of the plain of the Po, the only Italian river of importance. The Savoyard Duchy, astride the Alps, was half Italian and half French. Some minor units, such as Modena and Parma, would complete the list.

These city-states represented a deviation from the feudal practice that has been sketched. There would be rival lords or wealthy merchant families competing for control within the city, but above the city government no higher allegiance really existed. In the Netherlands and in Flanders, where also there were cities or communes with considerable wealth, derived as in Venice and Florence from trade, communal life was strong. The power of this wealth caused many a unit, small by territorial standards, to play an important role in the Empire, in Italy, or even beyond.

C.   Eastern Europe

When we come to the eastern, primarily Slavic part of Europe, the situation differs again. Hungary and Bohemia have been mentioned; in a sense they might be put in the category of national monarchies, save that their crowns, passing to the Habsburg House, inevitably embroiled them in the affairs of that House and of the Empire generally.

Still further east, Poland was a very large state in 1500, or perhaps one should say Poland-Lithuania, for the two had been joined in personal union since 1386. The state, though large, was weak and not properly integrated. It had played an important role, tending to expand eastward into present Ukraine, and overshadowed at this time small, rude, and backward Muscovy.

This last mentioned small central core was just in process of emerging from the Asiatic control of Mongol conquerors and beginning to lay the bases of a state. This work may be credited to Ivan III (1462-1505). Muscovy had received its Christianity from Byzantium; with the final demise of the Eastern Roman Empire, the Russian rulers descended from Ivan III and the daughter of the last Byzantine emperor began to lay claim to the imperial succession. Ivan IV, the Terrible, grandson of Ivan III, assumed in 1547 the title of Tsar (Caesar). Old Rome, center of world empire, having passed through Constantinople, would now revive in Moscow. In the sixteenth century, the claim was at least premature.

D.   The Ottoman Empire

The year 1453 saw the Turks in Constantinople. These Turks, the Ottomans, after emerging in control of Asia Minor, had crossed the Straits in the fourteenth century and overrun the Balkans long before Byzantium was reduced. The fall of Constantinople in 1453 made a profound impression upon Christian Europe. The date used to be given as marking the close of the Middle Ages, much as 476, when Rome fell, was given as their opening.

The conquering Turks restored the unity of the old Eastern Empire, for their control extended over Asia Minor as well as the Balkans. Their expanding vigor did not abate during the fifteenth and sixteenth centuries. The Danube was crossed and Hungary overrun and secured after the disaster of Mohacs (1526). The tide of conquest reached Vienna, which it failed to capture in 1529. The Black Sea became a Turkish lake, while in the east and south Ottoman power was spreading over nearly the same lands that the initial Arab conquest had overrun. Of North Africa, Morocco alone managed to remain a distinct entity.

For a time it looked as if there were to be a repetition of the huge pincer movement that had threatened to overrun all Europe in the early days of Islam. The earlier attack had eventually been held at the line of the Bosporus and of the Pyrenees. The later wave did not quite reach Gibraltar and could not master Vienna. When an equilibrium was reached the Ottoman state was well entrenched in Europe, in the subsequent history of which, whether vigorous and aggressive or decadent and retreating later on, it was to play a very important role.

Most significant, the Ottoman state was not Christian but Moslem. Though not religiously fanatical—rather less so in fact than Christians—Moslems looked upon Christians and Jews (the people of the book) as a less perfect breed. For the most part the Christian populations whom they had overrun in Europe retained their Christian allegiance, a small section along the European side of the Straits—roughly modern

Turkey in Europe—alone becoming "turkified."

The Turks were essentially a military people. While they controlled the land and the administration at the upper levels, the meaner cares of cultivation, ' of such trade as survived, and even much of the administration, were left in Christian hands. Their state retained its vigor only so long as its military arm kept its effectiveness.

There was an important peculiarity about the Ottoman state that set it apart from the rest of Europe, stemming also from the fact of religious difference. In Islam the Koran is the basis of law. The state is theocratic and the issue of relations between church and state, between Emperor or King and Pope, that fills so large a part of the annals of the Christian west, simply did not exist. The assumption by the Ottoman Sultan of the title of Caliph of Islam gave expression to this state of affairs. It was as if the imperial and papal dignities had in the west been merged in the same person.

Accordingly, the Turks came to regard religion as the basic element of distinction among peoples. Not being Moslems, Christians could not be subject to Moslem law, but must rather adhere to their own. The Greek Patriarch of Constantinople was normally regarded by the Sultans as the head of their Christian subjects. Similarly, from 1535, the French king became the protector and representative of Catholics whatever their national allegiance.[8]

A sketch has been presented of the basic elements of the European scene at the opening of the sixteenth century: the chief and permanent features of the land, the peoples and their differing degree of "national" consciousness, their institutions and beliefs, the structure of society, and the political divisions under which they lived. We must turn next to some of the great movements, sources of basic change, that make the sixteenth century the great transition that it was.

---

[8] This was the result of political expedience taking precedence over religious fervor. The Christian French king and the Moslem sultan were brought together by their common enemy, the Emperor.

CHAPTER 2

The Renaissance

THE RENAISSANCE AND ITS ROOTS

The term "Renaissance," often carelessly used, expresses a reality, yet conceals a distortion. Some historians have stressed the factor of continuity, before and after 1500; some have spoken of twelfth-century, or even earlier, Renaissances. This is legitimate enough, for we are dealing with a phenomenon that is primarily cultural, the manifestations and especially the roots of which are fit objects for debate and interpretation. Yet the nature and degree of some of these manifestations warrant the commonly accepted association of the word with the opening of the "modern" age in the history of Europe. It will suffice to realize that the use of both terms, "Renaissance" and "modern," has been questioned and that they have a relative content which is the basis of the questioning.

However that may be, there is little question that from about the eleventh century recovery in all its forms began to manifest itself in Europe. But the East, whether Byzantine or Arabic, was still during the later part of the Middle Ages the seat of higher civilization than the West. Recovery in the West went hand in hand with increasing contact with and influence from the east.[1]

---

[1] The terms East and West are, strictly speaking, geographically incorrectly used. The East includes Moslem and Arab, covering the entire African shore of the Mediterranean and part of Spain. But the use of these terms is consecrated by convention.

I.   THE RENAISSANCE IN ITALY

Of these contacts, Italy was logically the center and the
first and greatest beneficiary. Also, in Italy lies Rome, and
the memory of "the glory that was Greece and the grandeur
that was Rome," however distorted and dimmed, remained,
naturally enough, more alive in Italy than elsewhere. But, in
addition, increasing trade meant wealth and urban centers,
elements which are found in Italy earlier and to a greater
degree than elsewhere in Europe.

A.   Italy, Mother of the Arts

The various aspects of the Renaissance all flourished in
Italy, but in the realm of the arts Italian primacy was unchallenged. The connection between wealth and culture has
often been debated. Undoubtedly, the existence of wealth,
making it possible for society—whether through wealthy individual patrons or the state—to support an economically un-
productive group, is favorable to artistic production. But, by
itself, the possession of wealth is no more warrant of sound
artistic taste and judgment than the enjoyment of leisure is
of superior performance.

1. Nature and Conditions of the Italian Renaissance.
There were in Italy those enlightened patrons—Roman Popes,
Florentine Medici, Milanese Sforzas, and many others—who
understood and supported the arts, but this was also one of
those periods when there occurred that which wealth alone
cannot conjure, the appearance of a galaxy of executants of
the highest order of ability. We may be content with registering the fact that, in recorded history, there have been times
and places where a high concentration of talent has made its
appearance. The Renaissance in Italy is one of these high
peaks of man's endeavor, and the common association of art
with Renaissance in Italy, if somewhat oversimplified, is
warranted.

2. The Plastic and Pictorial Arts. The *Quattrocento*, or
fifteenth century, saw a remarkable flowering in Italy of the
pictorial and plastic arts. In the case of the former, this was
but a continuation of a development that can be traced to the

primitives, but there was now a new freedom in conception and execution, away from medieval formalism of style and from exclusively religious subjects, which is typical of Renaissance art. Much of its inspiration, in sculpture and in architecture, was derived from the models of classical art freely strewn about Italy. The contrast is striking between this new art and medieval Gothic, which began to be discarded and to be looked upon as symbol of a more barbarous age. The huge pile of St. Peter's in Rome is one of the most impressive, if not most beautiful, samples of this art. Ghiberti's (1378-1455) doors for the baptistery at Florence better deserve the qualification of superb. So judged them Michelangelo (1475-1564).

Michelangelo, apart from his outstanding quality, provides in his career a good example of the Renaissance artist by the catholicity of his endeavors: sculptor and painter, his craft included also architecture and poetry.[2] The list would be long of great names. Rather than give one such, the student may best get an inkling of the quality and magnitude of the achievement by leafing through an illustrated edition of such a work as Burckhardt's *The Renaissance in Italy*. But the name of Leonardo da Vinci (1452-1519), painter, sculptor, engineer, scientist, jack of all trades and in all outstanding, must at least be mentioned.

a. THE PLACE OF FLORENCE. Florence was the home par excellence of this movement, and the Medici as much as anyone its patrons. The Medici, whose coat of arms, the three pawnbroker's balls, recalls the mercantile beginnings, became a princely family, virtual rulers of Florence. They are a perfect illustration, but only one, of this close integration between wealth, art, and culture. To this day, Florence and Florentines bear the stamp given them by the Renaissance. But if Florence was the capital of the movement, the whole peninsula shared in it. The Popes became its sponsors, and Rome, sunk to the low estate of a town of some thirty thousand in the fourteenth century, became the great capital of which St. Peter's was the fitting symbol.

3. *Italian Culture and its Influence.* Not only were the

---

[2] The decoration of the Sistine Chapel, the heroic statue of David, the tombs of the Medici, are among some of his best known works. Michelangelo also assisted in the building of St. Peter and of Florence's cathedral.

arts more advanced in Italy earlier than elsewhere in Europe, but the general tone and manner of life was more urbane and softer. Castiglione's *Book of the Courtier* is the code of the civilized gentleman. And from Italy the influence flowed across the Alps. When the French kings began in 1494 their long series of Italian incursions, their armies, if militarily more effective, were looked upon as uncouth barbarians. As in Palestine some centuries earlier, the Franks discovered the amenities of a higher culture. Another French king, Francis the First, made a deliberate attempt to import at home Italian ways and culture: Leonardo died his pensioner in France, and the Medici provided queens for that country. The influence penetrated other parts of Europe as well as France, and Italy was universally regarded as a land of more advanced culture than the rest of Europe.

The arts were emulated also. French châteaux, as on the Loire, for instance, began to supersede with airy grace the gloomier piles of medieval castles, and some outstanding artists, though relatively few, also appeared outside of Italy. The names of El Greco in Spain, of Dürer and Holbein in the Empire, may be mentioned. Music was also much appreciated, cultivated, and developed, though its great flowering is of a later date. Here again, Palestrina (1524-1594), the outstanding name, is Italian.

II.   LITERARY ASPECTS OF THE RENAISSANCE

A.   Humanism

1. The Rediscovery of the Ancients. The influence of ancient models on the plastic arts has been mentioned. But this influence went far deeper than art in the narrow sense. If the view is no longer held that the fall of Constantinople to the Ottoman Turks in 1453 precipitated an exodus from that city as the result of which classical manuscripts and a knowledge of ancient Greek and Roman literature were brought to the West, the fact remains that around this time the interest in and search for such knowledge were being revived in earnest. Here also, Italy might be expected to play a prime role, and in fact she did. Petrarch (1304-1374) has properly been called "the father of humanism," but this movement was less exclusively Italian than its artistic counterpart. The prince of humanists, Erasmus (1466-1536), came from Rotterdam.

Here again there is continuity with the past, nor was the knowledge of the ancients wholly novel. Thomas Aquinas had made good use of Aristotle, to cite but one example. But this knowledge was both incomplete and imperfect, coming as it often did by the circuitous route of translations brought by the Arabs around the southern Mediterranean. Petrarch, apt representative of the new interest, spent much of his energy in the search for authentic versions and in the effort to restore ancient texts to their initial purity and to bring back into usage the presumably purer Latin of Cicero. He and his emulators had much success in this, as witness the dead language that is now studied as Latin. Much of their work was scholarship, of which Lorenzo Valla, searching through Vatican archives, gave an early and interesting example with his exposure of the fraudulent Donation of Constantine.

2. *The Invention of Printing.* It is in the midst of this activity that an invention was made the influence of which must be counted among the most far reaching. Gutenberg of Mainz is usually credited with the invention of printing, meaning by this the use of movable type, about the middle of the fifteenth century. In combination with this, contemporary improvements in the art of papermaking made it possible to create the modern book. Before the century was out, printing presses were busily operating in a number of European cities. The ease, cheapness, and dependability of the new process by comparison with the laborious task of copying manuscripts by hand is obvious. Here was clearly a powerful tool for the spread of ideas. The Aldine press in Venice put out as fine editions as were to be found, but printing was not an Italian invention, and in this case, as with the humanist movement in general, there was no Italian primacy or monopoly.

3. *The Spirit of Humanism.* Humanism covers a broader range than the revival of ancient literature and language.[3] Beyond the texts there was the spirit: Athens and Rome in their heyday were pagan and not Christian. As a group, the humanists did not lead a revolt against the Church of Rome;

---

[3] The knowledge of Greek had virtually died out in the West. The study of it was now taken up with eagerness by the humanists.

rather the Church itself, for a time and in the upper levels of its hierarchy, was permeated by the movement. Pope Alexander VI, and the so-called Renaissance Popes in general, took greater interest in political and cultural matters than in the affairs of the Church in their narrower religious and spiritual scope.

And the spirit that widely prevailed was unquestionably antithetic to that of medieval Christianity. The earthly passage need not be a journey through a vale of tears, forever darkened by the threat of the malignant powers that endangered the prospects of salvation hereafter. Life here and now could be lived and enjoyed for its own sake and worth. Lorenzo de Medici discoursing about Plato in the gardens of his Florentine villa represents the more urbane aspect of this hedonistic outlook; Benvenuto Cellini in his autobiography gives glimpses of its more lusty and cruder manifestations. Rather than prostrate himself in the dim shade of a cathedral, the individual could now assert himself in the broad radiant light of day.

It would be losing a sense of proportion to forget that such a movement affected but a relatively small fraction of society, the overwhelming bulk of which, the peasantry, went about its accustomed tasks in the wonted routine. But the stress on the humanist movement is warranted, for it contained the seed of future change. To this time and movement can be traced the tradition, only in our own day challenged, that the humanities constitute the best foundation for the proper education of man.

B. The Political Thought of Machiavelli

This sketch would not be complete without mention of Machiavelli, often regarded as the founder of modern political science.

The multiplicity of states in the Italian peninsula offered a small-scale replica of the larger European scene—just as the Europe of our day may be regarded as a miniature edition of the larger world picture. As Italy was more advanced in culture, so likewise the art of government may be said to have been more intensely cultivated in the microcosm of the multiplicity of her rival political units. It was in Florence again that Niccolò Machiavelli (1469-1527) flourished. Associated in relatively minor tasks with the government of his city under Medici rule, his fall from favor, along with their temporary eclipse, provided him with the leisure in which to set down the fruits of his experience and his thought. His little book *The Prince* is to this day the source of fame and controversy, but his *Discourses on Livy* are not less worthy of mention.

Machiavelli addressed himself to the question: how best— meaning most efficiently—govern the state? The problem of power lies at the center of his analysis, and the significance of Machiavelli is that, innocent of moral values and considerations, he views the problem as a limited technical one. The state is an earthly creation, an end in itself; man is essentially evil, or at least weak, and he may best be governed by exploiting this fact. Those means are good which further the power of the Prince—or state. Machiavelli's approach may be described as scientific—or amoral. Ruthless, unscrupulous, and for a time successful, Cesar Borgia, son of Pope Alexander VI, was his model.

As much as theorizing, Machiavelli was analyzing the methods and techniques of statecraft in Renaissance Italy. His admirers and his detractors alike would have to grant that this outlook has been, in actual practice, that which in the main has guided the conduct of the modern state. If order, law, and power were the highest aims of mankind, the admiration for Machiavelli could be unqualified.

C. Literature and Language

The language of the Church was Latin, and it was also that of literate Europe. Medieval Latin was a living tongue and there is irony in the fact that the humanists' endeavors succeeded in restoring Latin to its earlier Virgilian and Ciceronian purity but in the process killed it. A wide variety of vernaculars, derived from Latin or from other roots, were in common use, but only now began to achieve the dignity of literary media.

Dante's (1265-1321) *Divine Comedy*, a medieval synthesis, deserves much of the credit for making the dialect of his native Florence the modern language that has become Italian. Boccaccio's *Decameron* and Petrarch's *Sonnets* confirmed the change. *The Prince* was written in Italian, as well as Guicciardini's *History* and Vasari's *Lives*.

The same phenomenon occurred outside of Italy, and in fact the literary may be said to have been the chief manifestation of the Renaissance in the rest of Europe. The golden century of Spain produced Cervantes' (1547-1616) *Don Quixote*. Calvin's *Institutes of the Christian Religion* is a model of the French language. Almost contemporary with him was Rabelais (1490-1553) whose colossal burlesque *Gargantua and Pantagruel* still lives, as well as the more urbane *Essays* of slightly later Montaigne (1533-1592) and the work of a number of poets such as Ronsard. In the *Lusiad* Camoens produced Portugal's national epic.

Poetry flourished in England too, especially in the Elizabethan age, as witness Spenser's *Faerie Queene* and, most of all, the Shakespearean classic. Sir Thomas More's *Utopia*, originally written in Latin, appeared in English in 1551. Luther's translation of the Bible is one of the earliest monuments of the modern German tongue.

This literary activity, cause and effect at once, went along with the rise of distinct national consciousness and coincided with the great religious break in Christendom that will be surveyed in a later chapter.

III.   THE BEGINNINGS OF MODERN SCIENCE

A.   The Issue of Authority

The iconoclastic approach of antiquity-loving humanism, where medieval shibboleths were concerned, had consequences also in a different field, that of scientific development. To a considerable extent, these Renaissance humanists shared with the medieval age the worship of authority. It was merely a different authority: newly discovered Plato was not only worthwhile for his own sake, but equally useful as a stick with which to belabor Aristotle. This approach is very different from the essential characteristic of the scientific spirit, highly antithetic to the worship of *any* authority.

The sixteenth century, like our own, was not a scientific age in its temper, but rather one of intense feelings and ideological wars. Nevertheless, the questioning of one authority was useful as a wedge toward the questioning of authority in general. Some individuals, still exceptional, isolated, and untypical at this time, began to plant the seeds of that development, the growth and flowering of which were destined to fill an ever larger place on the historic canvas.

The significance of this cannot be overstressed, for science and its applications, now taken by us for granted, are a new phenomenon characteristic of the modern age. To be sure, the ancient Greeks had initiated an important development, most markedly successful in mathematics; but the Greek and Hellenistic phenomenon was short lived. The Romans, engineers, lawgivers, and administrators, showed little interest in or talent for abstract speculation, and in the succeeding medieval period much of the accumulated store of knowledge was lost. What was salvaged of it passed mainly to the Arabs, while the West sank into barbarism. Byzantium evinced no interest in the scientific aspects of Greek thought.

The Arabs made some contributions of their own, but they were mainly assimilators, preservers, and carriers of other cultures. With recovery in the West and through contact with Arab civilization, especially in Spain and in Sicily, some ancient Greek science was also reintroduced into this West. Greek knowledge followed the tortuous circuit of translation into Syriac, thence into Arabic, and finally into Latin. But not until the sixteenth century do we find a really autonomous and thereafter uninterrupted growth.[4] Most significant of all, perhaps, is the change in outlook: that of medieval Christianity was not so much inimical as indifferent to scientific endeavor, in its eyes without significant purpose.

B.   The Copernican Revolution

The generally accepted view of the structure of the universe was that drawn by Ptolemy in the second century B.C., wherein

---

[4] This statement, though basically correct, somewhat misrepresents the situation through oversimplification. Much work has been done recently in tracing the seepage into the West of the knowledge conveyed by the Arabs and of the early cultivation of medicine and mathematics in the medieval West.

It should be pointed out that the humanists had little interest in science, to the revival of which their contribution was indirect and accidental through their general interest in Greek culture.

the earth was the center around which the sun and the planets revolved. This view had superseded the earlier heliocentric scheme and it is of interest and in keeping with the time that Copernicus (1473-1543), a Polish-born priest and astronomer, should have been brought to question Ptolemy after perusing some earlier Greek sources.

His studies and calculations—he did little observing himself —led to the publication in 1543 of a Latin work, *On the Revolutions of the Celestial Bodies*, that expounded a heliocentric theory.[5] The book was dedicated to the Pope, played down the revolutionary nature of the theory, and created little stir at the time. But the seed was planted, and a line of successors, Danish Tycho Brahe (1546-1601) collecting observations, German Kepler (1571-1630) applying his mathematical genius to the formulation of precise laws, established the Copernican view on firm foundations.

The implications of this view were far reaching. By it the earth and man were reduced to relative insignificance in the universal scheme, and Galileo (1564-1642) ran afoul of the Church, by whom he was tried and compelled to recant, for his advocacy of it. Yet it was a Pope, Gregory XIII, who in 1582 caused the reform of the Julian calendar, which by that time had fallen out of order by ten days. Gradually, the Gregorian calendar has come to be universally accepted.[6]

C. The New Learning

1. Galileo. Galileo stands out in this development, because of the magnitude and quality of his own achievement. Not only did he contribute to astronomical knowledge, being the first to make and use a telescope with which he studied the moon, the sun, and the planets; he was also a physicist and studied the laws of motion, paving the way for Newton. Most important in some respects, Galileo was conscious of the

---

[5] Copernicus himself provides a good example of the gradual and transitional emergence of modern science. His own motivation was hardly "scientific" in the now currently understood sense, but the imperfect circularity (eccentric) of the Ptolemaic system was to him one of the weaknesses of that theory.

[6] The eastern Church did not accept the change with the result that the new calendar was not adopted in Russia until afer the 1917 revolution.

nature of the new path on which he had embarked as his *Discourse Concerning Two Sciences* shows.

2. *Bruno, Bacon, and Harvey*. The new knowledge and the manner in which it was obtained inevitably led to speculation about its nature and the processes that led to it. Giordano Bruno (1548-1600) in Italy took up with perhaps uncritical enthusiasm the advocacy of the new. His undiscriminating attacks led him into numerous difficulties, and finally the Inquisition, into whose hands he fell, caused him to be burned at the stake in Rome. By the end of the sixteenth century, the Church had become alive to the danger inherent in the new spirit of open-minded criticism inseparable from the scientific endeavor.

More sedate than Bruno, Francis Bacon (1561-1626) in England, in addition to a stormy political career, contributed some of the most important early philosophizing in the movement, especially in his *Essays*, his *Advancement of Learning*, and his *Novum Organum*.

To the theoretical development of astronomy and physics mathematics is essential. Though still at the stage of evolving a suitable set of symbols,[7] this science too began to grow. The names of Cardan and Vieta must be mentioned at this point. It will be noticed that the earlier and most striking achievements belong to the simpler exact sciences.

The more complex natural sciences did not as yet attain similar status. But the invention of the microscope in Holland introduced a powerful tool for observation. It was a Netherlander, Vesalius (1514-1564), who went to Italy and, while professing medicine at Padua, brought out the results of his studies in his justly famous *Treatise on Anatomy* (1543). William Harvey (1578-1657) also studied in Italy; returning to his native England, he established and announced his discovery of the circulation of the blood. Ambroise Paré in France was famed as a surgeon.

Medical practice still drew heavily upon ancient lore, especially that of Galen. Art as much as science, medicine

---

[7] The fundamental importance of notation and symbols may easily be appreciated by trying to perform the simplest arithmetical operations with Greek or Roman notation. The introduction of zero, brought to the West by the Arabs, constituted a very major contribution.

carried with it a large admixture of magic practice. None better than Paracelsus (1493-1541) exemplifies the combination of quackery with novel and valuable insight. The connection between science and magic is close at this time and they were often inextricably entangled. Tycho Brahe was astrologer as well as astronomer; chemistry gradually emerged from alchemy. Even numbers, as with Pythagoras, had magic properties; the "music of the spheres" was meant as more than a figure of speech. But the significant thing is that the process of disentanglement of what we regard as authentic science had begun. With such men as Galileo and Harvey modern science was born and launched upon its path of unlimited success and accomplishment.

IV.   FROM RENAISSANCE TO AGE OF REASON

A.   When Did the Renaissance End?

The frequent association between the term "Renaissance" and artistic and literary endeavor, while too exclusive and narrow, nevertheless has some justification. The closing date of the Council of Trent, 1563, has sometimes been suggested as a fit closing for the Renaissance.[8] A case might be made for this on the strength of the claim, largely correct, that the Counter Reformation was also Counter Renaissance in spirit. Even Erasmus' work had achieved the distinction of the Index in 1559. Nor were successful Lutheranism, and even more Calvinism, very friendly to the arts and to the outlook of humanism.

Yet, even in the limited field of the arts alone, Venetian painting might be cited, as well as the marvelous blossoming that took place in Holland and Flanders; individual taste must decide issues of primacy between Michelangelo or Raphael and Rembrandt. Even more, the literary golden age in both England and Spain straddles the turn of the sixteenth to the

---

[8] This is no place for a discussion of this issue. For the sake of convenience, and in view of the general organization of the present outline— using the date 1660 as dividing point—it has been found best to anticipate some of the developments treated in subsequent chapters and to deal with the story of the seventeenth-century intellectual development at this point. The student is therefore advised to refer to the following chapters in connection with this last section of the present one.

seventeenth century.[9] The prolonged·period of religious warfare on the other hand, culminating in its most destructive
phase of the Thirty Years'War, and of which the Empire was
the main battlefield, was clearly a climate inimical to cultural
pursuits.

But an aspect of the Renaissance has been mentioned which,
while not most characteristic, was for the future most important and fruitful. The name of Galileo best expresses it.
Galileo was born at the time of the close of the Council of
Trent and lived on to the middle of the next century. The
significance of his figure, beyond his place in the story of
the Copernican revolution, lies in the larger fact, already
mentioned, that he presides over the birth of modern science.
With him stands his contemporary Francis Bacon, exponent
of empiricism and of the virtues of the experimental method.
Bacon, however, unlike Galileo, had little to contribute to
specific knowledge, remaining primarily a philosopher of
science.

B.   Descartes and Pascal

A younger contemporary of Galileo and Bacon, René
Descartes (1596-1650) may be said to serve as bridge between
the initial period of scientific organization and the true opening of the floodgates of the modern development of science.
In the specific field of mathematics, the name of Descartes
holds high rank, and other sciences also held his attention. But
his single best known title to fame is his *Discourse on Method*,
published in 1637. The purpose of the method was "the
proper conduct of reason and the search for truth in the
sciences." The little book has properly been described as
the last battle of experimental science against aristotelianism.
The issue may be considered settled from this time between
authority and reason in the field of science.

This last aspect may serve as a link between Descartes and
the questioning spirit that the Protestant Reformation, perhaps

---

[9] There had been considerable freedom of thought in Spain. Despite the
Counter Reformation, the Inquisition, and Philip II, the impulse of intellectual vigor took a long time to die. It is equally interesting to consider
and contrast in England the simultaneous flowering of literature and the
progress of Puritanism.

unwittingly, had fostered. Yet Descartes was no Protestant but rather a careful conformist to Catholic doctrine. He resorted to a compromise, or dichotomy, which Pascal even better exemplifies.

The figure of Pascal (1623-1662) is both highly attractive and intriguing. A precocious and first rate mind, and a scientist in the narrower sense, physicist and mathematician, Pascal was also a sincere and devout believer. But for him the later conflict between religion and science did not exist: there were to be no fetters on the use of human reason, but there were also things that passed the capabilities of human understanding; it would be as unworthy to limit the exercise of reason in scientific search as it would be presumptuous for reason to seek to penetrate the mysteries of faith.

Descartes and many others at this time, if they would not put it in the form *credo quia absurdo,* would resort to the same dichotomy as Pascal. Descartes indeed, starting with his *cogito, ergo sum* went on to adduce "proof" of the existence of God, but this God was remote and rational and would not interfere with the exercise of the human rational faculty, which thus remained free to operate unhindered in the domain of experience. This stress on reason, this rationalism, incidental fruit of Renaissance and Reformation, was the greatest boon to the development of science. As to the ancients, they were indeed great and worthy of respect, but, "standing on their shoulders" and enjoying the benefit of their own accomplishments, men now could see farther horizons and surpass these achievements. The characterization Age of Reason applies to the seventeenth century perhaps better than to the eighteenth, more advanced in actual knowledge and more "enlightened," but in some ways also more naively uncritical.

C. Scientific Development in the Seventeenth Century

The spread of scientific activity is another important manifestation of this time. Not so much in the universities, generally retrograde and conservative, as in the network of exchanges among individuals. Father Mersenne in France conducted a huge correspondence and filled the role of central agency of information. Competition was keen and disputes over claims to priority bear witness to it.

1. Italy. In 1609, a group organized earlier in Rome, became the *Accademia dei Lincei*, an organization dedicated to the interchange of information and the fostering of search in all branches of knowledge. This early model of scientific societies was to be widely emulated elsewhere after the middle of the century. It was fitting that this first instance of scientific organization should see the light of day in Italy, and Italy long continued to hold an honorable place in the field of scientific discovery.

But the burning at the stake of Giordano Bruno in 1600 and the enforced recantation of Galileo in 1632 did not betoken a favorable climate for the use of reason and experiment. The *Accademia dei Lincei* passed out of existence in 1657. If the roster of scientific achievement continues to hold many Italian names, it remains broadly speaking true that the leadership in this development passed to the countries beyond the Alps.

2. Holland. It was in little Holland, scene of intense political and religious controversy during the first half of the century, that the most favorable climate existed for the free exercise and expression of thought. It was there that flourished the philosopher Spinoza (1632-1677) who sought to give metaphysics the logical rigor of geometric science. Descartes himself resided mainly there during his most active period, from 1628 to 1649. It was in England, however, where controversy had broken out into violence, that Milton penned his defense of freedom of expression.[10]

3. Intolerance and Superstition. Yet, to keep things in their proper perspective, it must be realized that there was much intolerance abroad, and that religious belief had an intensity unfamiliar to our own age. Of the English Puritans and Independents we shall speak. Pietism flourished on the continent, and the Jansenists, especially in France, attracted some of the best minds and individuals of the time, until their inclination, too akin to the tendencies that had presided at the birth of Protestantism, caused them to be condemned and

---

[10] Across the Atlantic, the settlement of Rhode Island by Roger Williams dates from this time. It provides an interesting illustration of intense interest in both religion and freedom. The Quakers may be put in the same category of development.

disbanded.[11] The belief in witchcraft was common, and suspected practitioners of the black arts were widely persecuted.

D. Developments in Political Theory

A subsequent chapter will trace the contrasting internal developments of France and England during the first half of the seventeenth century.[12] It is well to bear in mind that political theory often follows practice, of which it is a rationalization, and, as in the case of religious difference, it might be expected that theoretical disputes would accompany political divergence.

A century earlier, Machiavelli had discoursed on the best means for the governance of the state. But Machiavelli's approach was essentially the pragmatic and mechanical one of efficiency, minimizing therefore either morals or abstract principle. Machiavelli was an acute observer of the world that is; all politics, to a degree, may be called machiavellian. But, apart from the usefulness of his maxims in practice, there was now a more abstract and theoretical interest in the proper foundation of the state.

1. The Background of Absolutism. The English·revolution may be called premature, in so far at least as the monarchical idea, too deeply rooted to be effectively shaken, was concerned. Also, except for Holland, the English case may be regarded as exceptional in the context of seventeenth-century Europe, where Spain is rather the model.

The monarchy of Philip II had the earmarks of absolutism and divine sanction. Under that system, Spain continued to operate, and neighboring France under Richelieu and Mazarin was embarking on a similar path. The revolution in England was precipitated by the Stuart attempt to enforce in that country the theory as well as the practice of absolutism. Both Charles I and James I held to this view. The practice might

---

[11] Pascal had for a time Jansenist leanings. A measure of the prevailing temper of the time may be gathered from his *Provincial Letters,* a violent attack against the Jesuits.

[12] The attention of the student is again called at this point to the statement in footnote 8 above.

indeed have succeeded had they been as skillful managers as their Tudor predecessors, but the combination of managerial ineptitude and arrogant theorizing brought them to grief.

Yet it is in England that Hobbes' *Leviathan* was published in 1651. From his assumptions about human nature Hobbes was led to a virtual divinization of authority as necessary to the functioning of society. The opposite and premature republican views of James Harrington caused him to run afoul of Cromwell.

2. Grotius. It is again in Holland that some of the most interesting and important developments occurred. Hugo Grotius (1583-1645) is often credited with the foundation of international law. His early interest grew out of the maritime conflict between Spain and his own country, and led him to assert the doctrine of the free seas against the Spanish, later English, claim to rights of seizure on the open seas. But his fame rests on his better known *De Jure belli et pacis*, which grew out of his witnessing the horrors of the Thirty Years' War and a desire to mitigate them by the introduction of some rule of law even in warfare.

The concept of "natural" inherent rights, *jus gentium*, deriving from the simple fact of humanity, is worth comparing with the views of the Spanish Jesuit Suarez, who wrote at the beginning of the century and drew conclusions to comparable effect from divine origin instead of natural circumstances.

We shall also trace the disintegrating effect of war on the Empire. The central authority was to be essentially destroyed at Westphalia, but the individual princes were ready to grasp the full attributes of sovereignty. By 1660, whether in terms of power among other powers, or as a model to emulate for the internal organization of the state, France was about to emerge in a position of dominance and leadership. Her king, about to come of age and to assume in fact the reins of government, destined to the longest European reign on record, has given to the age his name in history.

ADDITIONAL READINGS

Allen, J. W., *History of Political Thought in the Sixteenth Century* (1928);
Allen, P. S., *The Age of Erasmus* (1914); Burckhardt, Jakob, *The Civiliza-
tion of the Renaissance in Italy* (new ed. 1944); Burtt, Edwin A., *The
Metaphysical Foundations of Modern Philosophical Science* (1948); Fergu-
son, Wallace K., *The Renaissance in Historical Thought* (1948); Mellone,
Sidney H., *The Dawn of Modern Thought: Descartes, Spinoza, Leibniz*
(1930); Ornstein, Martha, *The Role of Scientific Societies in the Seventeenth
Century* (1928); Phillips, Margaret M., *Erasmus and the Northern
Renaissance* (1950); Randall, John H., *The Making of the Modern Mind*
(1940); Robertson, James M., *Short History of Free Thought, Ancient and
Modern* (1936); Smith, Preserved, *A History of Modern Culture* (2 vols.,
1930-1934); Smith, Preserved, *Erasmus: A Study of His Life, Ideals, and
Place in History* (1923); Taylor, F. Sherwood, *Galileo and the Freedom
of Thought* (1938); Wolf, Abraham, *A History of Science, Technology and
Philosophy in the Sixteenth and Seventeenth Centuries* (1935).

CHAPTER 3

The Age of Discovery and the Commercial Revolution

I. THE FOREIGN TRADE OF EUROPE

Humanists and scientific searchers, however different their approach and their activities, had in common a spirit of inquiry, and shared in the elation of discovery, whether of old or new.

A. The State of Geographical Knowledge

The astronomical revolution has been mentioned. Alongside it, on a smaller scale, went on a revolution in geography. Belief in the sphericity of the earth had never wholly died out, though it was not widespread. Europe's ideas of geography were primitive, limited, and distorted. The Mediterranean was still the center of the world. The Arabs acted as connecting link between Europe and the East. Some Europeans had indeed gone to and returned from the realm of the Great Kahn, far off Cathay or China. Africa was known in part. These same Arabs had contributed much to the art of navigation, for which the compass that they brought to Europe is clearly invaluable.

B. The Place of the Mediterranean

Arab maritime trade was largely in the Indian Ocean. Mediterranean trade was mainly in Italian hands. Out of it Venice had built herself into *the* great trading and naval power of the day, though others still, Genoa, Marseilles, Barcelona, also participated in sea borne trade. From the Levantine ports, from Constantinople and Egypt, the luxuries and spices of the East were brought to such points as Venice whence they became distributed into the rest of Europe. With the general recovery that made itself felt from the eleventh century onward, the demand for these eastern products kept growing, though Europe as a whole found difficulty in furnishing suitable goods in exchange. There was a steady drain on Europe of its precious metals which were difficult of replacement.

1. The Coming of the Ottoman Turks. The fall of Constantinople to the Turks in 1453 and the extension of their control to Egypt at the beginning of the sixteenth century were hard blows to Mediterranean trade. The Turks, unlike the Arabs, were not sensitive to the worth of commerce, which they despised and looked upon as a fit object for taxation—and plunder.

II. EXPLORATION AND DISCOVERY

A. General Background

The Italian monopoly of Mediterranean trade, which other peoples resented and would have gladly broken, the coming of the Turks, technical improvements in the art of navigation and the construction of ships, the prevailing spirit of restlessness and inquiry, all these together created the suitable combination of circumstances for the great chapter that was about to open in European annals: the discovery of the world by Europe resulting in the ultimate conquest of this world— taking the word conquest in the same broad sense indicated before. It is one of the capital facts, not only of European but of world history, that it was Europe that discovered the rest of the world rather than the reverse. Coincidentally with this, and by-product of it, there took place the displacement of the Mediterranean by the Atlantic, a change fraught with the seeds of far-reaching readjustment within Europe itself.

In view of their maritime primacy, it might be expected that Italians would play a large role in the story of exploration and discovery. And in fact they did, but only as individuals, for the Italian states, as political units, were too involved in their mutual rivalries and quarrels, too bent, as

Venice for example, in preserving what could be saved of their former trade, with the consequence that they left to others, the larger and rising national monarchies consolidating along the Atlantic, the burden and the profits of the new development.

B. The Portuguese and Spanish Explorations

1. Portugal and the Route to India. Portugal was the first among these. During the fifteenth century, a member of her ruling house, Prince Henry (1394-1460), since dubbed the Navigator, created the then equivalent of a modern institute or foundation. Individuals interested in navigational and geographical techniques and lore gathered in Sagres, whence ships set forth on searching expeditions. Logically, they first went down the Atlantic coast of Africa, knowledge of which was pushed farther and farther south.

No sea monsters were met and the ocean did not boil at the equator, thus exploding some popular legends. In 1488, Bartholomew Diaz reached the "Cape of Storms," southernmost point of Africa, shortly renamed Cape of Good Hope. Ten years later, another Portuguese, Vasco da Gama, having rounded the Cape and with the aid of Arab pilots crossed the Indian Ocean, landed at Calicut in India in May, 1498. His return to Lisbon, bringing directly to Europe by an all-water route a cargo of eastern wares, marks the beginning of a new era for Europe, economically as well as politically.

2. Spain and the Discovery of America. Spain did not lag far behind Portugal. It was the rulers of the newly consolidated kingdom, Ferdinand and Isabella, who finally sponsored the expedition that the Genoese Cristoforo Colombo wished to undertake. The purpose was the same as Portugal's —finding a direct route to the East—but, staking his adventure on belief in the earth's sphericity, Columbus would sail westward. This he did finally in August, 1492, putting out from Palos with three small ships. After three months and much discouragement, land was finally sighted. Columbus had discovered island outposts of the American continent, but, mistaken in his estimate of the size of the earth, believed that he had reached the eastern Indies. The new continent was destined to be named after another Italian, Amerigo Vespucci, who later claimed discovery and whose claim found its way on early maps.

It took some time before it was realized that a vast new expanse of ocean lay between the newly discovered land and the true East.[1] Balboa, in 1513, crossing the isthmus of Panama, was first to gaze upon the wide Pacific. The business of exploration was actively pursued during the early part of the century. In 1500, Portuguese Cabral was accidentally blown to the Brazilian coast. Another Portuguese, Magellan, but in Spanish employ, from 1519 to 1522, rounded the Horn, crossed the entire Pacific to the Philippines, where he met death, leaving the remnants of his crew to rejoin Europe by way of the Indian Ocean and the circuit of Africa. The first complete circumnavigation of the globe had been effected.

The Portuguese were mainly active in the East, pushing from India to the Spice Islands and even to Japan. Meanwhile Spanish activity continued centering on the Americas. Cortez in 1519 landed in Mexico, where he proceeded to subdue a more advanced Indian culture than had been found on the Caribbean islands. A similar performance was enacted by Pizarro who, sailing from Panama in 1531, proceeded to discover and conquer the Inca civilization of Peru. From Florida to Cape Horn, the American continent was discovered.

3. Other Early Explorations. As early as 1497, another Genoese, John Cabot, commissioned by King Henry VII of England, had sailed to Nova Scotia, but the bleak northern climate did not invite important English settlement for another century. Jacques Cartier of France discovered the mouth of the St. Lawrence River in 1534. Cabot and Cartier were both looking for a northwest passage, a route to the Far East around the American obstacle, for a long time the object of explorers' search.

C. The Early Colonial Empires

The motivation of these voyages of discovery was commercial. But as the European powers came into contact with

---

[1] Columbus' and other calculations of the time assumed the earth's dimension to be smaller than it actually is. One difficulty lay in the fact that the lack of accurate clocks made it difficult to estimate longitude with accuracy.

new or older lands, they tended either to establish themselves in outright possession or at least to exert considerable political influence among the states and rulers that they found established.

1. The Treaty of Tordesillas. As early as 1494, the Portuguese and the Spanish, initial participants in the colonial or imperial contest, had the Pope, Alexander VI, arbitrate their differences. The Treaty of Tordesillas divided the entire globe in two by a meridian which cut off the easternmost bulge of South America.[2] East of this line Portugal would have prior claim, Spain to the west of it. Save for Brazil, the bulk of the American continent and the Pacific fell in the Spanish zone; the Atlantic, Africa, the Indian Ocean, and the Spice Islands of the Archipelago were Portugal's. The results of this early partition have left traces visible to our day.

2. Portugal's Commercial Empire. The Spanish and Portuguese empires were, from the first, wholly different in their natures. It was the Portuguese quest which had been successful by the test of its initial purpose. The Portuguese did not penetrate into Africa, being content with bases along its coasts, but concentrated on the resources, wealth, and trade of Asia and the islands. Trade was the lifeblood of their empire, but it led them to active participation and intervention in the affairs of India, for example, though India was not conquered. Asia as a whole was too densely peopled and too advanced in culture for any appreciable European settlement to be possible.

3. The Spanish Empire. By contrast, the Spanish search seemed at first a failure. In two places, Mexico and Peru, there turned out to be both developed civilizations and large quantities of precious metals. But for the rest, the American continent was relatively sparsely occupied by peoples in a primitive stage of civilization. The situation offered little scope for trade, but much of the land was suitable for settlement and cultivation. As to the gold and silver, they could of course be appropriated and carried off to Spain.

In any case, be it Portugal or Spain, superior force was an

---

[2] After some time the line was shifted farther to the east, but the arrangement remained.

important factor. After the initial conquest, the American Indian, whatever the stage of his cultural development, was to a large degree enslaved. Many were put to work in the mines, many became the peons of our time, the land having been pre-empted by the Spanish settlers, who established themselves on the American continent and gradually gave it the cultural and political shape that it has assumed. Europeans could settle, and even came to predominate, in temperate regions such as modern Argentina and Chile or in high land in the tropics. Elsewhere the original stock continued to prevail.

Quite early, it appeared that the native labor supply was insufficient. Out of this situation the trade in Negro slaves from Africa developed and prospered, thus introducing a substantial Negro element in the population of the large region stretching as a great arc from Brazil to the southern United States.[3]

4. Missionary Activity. There was much ruthlessness and brutality in the process of conquest and subjugation, whether Portuguese in India or Spanish in America, to say nothing of the African slave trade. Yet the conquerors carried the cross along with their arms and greed, and the fact may not be dismissed as mere sham. In the Iberian peninsula, much of whose history was the story of Christian reconquest of Moslem-held territory,[4] the spirit of crusading was strong, and the hope of converting the heathen sent many a missionary in the track of the *conquistadores*. Bishop de las Casas is a case in point in the Spanish domain. St. Francis Xavier went to India and as far as Japan.

The Jesuits became very active in this work after the foundation of their order in Europe. Much of Europe's early knowledge of China derives from their *Relations*. In

---

[3] Whether the lot of the Indians was worsened as the result of the introduction of Spanish rule is debatable. Cruelty there was, but the prior condition of the Indians, even in such advanced civilizations as the Aztec and the Inca, would not seem, for the common lot, to have been any softer.

Negro slavery did not play as important a role in the Spanish as in the later English possessions of North America.

[4] The same year 1492 that saw the discovery of America by Columbus was also the one when the Moors lost their last foothold in Spain with the fall of Granada.

North America they ventured beyond the area of settlement and became the initial discoverers of much of the present United States and Canada.

5. *Dutch, English, and French Overseas*. The process of overseas discovery and empire building was at first a Portuguese and Spanish monopoly. Nothing came at the time (1497) of Cabot's voyage in behalf of Henry VII; not until the turn from the sixteenth to the seventeenth century did England begin to consider seriously the possibility of overseas settlements and acquisitions. But, before that, England during the sixteenth century had laid the bases of her maritime power. The great sea captains of the Elizabethan age, men such as Drake and Hawkins, gained their experience and spent their activity in the process of encroaching upon the trade monopoly of Portugal and Spain. By them many a Spanish treasure ship, bringing home American gold and silver, was plundered.

The Dutch engaged in similar activities, likewise becoming in the process a great maritime and trading people. They made small lodgments in the New World, but their attention was chiefly attracted by the Far East, where they were to fall heirs to much of the Portuguese empire, mainly in the Archipelago.[5]

Jacques Cartier had planted on the banks of the St. Lawrence River the seeds of a future French empire, which the work of a small band of men, explorers, missionaries, fur traders, and some settlers, was to establish in North America.

In the seventeenth century, the national monarchies bordering on the Atlantic, Portuguese, Spanish, French, Dutch, and English, were the contestants in a struggle that was in time to range over all quarters of the globe.

III.   THE COMMERCIAL REVOLUTION

A.   New Commodities and Trading Centers

The effects of this European expansion to the far corners of the earth were, for Europe itself, numerous and far reaching, though spread in uneven fashion. Apart from increased

---

[5] From 1580 to 1640, that is during the period of Dutch emancipation from Spanish rule, Spain and Portugal were temporarily united under a common crown. Dutch activity was thus directed against both.

knowledge of the planet, the very mode of life was noticeably altered by the introduction of hitherto unknown commodities. To take illustrations only, the lowly potato has played an important role in history; tobacco and cotton have hardly been less significant,[6] to say nothing of the influence of cultural contact.

When Vasco da Gama returned from India with a cargo of spices, short-circuiting the numerous middlemen involved in the former usual route of travel, their price in Lisbon was but a fraction of what it used to be in Venice. In modern parlance, the bottom dropped out of the pepper market. For Venice this was a calamity of the first order of magnitude. In the sixteenth century begins the decline of Italy, simultaneous with the opening of the Atlantic. Lisbon for a time, then Antwerp and Dutch Amsterdam, rose to commercial prominence.

B. Capitalism

Despite rising commercial activity, Europe was chronically short of specie during the period prior to the great discoveries. Money as such, as a commodity, had been acquiring increasing importance despite the Church's ban, well honored in the breach, on usury or money lending. In this activity, as in many others, the Italians had been foremost. The Medici were bankers, a calling the early practice of which was to a large degree in Italian hands.

1. The Influx of Specie from the New World. The result of Spain's New World discovery and acquisition was the influx of a large quantity of gold and silver. Save for what might be plundered in transit, this of course went to Spain. This wealth had much to do with sixteenth-century Spanish power: gold can buy armies. But, apart from this, Spain, lacking the background and experience of Italy or Flanders, did not develop into an important commercial state. The handling of trade in Spain was, to a large degree, in foreign

---

[6] Cotton is of Asian origin rather than American, but its cultivation assumed increasing and eventually enormous importance in the North American economy, which came to supply a large part of the European demand.

hands, and Spanish gold in various ways found its way to other parts of Europe.

This influx of precious metal in Europe was useful in accelerating the transition to a money economy and to the rise of what is generally described as capitalism. Around the middle of the century, Antwerp,[7] strategically situated at the cross roads of various trade currents, was the chief center of exchange until political developments brought about its downfall. In 1531, the first stock exchange had been established there. Like the Florentine Medici and other Italians, the great house of Fugger, originating in Augsburg, was prominent in these activities. The Fuggers played an important role through their accumulating wealth, being called upon to finance the imperial election and then the wars of Charles V.

The Fuggers, among other things, financed much of the Portuguese trade with the East and had interests in the Americas. Such large scale operations called, not only for bankers, but for entrepreneurs operating on a new scale of magnitude, other than that with which local town guilds had been equipped to deal. The latter tended, consequently, to become weaker in the changing economy.

2. The Price Revolution. The great and rapid influx of specie into Europe had the usual effect that the appearance in large quantities of any commodity has, that is, to cheapen its value. The cheapening of money, inflation as we call it now, manifests itself through a rise in prices. It is generally calculated that the sixteenth century witnesses a fourfold increase in prices. Though such a figure must be regarded as very rough average and approximate, the central fact of a large price rise is unquestioned.

The social effects of inflation are always far reaching, and so they were in the sixteenth century. "The debtor gains what the creditor has lost," remarked a French observer in 1620. In western Europe, by 1500, the peasantry had to a large extent obtained a money commutation of its feudal dues. Inflation worked to its advantage and to the corresponding detriment of much of the landed gentry. But rising prices had the opposite effect in eastern Europe, where the peasants had so far failed to secure as good a position as in the west,

---

[7] Antwerp, with the Low Countries, was a Spanish possession.

and found their condition further depressed while the land-owning class increased its advantage and strengthened its hold. The significance of this divergence in the history of Europe to the present day can hardly be overstated.

C. Mercantilism

1. The Favorable Balance of Trade. The state did not ignore the significance of economic change. The aim of its economic policy was the enhancement of the nation's wealth. Mercantilism describes the generally accepted view of this policy. It was based on the concept that it was desirable to increase the amount of bullion existing within the state, and that this could be achieved through the agency of a favorable balance of trade. With this in view, trade should be appropriately regulated. It was also believed that the total existing wealth was a static quantity, hence that one's gain was another's loss.

2. State Regulation of Commercial Activity. Mercantilistic policy long remained the prevailing practice of European states. Monopoly of trade was one aspect of it. Spain alone could trade with the Spanish possessions; England and France acted similarly once they acquired possessions of their own. The English Navigation Acts of the seventeenth century are perfect expressions of the mercantilistic outlook which, however, did not confine itself to matters of foreign trade but dealt with elaborate and minute regulation of domestic manufacture as well. Colbert in France, also in the seventeenth century, well exemplifies this aspect.

For the purpose of long distance foreign trade, chartered companies, associations sanctioned by the state from whom they received wide privileges and rights of administration, became the accepted practice. England, Holland, and France had chartered companies for trade with India, with the West Indies, the Levant, and elsewhere. The seventeenth-century English settlements along the North Atlantic coast in various forms originated from royal grants of charters.

ADDITIONAL READINGS

Abbott, William Cortez, *The Expansion of Europe* (2 vols., 1918); Ehrenberg, Richard, *Capital and Finance in the Age of the Renaissance: A Study of the Fuggers and Their Connections* (1928); Hannay, David, *The Great Chartered Companies* (1927); Haring, C. H., *The Spanish Empire in America* (1947); Heckscher, Eli, *Mercantilism* (2 vols., 1935); Madariaga, Salvador de, *Rise of the Spanish American Empire* (1947); Morison, S. E., *Admiral of the Ocean Sea* (2 vols., 1942); Packard, Laurence B., *The Commercial Revolution, 1400-1776* (1927); Roover, Raymond de, *The Medici Bank: Its Organization, Management, Operations, and Decline* (1948); Tawney, R. H., *Religion and the Rise of Capitalism* (1947); Weber, Max, *The Protestant Ethic and the Spirit of Capitalism* (1948); Williamson, J. A., *The Ocean in English History* (1941).

CHAPTER 4

The Reformation

I. WESTERN CHRISTIANITY IN 1500

A. Its Extent and the Structure of the Western Church

From Sicily to Finland and from Poland to Iceland and to Spain, European mankind in 1500 religiously was one. The historic role and position of the Church, whose head was the Roman Pontiff, have been indicated in the first chapter of this survey. The universality of the belief in this version of Christianity may be stressed again. Part of the belief consisted in acceptance of the necessity of the institution that was the Church, which moreover was closely integrated with the state, by contrast with the widespread later practice of separation of church and state. Heresy or erroneous belief was not merely a matter between the individual and his maker or his conscience, but a concern of the civil power as well. The Church would judge the heretic whom the secular arm might extirpate, through execution if necessary.[1]

In the course of the centuries, the Church had come to take the shape that it had attained by 1500. The long struggle between Pope and Council, for allocation of authority, had resulted in final victory for the former, confirming the monarchical and authoritarian aspects of the institution.

[1] This practice, long repudiated in the western world though lately regaining favor, may perhaps best be understood in the light of another modern and non-controversial practice. The segregation of cases of infectious diseases is now generally taken for granted. The danger of infection from pernicious ideas that might endanger the soul's salvation is obviously —granted the premise—a much more serious matter that calls for protection by all available means.

B.   The Sacramental System

The priesthood was the agency through which the Church performed its earthly function, and the priest was endowed with sacred character and powers to perform his task. This character was conferred upon him by ordination. Ordination is a sacrament, meaning a special endowment of divine grace made manifest by a ceremony which is its outward symbol. The sacramental system is fundamental in the Church of Rome, and there are seven sacraments.

In view of the importance of this system, which was to be one of the chief foci of controversy in the subsequent story, they may be enumerated. They are: (1) baptism, which removes the stain and disability of original sin; (2) confirmation, which confers the Holy Ghost; (3) penance, or the forgiveness of sin—not its exoneration; (4) the Eucharist, whereby during the ceremony of the mass, the miraculous—and literal, not symbolic—transformation takes place of bread and wine into the body and blood of Christ, of which the faithful may then partake; (5) extreme unction, the preparation for the departure for the after life; (6) holy orders, previously mentioned; and (7) matrimony, the consecration of wedlock, hence indissoluble by human agency.

C.   Corruption and Abuses in the Church

It has also been pointed out that, in the course of time, the Church had gone through a series of declines and renovations which, however, did not affect its doctrine, whatever estimate they may have caused to be held of the personnel of the institution. Nor had these crises caused a disruption of unity.

1. The Leadership. The period immediately before the sixteenth century was one of these times of decline. The long Babylonian captivity, when the Popes had resided in Avignon and been to an undue degree under the influence of the French crown, the spectacle of rival claimants to the papal throne, could hardly redound to the credit of the institution.[2] But there was also at this time laxity and corruption of a simpler

---

[2] To a considerable extent these developments were confined among the upper strata of church and state, which is why the mass of believers and the structure of the institutions was little affected.

but cruder sort. The worst of it was at the very top, in the papacy itself. The so-called Renaissance Popes, men like Alexander VI or Julius II, may have been generous and discriminating patrons of the arts, but the phrase "let us enjoy the papacy while God has made it ours," attributed to one of them, expressed their outlook. Along with their artistic tastes they were interested in the material goods that wealth can purchase, and in power. Living was high and morality correspondingly low at the papal court, into whose coffers the faithful poured their contributions—to increase which many abuses were resorted to. These Popes would provide handsomely for their kin and their children, if any. They participated with gusto in the complex politics and intrigues of the microcosm that was Italy where their interest largely centered.

2. The Lower Clergy. This is not to say that the whole clergy was corrupt. If in its upper reaches, among bishops and cardinals, instances of the Roman state of affairs could easily be found, the papal example was not necessarily followed by many a parish priest who faithfully performed his duties and shared in the simple, and meager, life of his flock. Among this lower clergy, the deficiency was often due to laxity of standards in their education and training. Of monks and nuns, much ribald literature bespeaks less than high regard in the popular eye.

3. Special Conditions of the Sixteenth Century. Such conditions had occurred before. They could be transitory and remediable, and, by themselves, need not have caused a breach in Christianity any more than they had on earlier occasions. But they now happened to exist at a time characterized by the questioning restlessness of mind which has been noted under the rubric Renaissance. Reformation and Renaissance are often looked upon as antithetic terms. In many ways they are. Yet they may also be regarded as not unrelated manifestations of the same spirit of inquiry that prevailed at this time. In unexpected, unintended, and often devious ways, both have contributed to that phenomenon, for good or evil characteristic of the modern age, the emancipation of the spirit of man.

II. THE PROTESTANT REVOLT

The word "Protestant," initially of limited application,[3] has come to cover a variety of persuasions, widely varying in their doctrine, but having the common denominator of belief in Christ but refusal to recognize the authority of the Roman Pontiff.

A. Lutheranism

1. Martin Luther. First among these in time was the revolt that occurred in the Empire and is associated with the name of Luther.

Of humble origin, Martin Luther (1483-1546) had become a monk, and through ability had risen to the position of professor of theology at Wittenberg, where his teaching was popular. An intense nature, the central problem of salvation was to him very real, and he found himself attracted by the views of St. Augustine and St. Paul, with the consequence that he came to put greater emphasis on the aspect of "justification by faith," deriving from the stress on the depravity of man, by contrast with the more tolerant view of human frailty which had caused to magnify the value of "good works" and external practices.

2. The Issue of Indulgences. It is at this point that the abuses that Rome had allowed to develop come into the picture, specifically in the matter of indulgences. The theory of indulgences was old, and reasonable enough; they were a typical illustration of the value of "good works." For some such deed, a pilgrimage, a money contribution to a worthy cause, and if in addition the recipient was in the proper mood of repentance, the Pope, by virtue of his God-given powers, claimed the right to confer, not a remission of sin, but an alleviation of the penalty for such.

Obviously, an indulgence could be no object of money purchase, but to assist financially in the building of the glorious pile of St. Peter might well be classified a meritorious deed, and with increasing pressure for greater revenue, in

---

[3] The name originated from a group of princes "protesting" the decrees of the Imperial Diet and did not have initially the subsequent broad connotation.

the hands of the sixteenth-century version of efficient "sales-
men," a situation could easily develop where, in the eyes of
simple folk, the line might become dim that separates proper
theory from illegitimate practice. To all intents and purposes,
in 1517, a wide campaign was being conducted to raise money
through the "sale" of indulgences, though the endeavor to
tar the Church of Rome with acceptance of the theory of
sale would be absurd futility. Here was another illustration
of the frailty of man. Unfortunately for Rome, morally frail
men conducted her affairs under the claim of divine dispensation.

a. LUTHER'S NINETY-FIVE THESES. Here is the immediate
and specific occasion of the Lutheran rebellion. To see in it
the sole cause would be historic falsification. The quarrel over
indulgences must be seen in the broader context of the circumstances of the time. At all events, in 1517, Luther posted on
the church door at Wittenberg his ever since famous ninety-
five theses—statements or assertions—in regard to indulgences,
and issued a challenge to debate. Such a debate took place, in
1519, and Luther's opponent, John Eck, drove him to admit
that which was implied in his views, a challenge to the basic
claim of the Church that it was the divinely appointed institution charged with the task of man's guidance on earth and of
mediation between him and the deity. Luther's position was
tantamount to questioning the very *raison d'être* of the Church.

3. The Shaping of Lutheranism

a. LUTHER'S SUCCESSFUL DEFIANCE. For such doctrine John
Huss had been declared a heretic and burned. Luther did not
submit, nor was he burned, but lived instead to found another
Christian Church. His three pamphlets of the following year,
An Address to the Nobility of the German Nation, *On the
Babylonian Captivity of the Church of God*, and *On the Free-
dom of a Christian Man*, consummated his break with Rome.
In 1521, Luther was excommunicated by the Church and out-
lawed by the Imperial Diet at Worms.

What saved Luther was the political situation in the Empire. For all that he had been outlawed, he had powerful
allies and protectors, particularly the Elector of Saxony. Apart
from those who agreed with his challenge of Roman abuses,

his more far reaching questioning of the very function of the Church appealed to many, princes who saw an opportunity of gain in appropriating Church lands and revenues, burghers who resented the flow of German wealth across the Alps in support of an Italian hierarchy. The conjunction of authentic devotion and material greed made a powerful combination, destined to be successful.

b. THE PEASANTS' REVOLT. During the decade of the twenties, Lutheran doctrine was to take shape, in doing which contemporary events had a strong influence. The implicit challenge to all existing authority was taken up with enthusiasm by the lower class, which had grievances enough, not only against the Church of Rome, but even more immediately against its immediate lay lords. Untroubled by fine points of theological distinction, the peasants rose against their masters. The Peasants' Revolt in 1524-1525 was crushed with much brutality and bloodshed. Faced with an unforeseen dilemma, Luther aligned himself unequivocally with the established powers and even used the most violent language in advocating ruthless suppression.

By 1526, the Lutheran party was strong enough among the princes to force leaving the issue in suspense at the Diet of Speyer. The Emperor's attempt to enforce the suppression of heresy three years later was a dead letter, and his intention to use force produced the Schmalkaldic League, an alliance for mutual defense of Lutheran princes in 1531.

c. THE CONFESSION OF AUGSBURG. Meantime, Philip Melanchton, a humanist colleague and friend of Luther, but of a gentler and less intransigeant disposition, produced a statement of doctrine in an effort to reconcile divergent parties. The compromise did not succeed, but under the name Confession of Augsburg became the statement of Lutheran faith. The Lutheran Church, when organized, retained the Roman episcopate though minimizing its importance. The sacramental system was also retained, but sacraments were reduced to three: baptism, the Eucharist, and confirmation. The miracle of the mass was denied, a somewhat metaphorical doctrine of "real presence" taking its place. By comparison with the Roman structure of hierarchy and ceremonial practice, consid-

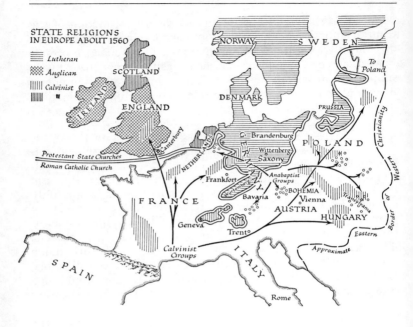

It is not possible to draw a religious map of Europe during the Reformation because persons of different religious belief were intermixed, and each group still labored to convert others to its position. Legally, however, by 1560 or 1570, the churches were as indicated above. Many Catholics lived north of the double line, especially in Ireland, and many Protestants south of it, especially in France, Bohemia, and Hungary. The Germans, because of political disunity within the Holy Roman Empire, were the one large people of Europe to emerge from the Reformation almost evenly divided. In the other large countries one side or the other, Protestant or Catholic, was ultimately reduced to a small minority.

erable simplification had been effected. Also, and in contrast with the Church of Rome, Lutheran churches were much more intimately attached, and even subservient, to the state.

4. *Religious Wars in the Empire.* With the formation of the Schmalkaldic League a period of internecine war began in the Empire. Charles V himself retained the allegiance to Rome, but his involvements elsewhere in Europe prevented his devoting single minded attention to the religious break within the Empire. Inevitably, civil and foreign war became entangled,[4] until after a quarter of a century of inconclusive struggle a compromise was achieved.

a. THE PEACE OF AUGSBURG. The Peace of Augsburg in 1555 is an important landmark in this story. Its chief provision was the adoption of the principle *cujus regio ejus religio*, meaning that each prince could choose his religion, which would then become that of his subjects, save that Lutheran subjects of ecclesiastical states could retain their faith. The choice, however, was confined to Catholicism and Lutheranism, no other form of Christianity being tolerated. The status of church property was to be frozen as of 1552. The clause known as "ecclesiastical reservation" provided that an ecclesiastical prince must yield his see upon becoming Lutheran. The settlement did not prove final; another century was to elapse and much violence to occur before a lasting compromise was effected.

5. *The Spread of Lutheranism.* The attraction of the Lutheran example in the Empire made itself felt beyond its confines, though in limited areas. The three Scandinavian Countries, Denmark, Norway, and Sweden were united under King Christian II (1513-1523). Upon his death, Swedish national sentiment asserted itself under the leadership of the house of Vasa. Gustavus Vasa became king in Sweden, while Frederick II succeeded his nephew in Norway and Denmark. In both cases, the royal house followed a policy similar to that of those German princes who had thought to increase their power by espousing the Lutheran faith. By 1536, Christian III was able, despite some protest, to make good the change in Denmark and Norway, while Gustavus Vasa did the same in Sweden following upon a quarrel with the Pope over the appointment to the see of Upsala. The Scandinavian countries gradually became and have remained almost exclusively Lutheran.

---

[4] See below, p. 75.

B. Calvinism

Another form of the Protestant revolt, less involved with
the power of princes, was destined to a wider spread than
Luther's.

1. Zwingli. In the Swiss cantons, nominally under Imperial
allegiance, but in effect virtually independent little republics,
there appeared Zwingli, who increasingly came to attack
Catholic practices. Zürich was his stronghold, where he
preached in the cathedral. Zürich's refusal to submit to a
papal request to abandon Zwingli in 1523 marks the first
formal break with Rome, after which the movement spread
among the cantons. Warfare resulting from an attempt to
convert by force some Catholic cantons led to Zwingli's death
in the battle of Kappel in 1532. The movement was left leader-
less, especially as the effort to bring Zwingli and Luther together had failed over the inability to reconcile their divergent
views of the Eucharist.[5] But only four years after Zwingli's
death his succession was taken by the more famous Calvin who
appeared in Geneva in 1536.

2. John Calvin. John Calvin came from France, where he
was born Jean Cauvin in 1509. He spent some years in Paris,
studied law, and, having experienced a "conversion," came
under the influence of the religious unrest of the time, which
was also felt in France. In Basel he became acquainted with
Zwingli's work, and in 1536 wrote *The Institutes of the Christian Religion*, an exposition of the Protestant position which
brought him wide repute.

Calvin was, temperamentally, the very antithesis of Luther,
whose doctrine he did not adopt. His *Institutes*, a well-
organized and closely reasoned work, had great influence on
the course of Protestant thought and doctrine, but failed to
produce unity.

The same year 1536 found Calvin in Geneva. The troubled
situation of that city, in revolt against the authority of the
Duke of Savoy as well as that of its bishop, brought Calvin
the appointment as chief pastor. This position Calvin re-

---

[5] This was attempted at the so-called Marburg Colloquy and is an
instance of the importance of the purely theological aspects of sixteenth-
century religious controversy.

tained, save for a brief interim of exile, until his death in 1564. During this period, Calvin was real ruler of Geneva, making its government a virtual theocracy managed with an iron hand and an uncompromisingly intransigeant spirit. Calvin's outlook was dour and his doctrine austere. He saw to it that sin was ferreted out and punished; the pleasures of life were banned, and, outwardly at least, Geneva settled under a mantle of virtue and of gloom.

3. The Spread of Calvinism. Calvin's intellectual ability and his indefatigable energy spread his doctrine far and wide. Unlike Lutheranism confined to the Germanic world, Calvinism shared with Catholicism the quality of universality in its appeal, and Geneva was rightly dubbed the Protestant Rome, wherein Calvin was the Protestant Pope.

Besides Switzerland, where it absorbed the Zwinglian influence, Calvinism made a considerable impression in neighboring France, especially among the upper layers of society. The result was warfare, civil-religious, that filled much of that country's history during the second half of the century.

It penetrated the Empire also, but the Peace of Augsburg found Catholics and Lutherans united in checking its spread. In the Netherlands, however, it was eminently successful. The Dutch Reformed Church came to command the allegiance of the majority of the people in the northern (Dutch) provinces. Eastward from Switzerland, in Hungary and Poland, Calvinism achieved important, if temporary, success.

In Scotland, John Knox (1515-1572), initially a priest, found himself in sympathy with the reforming tendencies of the age. A sojourn in Geneva brought out his fundamental agreement with Calvin. Returned to Scotland, the struggle for religious reform merged with the political issue centering around Catholic Mary Stuart. Knox won a complete victory and Scotland has since been essentially Presbyterian.

4. The Doctrine of Calvinism. Calvinist churches were permeated by the austere stamp of their founder. Like Luther, but to a much greater degree, Calvin put stress on "faith," to such an exclusive extent in fact as to develop a doctrine of salvation based on predestination. God would choose the "elect," unaware of course in life of their election. The sacramental system was reduced to a minimum, baptism and the

Eucharist alone being retained. As to the latter, it was no more than symbol and commemoration.

The organization of the church likewise was reduced to a minimum, almost eliminated. No episcopate was retained, and the priest was shorn of his sacred character, becoming the presbyter who would lead the congregation whose choice he was. The stress throughout was on simplicity. Elaborate ceremonial, images, artistic decoration, all smacked of pagan corruption; they were distracting elements to be eschewed in the bare unadorned and cold edifice of the temple, deliberate contrast with the Roman Church with its statues and paintings, its priests in gorgeous vestments, and its incense.

C. Anglicanism

England, like the rest of Europe, was affected by the ferment of the time, but the religious issue followed there a peculiar course owing to the influence of her ruler. The marital vagaries of Henry VIII would not alone have caused a schism; grafted on to the circumstances of the time, they resulted in the emergence of the Church of England.

1. Henry VIII. The king had no doctrinal quarrel with Rome. On the contrary, his attack on Lutheranism in 1521, *The Defense of the Seven Sacraments*, had earned him from the Pope the title of Defender of the Faith, still borne by English rulers. If Henry lost the faith he kept the title.

Henry was married to Catherine of Aragon, a marriage made possible by Papal dispensation, since Catherine was his brother's widow. After some eighteen years of married life, Henry had wearied of his wife, who moreover had failed to present him with a male offspring. Royal philandering was current and accepted practice, but Henry wanted to marry Anne Boleyn who, besides having caught his fancy, might thus provide him with a legitimate male heir. Could not one Pope undo what another had done, that is, declare invalid the earlier dispensation, thereby annulling Henry's marriage to Catherine and make him free to wed Anne? Such was Henry's reasoning, wholly divorced from doctrinal dispute, which led him to sue Pope Clement VII for an annulment.

a. THE "DIVORCE" AND THE BREAK WITH ROME. This was a

case in canon law, hard to keep wholly free, however, from extraneous political influences: the King of England on one side, on the other his wife, whose nephew was Emperor Charles V.[6] The Pope put off a decision, but Henry, never a patient man or one to brook opposition, wearied of these delaying tactics. Failing to procure a verdict by exercising financial pressure, in England and in Rome, he took the formal step of securing a declaration from Cranmer—by him appointed Archbishop of Canterbury—that the ecclesiastical authority in England was competent to judge the case. This challenge of Rome's authority was confirmed by Parliament's enactment, in 1534, that the king was supreme head of the church in England.

2. *Protestantism in England.* The breach had been consummated that proved to be irrevocable. In contrast with Luther and Calvin, no doctrine was challenged by Henry, the issue being confined to one of jurisdiction. Seizure of Church property, important and profitable though it was, did not affect essentials, which were instead rather confirmed by the "Six Articles" enacted into law by Parliament in 1539. Henry avoided extending the controversy beyond the one central issue.

a. EDWARD VI. But the influence of other aspects of the Protestant revolt could not be kept out of England, all the more since she had parted company with Rome. During the short reign of Edward VI (1547-1553), the substitution of English for Latin in the service, the adoption of the *Book of Common Prayer*, abandoning the Catholic view of the Eucharist, tended to give the Church of England a definitely Protestant tinge.

b. "BLOODY" MARY. Edward's half-sister and successor was Mary, daughter of "divorced" Catherine and a Catholic, married in addition to her cousin Philip II of Spain, prime champion everywhere of the Catholic cause. Mary sought to effect a restoration of Catholicism in England. But the change

---

[6] The fact that Emperor Charles V was a defender of Catholicism made it all the more necessary for the Pope to defer to him. It was in 1527 that the Imperial troops, though not by order of the Emperor, indulged in the sack of Rome.

had already struck roots that were too deep, her reign was too
short (1553-1558), and she merely succeeded in attaching the
epithet "bloody" to her name in English annals, owing to the
coercive measures to which she had resort.

c. ELIZABETH I. Henry's daughter by Anne Boleyn, Elizabeth, was next on the English throne. Elizabeth was not one to
be troubled by fine points of theological dispute, salvation,
grace, or the precise nature of the Eucharist. Her approach to
the task of ruling was basically political.[7] Shrewd judge of the
possible, she adopted a policy designed to minimize divergence
and avoid the disrupting strife of which neighboring France,
less wisely led, gave an example.

The breach with Rome persisted; the bearer of the English
crown would also be supreme ecclesiastical head, and the
Anglican Church was definitely Protestant in character. Cranmer's *Book of Common Prayer* was essentially retained, but
the doctrine defined in the "Thirty-nine Articles" enacted by
Parliament was calculated to leave room for ambiguity and
choice rather than stress sharp distinction. The policy was
successful. Within the broad limits of lenient interpretation
there must be uniformity: Catholic "papists" and radical
Protestant dissenters were alike persecuted. But England was
internally at peace under Elizabeth and, by the end of her
reign, was essentially Protestant.

D.   The Catholic Reformation or Counter Reformation

The establishment of Protestant churches, whose common
ground was rejection of the authority of Rome, represented a
revolutionary success. As with most revolutions, the origins
are to be found in the abuses and blindness of the established
authority, the success in a suitable combination of circumstances among which the political loom large. But the revolt
in this case did not wholly supplant or destroy the formerly
established order. The area of its control reduced, the Church
of Rome survived. This was, in part at least, due to the fact
that it embarked upon the task of internal reformation.

1. The Popes. This demand for reform was widespread.

---

[7] She had, however, a stake in adhering to her father's position, else her
very legitimacy would be questioned, as indeed it was by Catholics.

Men like Erasmus, who parted company with Luther, pointedly called attention to abuse and corruption in the Roman structure. Nowhere more than in Rome itself, at the papal court, were these conspicuous and flagrant.[8] Also, it was becoming clear as the century approached its halfway mark that the revolt was making serious progress.

In these circumstances, the papacy itself undertook the task of purification. Beginning with Paul III (1534-1549), a series of reforming Popes during the rest of the century restored the papal office to its proper function, rewarding virtue and competence rather than wealth and family connection. Their example and policy seeped down into the lower hierarchy.

2. Loyola and the Jesuits. But, as often the case before, reform came also from below. Ignatius Loyola (1491-1556), a Spaniard, was fighting in the armies of Charles V. He too experienced a "conversion," the effect of which was dedication to the service of the Church. While completing, or acquiring, his education he gathered together the small band that was to be the nucleus of the Society of Jesus, or Jesuit order.

The Society was military in the form of its organization. Its members had to undergo a long and arduous training, the factor of obedience was particularly stressed, and a special vow of allegiance to the Pope was required of them. Launched in 1534, the Society received papal sanction after some hesitation on the Pope's part. The Jesuits and their work have been painted in a variety of hues, ranging from the very darkest. Of their effectiveness and competence there can be little question. The initial intent of the order was missionary: some of their work, along this and related lines, outside of Europe, has been mentioned.

But their most important achievement lay in Europe itself. Here their training and their learning made them effective agents in stemming and even causing to recede the Protestant tide. Their tools were mainly two, preaching and education. In Hungary and Poland, in southern Germany, where the situation had not yet crystallized, they came to debate and

---

[8] The Protestant view must be stressed that what was being attempted was a restoration (Reformation) of Christianity to its initial purity of purpose and practice, from which it was Rome that had deviated.

reconvert. As teachers in the schools they were unsurpassed. As their fame grew, so did their influence, and they were to be found close to high positions of power, often advising princes.

3. *The Council of Trent*. There had been two aspects of the Protestant revolt: the attack on abuses and corruption, and the questioning of dogma. Of the two, the second was ultimately more serious. With both aspects in mind, a general Council of the Church was called. It met in Trent, on the geographical dividing line of controversy, intermittently from 1545 to 1563. The Protestants having declined to attend, its task was limited to matters within the Catholic fold.

Briefly, the Council's work may be summed up under two heads. On the score of reform and organization, the work already under way was confirmed and extended. Discipline, proper practice, sound education for the clergy, were reviewed and tightened. Abuses and wrongdoing were acknowledged and measures taken for their extirpation. On the doctrinal score, no room for compromise was found. Protestant views on grace and faith and sacraments were all rejected, and the theology of Thomas Aquinas reasserted. From Trent, the Church of Rome emerged purified and strengthened, but also inflexible and crystallized.

Along with the purification of its practice and the reorganization of its central government, the Church of Rome took measures to insure against future deviation. Revised and uniform editions of catechism and service books, as well as the Vulgate, Latin edition of the Bible, were part of this. In addition, an Index, or list of forbidden books, was prepared, and the medieval Inquisition was revived, especially in Spain and Italy.

III.   THE BALANCE SHEET

A.   The Divisions of Christianity

As the century drew toward its close, it was apparent that the Protestant revolt against Rome had made good its hold on a substantial part of Europe. The eastern, or Greek Orthodox, domain had been untouched by the upheaval, but western Christendom was irrevocably divided. Rome retained the allegiance, either in whole or in overwhelming measure, of the Latin countries, Portugal, Spain, France, and Italy. The southern Netherlands and some of the Swiss cantons were also Catholic, and, roughly, the southern half of the Empire, as well as Hungary and Poland. The rest of Europe, in one or other form, was Protestant. The line of demarcation was not absolute: there were Catholics in England, and there were Protestants in France and Hungary, but the religious composition of Europe has altered little after the sixteenth century.

B. Significance and Legacy of the Revolt

1. The Principle of Authority. The initial motivation of Protestantism was reform rather than rebellion. Disputation, the heat of controversy, and political factors, produced the formal break. But perhaps most important of all was the rejection, either asserted or merely implied at first, of the principle of authority embodied in the churchly institution. The consequences of this were not fully realized for some time; they were none the less profound and may be placed under two heads.

2. The Atomization of Protestantism. Luther in his questioning was led to exalt the Bible as his authority, a tendency largely shared by other Protestants. In the last analysis, that meant the Bible as understood by Luther. Theoretically, one might argue that the truth is one, the truth is in the Bible, hence this same truth will be found there by all. The naïveté of this reasoning need hardly be exposed. In fact, Luther and Calvin did not find wholly identical truths in the ultimate source.

The outcome was a compromise which is in essence logically weak. The unlimited resort to personal interpretation would be an obvious invitation to chaos. Something had to be retained of the Roman position of institutional authority for guidance and interpretation. Thus there arose Protestant churches, Lutheran, Calvinist, and Anglican.

But this could only be an intermediate stage. If Luther and Calvin could differ from the Pope and Rome, what was to prevent anyone from disagreeing with Luther and Calvin themselves? The Protestant challenge had in itself seeds of further challenge. And this is, in fact, what happened. From the time of its birth, the story of Protestantism has been one of increasing differentiation, of an ever-growing multiplicity of sects, retaining little more in common than the heritage of reverence for the figure of Christ and for the Bible, although the initial three main divisions have persisted in commanding the allegiance of large groups.

a. RADICAL SECTS. As might be expected, these multiplying sects tended to exhibit radical tendencies, stressing the factor of personal interpretation at the expense of authority. Some put great stress ón the emotional aspects of personal religious experience. The epithet "evangelical" has been used to describe this approach, of which Thomas Münzer's (1489-1525) Anabaptists and Mennonites are examples. In England, where the hierarchical structure was least disturbed, the radical approach stressing the egalitarian aspect of the membership gave rise to Congregationalism.

Just as the nature of the Eucharist had been questioned, so there soon appeared some to question the divinity of Christ. These were the Unitarians, among whom are distinguished names. Michael Servetus, whom Calvin had burned in Geneva, is one, and so are the Sozzini, Italians, much of whose activity is associated with Hungary and Poland. The process of atomization has ever since continued.

3. *Protestantism and Free Thought*. The question might be raised of how much is left of any religious content in Unitarianism.[9] If Christ is a purely human, though revered, figure; if the Holy Book is merely an important literary and historical work, much of it allegorical, then a dispassionate view, mainly rational and eschewing the supernatural, has been reached. This was not the prevalent view of early Protestantism, but its initial seed of questioning had made it possible to make the transition toward a position where dogma and divinity had vanished.

Protestantism is not free thought, but can easily serve as a bridge, through its flexible variation and fluidity, toward such a state. It will thus appear that while the Protestant revolt

---

[9] "Theological" would perhaps be a better term than "religious" here. This in itself bears witness to the decreasing importance attached to dogma in the evolution of Protestantism.

opened a path of ever further questioning, Rome had the precisely opposite reaction of rigidly defining and crystallizing its doctrine. Protestantism, itself a factor in giving the modern world its shape, has the asset of flexible adaptability which might conceivably lead to its own demise through ultimate disintegration. Catholicism has the asset of the logical consistency derived from clearly realized assumptions; this makes for strength and inadaptability, and a conceivably similar outcome.[10]

4. The Issue of Tolerance. This distinction, however, is not one that was clear in the sixteenth century. Luther's own outlook was essentially medieval; he had *the* truth, hence could not compromise and would even enforce its acceptance. On the score of the unicity of truth there was general agreement. If truth is one and all else false, yet there is no consensus, the step is short that will lead to the attempted enforcement of conformity. Our religiously emasculated age may have difficulty in granting the rationality of intolerance and in appreciating the intensity and violence of sixteenth-century religious feeling. Yet one should realize that the sixteenth century was an age of intolerance, in many ways akin to our own, though we now choose to call our differences ideological and stress political instead of theological content.

This temper is worth emphasizing, especially in view of subsequent interpretations of the Reformation. Allowing for the role of political and economic factors, the fact remains that the Reformation was first and foremost a religious upheaval. But if sixteenth-century men would with enthusiasm cut each other's throats because they differed on the Eucharist, it so turned out that their different views were in the end not able either to convince or to eliminate each other. After a time the weariness of stalemate produced *de facto* acceptance of the inevitable coexistence of difference; if intolerance is the more rational, tolerance may be the more expedient way.

a. THE EDICT OF NANTES. The Peace of Augsburg gave

---

[10] There will be occasion to consider the connection between the Protestant revolt and the subsequent evolution of thought to the eighteenth century Enlightenment.

The greater rigidity of Catholicism accounts for the much greater strength of anticlericalism in Catholic than in Protestant countries.

equal status to Catholicism and to Lutheranism in the Empire,
though both agreed that there was no room for Calvinism.
That settlement was far from being the end of religious
struggles in the Empire. But forty years later, in 1598, Henry
IV of France issued in that country the Edict of Nantes after
it had long been torn by religious strife.

Henry IV, like his contemporary Elizabeth of England,
was anxious to minimize the divisive effects of religious controversy. France was predominantly Catholic, but the Protestants, or Huguenots as they were known in France, were a
powerful faction. Having become a Catholic himself,[11]
Henry IV granted the Huguenots freedom of conscience and
the right of public worship in a number of specified towns.
Their books could be published, their civil rights were un-
impaired, and by way of guarantee, they were to have control
of some two hundred fortified towns. The Edict was inspired
by a genuine spirit of compromise. It put an end to civil
strife in France and may be said to have been the first important instance of true religious tolerance, the model of
which was destined to be gradually extended in Europe and
elsewhere.

5. Religion, Politics, and Economics. The consequences
of the sixteenth-century religious upheaval were associated
with all aspects of contemporary life. The stress on reform
and purification was at first inimical to learning, to art, and to
amenities in general. The main Protestant churches were established and associated with the state in closer union than had
been the case under the supranational aegis of Rome. Henry
VIII was supreme ecclesiastical head of the Anglican Church.
But Catholic Francis I, if he did not head a similar Gallican
establishment, obtained in 1516 a Concordat that gave broad
rights to the French crown in the affairs of the Roman
Church in Gaul. National monarchy was helped by this.

The confiscation of church property, in England and elsewhere, served to create a vested interest in the change once it

---

[11] Henry IV's conversion was naturally a controversial act. "Paris is well
worth a mass," is one version of it. There had been growing in France a
party of so-called *politiques,* represented by such men as Montaigne, whose
attitude toward religious difference was "live and let live," or alternatively "a
plague on both your houses."

had been enacted. The Calvinistic creed especially found wide response among the commercial class, to whom the economic changes of the day were giving increased importance. The contention that material success is outward sign of divine favor is one of the less attractive manifestations of the spirit of mercantile endeavor.

Eventually, and by indirection, the Protestant revolt was favorable to the spirit of critical, unfettered inquiry that was to culminate in the eighteenth-century Enlightenment. The same is true, to a degree, regarding the development of democratic institutions, though other factors also enter here.

Before tracing such changes we must turn for a time to the more purely political development of Europe in this age of violent turmoil and change.

ADDITIONAL READINGS

Janelle, Pierre, *The Catholic Reformation* (1949); MacKinnon, James, *Calvin and the Reformation* (1936); Murray, R. H., *Political Consequences of the Reformation* (1926); Palm, Franklin C., *Calvinism and the Religious Wars* (1932); Pascal, Roy, *The Social Basis of the German Reformation* (1933); Powicke, F. M., *The Reformation in England* (1941); Roth, Cecil, *The Spanish Inquisition* (1937); Smith, H. Maynard, *Henry VIII and the Reformation* (1948); Smith, Preserved, *The Age of the Reformation* (1920); Smith, Preserved, *Martin Luther* (1911); Troeltsch, Ernst, *Protestantism and Progress* (1912); Williston, Walker, *John Calvin: the Organizer of Reformed Protestantism, 1509-1564* (1906).

CHAPTER 5

The Spanish Century

It has been pointed out that one of the most significant features of the turn from the fifteenth to the sixteenth century, a development pregnant with consequences for the future, was the emergence of "national" monarchies along the Atlantic seaboard. The appearance of able and strong rulers evinced wide, if tacit, support in countries weary of the strife of rival lords and houses. This is especially the case in England and in France. In the former country, the house of Tudor, beginning with Henry VII (1485-1509), is rightly credited with laying the foundations of consolidation. The same applies to his contemporary Louis XI (1461-1483) in France. In Spain, Ferdinand of Aragon and Isabella of Castile, reigning jointly till 1504, cleared the newly formed country of the last Moorish remnants while laying the extensive Spanish claims in the New World. By 1500, in all three countries the crown was firmly planted in control, while the Empire and Italy were torn by the divisive multiplicity of a multitude of princes and states. In the east, huge but amorphous Poland was striving in an ultimately unsuccessful search for a unifying principle, and the Ottoman Turk was advancing from the southeast in his still successful conquering progress.

The Italian Wars. Of the various fragments of the Italian peninsula, the largest, the southern Kingdom of Naples, belonged to the Aragonese house, as well as the islands of Sicily and Sardinia. In the north, Milan, for whose rule struggled the rival families of Sforza and Visconti, was under loose allegiance to the Empire.

As the result of earlier marital connections, the French crown was in a position to advance claims to both Milan and

Naples. Charles VIII (1483-1498) and Louis XII (1498-1515) were less able rulers than their predecessor Louis XI, but they did not endanger the solid edifice that he had built. Rather they thought to use the strength and the resources of France to make good their Italian claims. In 1494, French armies appeared in the peninsula. The northern "barbarians" would not abide by the rules of a game played with comparative urbanity by the *condottieri*-led armies of Italy, of whom they easily disposed.

Moreover, there was no unity in Italy in opposing the French invaders. In the eyes of Florence, Venice, the Pope, and rival Milanese factions, this was merely a new element to be used in the pursuit of their own small-scale international politics, into the shifting combinations of which there is no cause to delve. What is of greater moment is the fact that French power collided in Italy with another power of comparable dimensions, the Spanish. For the first half of the sixteenth century, Italy was the battleground of France and Spain. France was fated to ultimate defeat, having wasted much substance in these Italian wars, but more important still, the contest over Italy turned out to be but a phase of a conflict of European dimensions.

I.   THE AGE OF CHARLES V

A.   The Domain of Charles V

1. Charles V's Direct Inheritance. It has been said of the Habsburg house that, while others used warfare to enhance their fortunes, it obtained these results through the use of marital policy. Dynastic marriages, always important, play at this point a crucial role.

Ferdinand and Isabella were rulers of Aragon and of Castile, respectively. When Isabella died in 1504, their daughter Joan ruled with her father. Ferdinand lived until 1516, when the whole inheritance would become Joan's. Meantime, however, Joan had married Philip Habsburg who, from his mother Mary of Burgundy, inherited the Netherlands. Philip's father was the Holy Roman Emperor, Maximilian I. Philip died in 1506, but from his marriage to Joan two sons were born, Charles and Ferdinand. Joan has gone down in history as Joan the Mad.

She was declared incompetent to rule, with the result that when his grandfather Ferdinand died, Charles found himself ruler of the whole united Spanish kingdom and of his father's Burgundian appanage as well. This is how Spanish rule came to be established in the Netherlands and in Franche Comté. Charles himself, born in 1500, from the locale of his early upbringing considered himself a Netherlander and was a stranger to his larger possession, Spain.

2. The Imperial Election of 1519. Three years later, in 1519, Charles' Habsburg grandfather died. The imperial succession was open, and though it had become the custom to bestow it upon a member of the Habsburg house it was after all elective. Henry VIII of England, and even more Francis I of France, thought it worth a substantial expenditure to vie for the position.[1] However, customary tradition prevailed, and Charles I of Spain was elected Holy Roman Emperor Charles V. Since the New World possessions went with Spain, Charles was thus truly lord of the first empire over which the sun never set.

3. Resources and Problems of the Domain of Charles V. The resources of the totality of Charles' possessions were immense, hence his power might seem overwhelming. That this was not the case was due to the disparity of his domains, which confronted him with a variety of disparate problems. His scattered lands, going their several ways, in some respects weakened rather than strengthened each other. Unlike France and England, where the monarchy drew its strength from a compact national domain, Charles' empire was merely dynastic, held together by an allegiance that was purely personal.

a. ADMINISTRATIVE PROBLEMS. The basic task of administration and management alone would have consumed much energy, even if it had not been interfered with by foreign complications. Charles could never reside for long in any one of his possessions. The Netherlands were his own and the brightest, and richest, jewel in his crown; but even they, divided into seventeen provinces, lacked a strong central

---

[1] Despite the advantage deriving from his family connection, Charles found it expedient to indulge in substantial expenditures before the election. These expenses were financed by the Fuggers.

government, while Franche Comté was geographically and politically separate.

In Spain he was a stranger, and his Netherlandish administrators and advisers caused some resentment there. Moreover, Spain and the Italian lands that went with her, were hardly integrated; Charles had to deal in Spain with a number of distinct units, each with its own *cortes* or parliament and ancient rights or *fueros*. Much work had to be done in organizing the administration and exploitation of the New World whose resources were beginning to pour into Spain in growing quantities.

At the other end of Europe, the management of the lands which were the Habsburgs' direct heritage, Austria proper and the neighboring provinces, was turned over to his brother Ferdinand. By marriage in one case, by election in the other, in 1526 Ferdinand added the crown of Bohemia and that of Hungary to the Habsburg collection. The Holy Roman Empire itself was beset by the problem of the religious schism and its potential ramifications. All this had to be dealt with in the midst of foreign involvements.

B. The Policies of Charles V

1. The Contest with France. A glance at the map will show that France was partially surrounded by Charles V's possessions. The reaction to such encirclement, then as on other occasions, is an attempt to break or to weaken the circle. This is the larger frame of the long contest between the houses of France and of Austria, a frame in which specific and limited issues fit as individual illustrations and occasions.

Francis I had come to the French throne in 1515. Flighty and attractive, lover of beauty in women and in art, the gentleman king of the Renaissance, he chose to revive once more the Italian claims of his predecessors. This, plus additional covetous glances toward Navarre and the Netherlands, added to the personal contest for the Imperial crown, to say nothing of the radical contrast in personality, gave ample grounds for conflict.

a. THE STRUGGLE FOR ITALY. The struggle opened in 1522 with Italy as battleground. The French came to Milan, from

which the Imperial forces drove them, and invaded France to
besiege Marseilles. New French armies turned the tide back to
Milan once more. But a decision to go on to Naples gave
the Imperial forces their opportunity. The battle of Pavia in
1525 was an overwhelming French defeat where the king
himself was captured. Charles was somewhat embarrassed by
his royal prisoner, from whom he extracted the Treaty of
Madrid in 1526, a renunciation of all French claims in Italy.

No sooner was he free and back in France than Francis did
the expected in denouncing the treaty signed under duress.
He raised a league of Italian states, fragile as most Italian combinations. War was resumed[2] and another peace, of Cambrai
(1529), once more confirmed French failure. Cambrai was
but a truce; war went on intermittently and the Italian issue
was not finally settled for another thirty years, after the death
of both Francis and Charles, while the north became a more
important theater of operations.[3]

2. The War with the Turks. A common enemy will produce strange alliances. In 1535, His Most Christian Majesty of
France was the first European ruler to join the infidel Turk
in friendship. This was the opening of a new chapter in the
long tale of French interest and action in the Levant. Immediate political necessity ignored the lifting of horrified Christian eyebrows in Europe.

The Turks were at this time reaching the heyday of their
power under the able leadership of Soleiman, called The
Magnificent (1520-1566). Continuing their triumphal progress into Europe, they constituted for the whole of it a threat
of the first magnitude, reminiscent of the Arabs' eighth-century
attack. Sweeping past Belgrade, Hungary was invaded. The
flower of Hungarian chivalry fell at Mohacs in 1526 and the
road to Vienna was open. The siege of Vienna in 1529 was
the high water mark of the Turkish advance, for Vienna
successfully resisted and some stability was reached. In 1547,
most of Hungary was recognized a Turkish province, the

---

[2] It is during this phase of the war, in 1527, that the Imperial armies,
in short supply of money and of victuals, proceeded to sack Rome, an
episode of thoroughgoing frightfulness that made a deep impression at the
time.

[3] Charles visited his Italian lands for the first time in 1530, on which
occasion he was crowned Emperor by the Pope at Bologna.

western fringe alone, and that under tribute, remaining in Habsburg hands. The Habsburgs at this time were playing a role as defenders of Christendom comparable to that of Charles Martel's Franks.

3. The Disunited Holy Roman Empire. This effort in itself, however, weakened Charles in dealing with the internal strife of the Empire. This Empire was overwhelmingly Germanic in its composition, and the central issue of this time was that between the centralizing and unifying principle of the crown and the divisive and pluralistic tendency of the princes. The Imperial position was also weakened in this contest by the adherence to an outworn claim to universality. It was to take three centuries before Emperor, princes, towns, knights, and peasants could effectively be brought together. The fact that in the intervening period division reigned supplies one of the keys to an understanding of the Germanic world and its history.

It is at this juncture that the Lutheran breach took place. The Emperor himself remained loyal to Rome, and his efforts at enforcing uniformity merely led to open revolt. The members of the Schmalkaldic League and the French king found in Charles a common focus of opposition. Thus a Catholic king helped Lutheran princes, who in turn would cooperate with him against their Emperor. The last ten years of Charles' reign saw the Empire a prey to civil war.[4] The provisional stalemate of the Peace of Augsburg (1555) has been discussed before.

C. English Affairs

The first half of the sixteenth century did not find England a very active or effective participant in the affairs of greater powers. England was a small state by comparison with Spain, France, or the Empire. The consolidation of the monarchy

---

[4] Prior to this a Council of Regency had been created in 1521. Its outlawry of Luther helped precipitate the so-called Knights' War in 1522. This movement failed and was soon followed by the Peasants' Revolt. The Knights' War was the final failure of the attempt to create a unified German state. By 1531, the Council of Regency, discredited by its failure, was abolished. In the same year the Schmalkaldic League was organized.

under Henry VIII and the break with Rome fitted in well with
the rising national feeling. Henry's continued marital vagaries
—he was legally married six times—did not interfere with the
growing prestige of the crown.

For a time, Henry's chief adviser, Cardinal Wolsey, an ambitious man given to intrigue and still a controversial figure,
thought to use the quarrel between the Empire and France to
further England's, and his own, advantage by holding a balance of power between the two. Wolsey's calculations, among
the shoals of Henry's religious and marital embroilments,
miscarried. England did not play an important role on the
continent despite a limited degree of involvement, and Wolsey fell in disgrace. The advent to the English throne of
Catholic Mary in 1553 made for better relations with Charles
V, but also had the consequence of losing for England Calais,
her last continental foothold, regained by France.

Emperor Charles, at fifty-six, was gouty, old, and weary of
the cares of power. Bidding farewell in Brussels to representatives of his own cherished Netherlands, he handed the Spanish
crown and all that went with it to his son Philip. His brother
Ferdinand succeeded to the Imperial dignity. Charles lived on
two more years in the shelter of a Spanish monastery. From
1556, two distinct branches of the house of Habsburg, stemming respectively from Ferdinand and Charles, ruled separate
domains. But the dynastic tie remained important for the
future politics of Europe.

II.   THE REIGN OF PHILIP II

For nearly half a century Philip II (1556-1598) was king of
Spain. Philip had been carefully nurtured for his role, which
he assumed and kept performing with conscientious devotion.
Philip worked hard at the kingly trade, too hard in fact, unable to delegate detailed authority and free himself for larger
purposes. Philip, unlike his father, was above all a Spaniard,
and as befitted a Spanish ruler, a staunch Catholic. To the twin
glories of Spain and of the Church his life was dedicated.
Since the Empire was no longer his responsibility, save through
the family connection, to that extent his task was simplified.
Yet Philip's reign was beset with troubles and failures.

A. The War with France and with the Turks

In view of Philip's staunch Catholicism, it may seem odd
that his reign should have opened with a conflict that found
ranged against him the King of France, the Sultan, and the
Pope. This last aspect was minor; by 1559 even the papal ex-
communication had been lifted.[5]

The French quarrel had deeper roots and was a mere continuation of an older contest. Even Paris was threatened for
a time, in 1557, but two years later the Treaty of Cateau
Cambrésis virtually put an end to the Italian phase of Franco-
Spanish rivalry. France was decisively evicted from Italy, but
her occupation of the bishoprics of Metz, Toul, and Verdun—
a gain at the expense of the Empire—pointed to the future and
more important scene of her activity, the northeast and the
Rhine.

1. The French Wars of Religion. In France, after Francis
I and Henry II (1547-1559), the country fell upon evil days.
Henry's three sons, Francis II (1559-1560), Charles IX (1560-
1574), and Henry III (1574-1589), reigned in succession. Incompetent and feeble as they were, their mother Catherine de
Medici dominated the scene. The lack of strong and above all
consistent direction from the crown made possible a revival
of the power and rivalry of the great nobles, and this in turn
became entangled with religious dissent.

The Huguenots had made significant inroads in some sections of the country, and, most important, among the upper
layers of society. The policy of the crown was hesitant, now
leaning on this faction, then encouraging the opposite, in a
mistaken application of the principle of divide and rule. For
thirty years, after 1562, the country was torn by religious
wars somewhat reminiscent of those of the Empire.

a. THE THREE FACTIONS. Two great families emerged in
leadership of rival factions. The house of Bourbon, headed by
the King of Navarre, to whom the crown would fall in the

---

[5] The fact of Philip's devotion to Catholicism must not be misunderstood
as implying of necessity smooth relations with the papacy. The old issue of
delimiting the respective spheres of control between civil and religious
power ever continued to trouble the relations between Popes and Catholic
rulers.

likely event that no male heirs would be granted the Valois kings, was Protestant. The Guises of Lorraine led the Catholic party. The duke of Guise had rendered valuable military service, and with his brother the Cardinal of Lorraine, wielded great power.

The Guises enjoyed the favor of Henry II but the queen mother feared their power. One episode attending her vacillating tactics was the massacre of Protestants on St. Bartholomew's night (August 24, 1572). That dark day in French annals merely served to increase mutual distrust and bitterness. In the prolonged deadlock, the very fabric of government seemed to disintegrate. Weary of strife, a third faction emerged, the *politiques*, of which Bodin was an example,[6] who saw nothing but loss to the country from the domestic struggle, hence favored a compromise of live and let live on the religious plane and of union on the national.

b. THE THREE HENRYS. This troubled situation was one where Philip II saw possibilities of profit for both himself and for Catholicism. In 1585, he entered in league with Henry of Guise whom he would help mount the French throne (Henry III had no issue) in exchange for a policy of French collaboration with Spain. The result was the so-called war of the three Henrys: Henry the king, Henry of Guise the aspirant, and Henry of Navarre the heir. Henry III caused Henry of Guise to be murdered in 1588 and himself met a like fate the following year.

This left Navarre alone in the field, but he had virtually to reconquer the country by force of arms. His military successes, followed by his acceptance of Catholicism in 1593, helped pacify the country. Henry's approach was both political and politic. Recognizing the predominantly Catholic character of the country, he issued the Edict of Nantes in 1598,[7] first genuine instance of modern religious toleration. The same year saw the death of Philip of Spain and the restora-

---

[6] Jean Bodin (1520-1596), a political philosopher, whose views stood in contrast with those of Machiavelli, is credited with the modern theory of sovereignty. He favored a limited monarchy in which the Estates General would have a significant role.

[7] See above, p. 67.

tion of peace with that country by the Treaty of Vervins, largely a confirmation of Cateau Cambrésis.

Henry IV, first ruler of the Bourbon line in France, pursued a wise and enlightened course that earned him the affection of his subjects and high rank in the roster of French monarchs. The resources of France were large; properly managed, the bases were now laid for launching her upon a career of greatness.

2. The Turks in the Mediterranean. Lepanto. At the other end of Europe the Turkish failure before Vienna had relieved pressure in that quarter. But the Turks were still actively expanding in the Mediterranean, the western half of which was largely Spanish waters. Their progress in the eastern section was mainly at the expense of Venice; by 1570, Crete and Malta alone were left in Christian hands, while the Balearics and Sicily were objects of their plundering raids.

At this juncture the Pope sought to revive the old crusading spirit. Venice and Genoa furnished the core of naval power, Spain further ships and the commander, Don John of Austria, Philip's half-brother. The naval battle of Lepanto on October 7, 1571 was a thorough disaster for the Turks. The southern pincer of the great enveloping movement with which they threatened Europe was permanently broken. This was one of the few successful undertakings in which Philip engaged.

B.   The Birth of Holland

1. The Situation in the Low Countries. If Philip's policy had failed in France it was partly because his resources were elsewhere occupied. In the Low Countries Philip was a stranger. So likewise were Spanish troops and administrators. This, and economic grievances, taxation, and restrictive practices designed to further Spain's advantage, were the initial sources of friction. Protestantism had also made inroads in the land, and the introduction of the Spanish Inquisition was much resented. Politics, economics, and religion became inextricably entangled in the quarrel between the Netherlands and Spain.

a. THE SPANISH POLICY OF SUPPRESSION. A petition for redress of grievances, in which both Protestants and Catholics joined, was presented to the Regent Margaret of Parma, Philip's half-sister. The contemptuous epithet *gueux* (tramps, beggars) applied to the petitioners was made by them a title of distinction. Outbreaks of violence in the same year caused Philip to send the duke of Alva to the Netherlands. His "Council of Troubles," locally dubbed "Council of Blood," was the instrument of ruthless suppression, the effect of which was mere exacerbation of Catholics and Protestants alike.

2. The Revolt of the Netherlands. Requesens superseded Alva in 1573. In the field, Spanish infantry, the best in Europe, was invincible. But the armies sometimes were diverted toward France and sometimes went unpaid for long periods, at which times they would engage in wholesale and undiscriminating pillage. Such an episode was the "Spanish Fury" in Antwerp in 1576, to which the answer was the "Pacification of Ghent," an agreement covering virtually the seventeen provinces to persevere in the struggle for redress.

a. THE DIVISION BETWEEN NORTH AND SOUTH. In 1578, Alexander Farnese, duke of Parma, was sent to govern the provinces. Meantime, in the leadership of revolt had emerged William of Orange, known to history, though erroneously, as "the Silent," one-time governor of Holland and Zeeland. Farnese was more supple than Alva. Capitalizing on the differences between the seven northern provinces, Dutch, Calvinist, and mercantile, and the ten southern ones, Catholic, partly French, and more given to manufacture, he succeeded in dividing the opposition. In 1579, the southern provinces joined in the defensive League of Arras, while the north formed the Union of Utrecht. Thus were laid the bases for the eventual division between modern Belgium and Holland.

The south was pacified and remained in Spanish hands, but in the north the struggle continued under William's able and stubborn leadership. The Act of Abjuration, rejecting Spanish authority, in which he induced the northern provinces to join in 1581, is the Dutch declaration of independence.

b. DUTCH INDEPENDENCE AND CONSTITUTIONAL DEVELOPMENT. William was murdered in 1584, but the struggle went on. Dutch assets were determination, the nature of the land, sea trade, and sea power;[8] also assistance from Protestants elsewhere and Philip's other simultaneous embroilments. Though unable to subdue the Dutch, Philip refused to the last to recognize them. A twelve year truce in 1609 was tantamount to this, however, but not until 1648, at Westphalia, did Spain formally recognize the long accomplished fact.

The seven provinces formed a federation under a common parliament, the States General, though each retained its government. The constitutional history of Holland is of the greatest interest and significance, antedating the corresponding development in better known, because larger and more powerful, England. Two struggles went on simultaneously in the United Provinces, one between the dominant unit, Holland proper, and the rest; the other between the governor, or Stadholder, and the States General. The Stadholderate became hereditary in the Orange family which, supported by the poorer classes, endeavored to develop monarchical institutions; the commercial aristocracy, represented in the States General, struggled against the increase of the central power. Holland was the early home of freedoms unknown to Europe until much later days.

C. Elizabethan England

1. England under Elizabeth.
The revolting Protestant Dutch, as their coreligionaries in France, had received help from England.[9] In English eyes especially, the Elizabethan era has taken on an aura of greatness. England, during the second half of the sixteenth century was a small and not very powerful state by European standards of the time. But one may rightly say that this was the period when the bases of her future greatness were laid.

Internally, England was soundly managed. Calculating and shrewd, Elizabeth knew how to avoid the religious strife that rent France. The ancient institutions of the state, crown and

---

[8] The "sea beggars" early began to prey upon Spanish trade, and Dutch maritime development became the basis of the Dutch Far Eastern empire and of the country's wealth. In connection with the struggle for Dutch independence, the closing of the Scheldt ruined Antwerp, whose place was taken by Amsterdam.

[9] The English assistance to the French Protestants never assumed the proportions of a major policy.

Parliament, thanks largely again to the skill of the former, continued to operate in harmonious league. The result was to enhance and strengthen the royal power, cautious however not to assert formal and abstract claims to precedence, and the English nation emerged conscious and proud of unity.

When Philip came to the Spanish throne he had been Mary Tudor's husband and had resided for a time in England. Her death in 1558 was a blow to his policy of joining the two countries. Nothing daunted, Philip would have married Anne Boleyn's daughter and striven to restore the Catholic cause in England. Elizabeth was very cool to the Spaniard's advances. Instead, England and Spain were soon embarked on a prolonged conflict. Frustrated but steadfast of purpose, Philip gave aid and encouragement to any and all who would have unseated the English queen. Sedition, conspiracies, assassination plots, were all devices in his armory. All failed, and Elizabeth outlasted Philip five years.

2. Mary of Scotland. The romantic and highly controversial figure of Mary Stuart intrudes at this point. Mary Stuart inherited the Scottish crown. Married to Francis II of France, she returned to her own country after the death of her French husband in 1560. Her rule in Scotland was tormented and brief. Mary was Catholic and although she did not attempt to persecute Protestants, John Knox did not reciprocate her tolerant outlook. A religious-political conflict ensued, and Mary was unable to dominate the unruly factions of rival nobles. She evidenced, moreover, less than wisdom in the management of her private affairs: her marriage to her cousin Darnley was followed by another wedding to Bothwell, thought to be involved in Darnley's murder. The possible implications were obvious, and Mary, hounded by her enemies, abdicated the Scottish throne and took refuge in England in 1568.

a. ELIZABETH AND MARY. England's Elizabeth and Scotland's Mary were both descended from Henry VII. If Elizabeth's legitimacy, hence right to rule in England, were questioned, as in the Catholic view it was, Mary would be the rightful claimant to the English throne. However that might be, Mary's son James was in any event the heir to both crowns if Elizabeth had no issue. The statement attributed to Elizabeth that "there is not enough room in England for two queens" aptly sums up the situation. Whether she would or no, Mary was the natural and inevitable focus of intrigues and plots such as Philip encouraged. After twenty years of virtual imprisonment in England, Mary was finally beheaded in 1587.

3. The Anglo-Spanish Conflict. The execution of Mary Stuart in England was a setback to Philip's policy, an episode in the intensifying struggle between rich Spain and rising England. In this as in other struggles in which he was involved, Philip was at the same time fighting against the spread of heresy and against the bold, and often successful, raiders that plundered his treasure fleet.

a. THE INVINCIBLE SPANISH ARMADA. Out of the Tagus River,[10] in 1588, there sailed the greatest accumulation of power hitherto gathered on the sea. The Invincible Armada was to collect the Spanish troops engaged in subduing the Netherlands, and with its own contingent, to effect a landing in England.

Not since the Norman conquest has England been invaded, and seaborne threats of landings have been few. This was one of them and it marks a high point in English history. The unwieldy Spanish fleet, encumbered by its slow and heavily laden galleons, suffered substantial losses in its northward journey to the Channel. From Plymouth and the southern ports, the sea dogs of England set out in smaller, faster, more maneuverable ships, technically far superior to the lumbering Spaniards in seamanship as well as in the use of fire. Badly injured by weather and Englishmen, unable to establish contact with the Netherlandish force, the Armada sailed on through the Straits, and returned to Spain after completing the northern circuit of the British Isles, during the course of which its strength was further depleted.

4. The Mounting Troubles of Spain. It was a sad day for Spain, and a correspondingly glorious one for England. To be sure, many a valuable lesson was learned and put to good use in Spain regarding naval practice. An ambitious English

---

[10] The crown of Portugal had been joined to that of Spain in 1580. Unlike the case of Aragon and Castile, the union did not become permanent, and Portugal re-emerged as a separate entity in 1640.

seaborne attempt against Spain—reverse version of the Armada
—was a failure. Spain continued to be the great power of
Europe, though the mounting troubles with which she seemed
incapable of coping were sapping her strength. Her policies,
if continued, would lead to decline, as in fact they did. For
England, the bases of sea power, foundation of her future
greatness, had been proved in the test.

Philip survived ten years the loss of his armada. As his life
and the century were drawing to a close, his record must
be written largely one of failure, whether in terms of Spanish
or of Catholic power. His, to be sure, was Spain's golden
century in culture. But neighboring France, now emerged
from sterile internecine strife, was about to embark upon a
long career of power. The French displacement of Spain is
one of the important developments of the next half century,
which will be presently surveyed. But first, a brief glance
must be cast at the condition of the east of Europe.

III. EASTERN EUROPE IN THE SIXTEENTH CENTURY

A. The Emergence of Sweden and Russia

Religious differences, national sentiment, and power rivalries became entangled in northeastern Europe no less than in
the west. By the Union of Calmar of 1397 the three modern
Scandinavian countries and Finland were joined under the
Danish crown. There was opposition in Sweden to this union,
which was broken in 1523 with the separation of Sweden-
Finland under the leadership of Gustavus Vasa (1523-1560),
founder of a new dynasty. The economic aspect of this
division is no less important: competition for the inheritance
of the Hanseatic League, or hegemony in the Baltic.

The contest was further complicated by the intrusion of
Russia, or Muscovy. Ivan the Terrible (1533-1584) may be
said to have laid the foundations of the modern Russian state.
Ruthless like some of his successors in that land, and still beset
by Tartar pressure and raids, he managed to reorganize the
state while extending it toward the west. The economic motivation in this push toward the Baltic seems clear; his dealings

with the English Muscovy Company (1567) penetrating Russia from the north are evidence to the same effect.

B.   Poland-Lithuania

The very large state of Poland-Lithuania could not but be involved with both Sweden and Muscovy. The Baltic shore of Livonia (Estonia) was the meeting point of these influences, and the death of Gustavus Vasa in Sweden was followed by a seven years' northern war (1561-1568) in which Denmark and Poland were aligned against Sweden and Muscovy. Poland, moreover, was endowed with a peculiar constitution which militated against the rise of a strong royal power, as did the fact that the elective principle continued to apply to the crown.

1. Poland's Domestic and Foreign Difficulties. With the death of Sigismund II (1548-1572) the Jagellonian dynasty came to an end in Poland. After the unsatisfactory experiment of a French king,[11] Stephen Batory, prince of Transylvania, was elected and reigned until 1586, to be followed by Sigismund III of the house of Vasa.

Sigismund had married into the house of Jagello, but to him came also the Swedish crown in 1592. This further experiment in personal union was also unsatisfactory, for while Sigismund lasted out his reign in Poland (to 1632), he became involved in the attempt to restore Catholicism in Sweden. The definite adoption of the Confession of Augsburg in 1593 set the seal on a separate Swedish church. Sigismund failed to reconquer Sweden, whose fight was led by his uncle Charles Vasa. In 1599, Sigismund was deposed by the Swedish Estates and Charles became king of Sweden as Charles IX. The stage was set for the spectacular, if relatively short-lived, career of Sweden among the constellation of great European powers.

C.   The Ottoman Power

The election of Stephen Batory to the Polish throne in 1574 had been a triumph of Turkish influence, already established

---

[11] Henry of Valois was elected king in 1573. After a brief sojourn in Poland, he fled back to his country and his French crown, becoming Henry III of France (1574-1589).

in Transylvania. The apogee of the Ottoman Empire was reached under Soleiman II, The Magnificent (1520-1566), and was due to the vigor, military skill, and progressive management of the Turkish state. Turkey, like Spain, was soon destined for decline, but her power was long to be felt as a menace. Even from the crushing defeat of Lepanto, Turkey recovered promptly, and, in alliance with Barbary corsairs, was able to extend her sway over the entire North African coast, exclusive of Morocco. But the Mediterranean was already set on the path of eclipse. The centers of power in Europe were shifting toward the north and west.

ADDITIONAL READINGS

Black, J. B., *The Reign of Queen Elizabeth, 1558-1603* (1936); Geyl, Peter, *The Revolt of the Netherlands, 1555-1609* (1932); Grant, Arthur James, *The Huguenots* (1934); Halecki, Oscar, *Borderlands of Western Civilization* (1952); McElwee, William L., *The Reign of Charles V, 1516-1558* (1936); Merriman, Roger B., *Suleiman the Magnificent, 1520-1566* (1944); Mowat, R. B., *A History of European Diplomacy, 1451-1789* (1928); Neale, J. E., *The Age of Catherine de Medici* (1943); Neale, J. E., *Queen Elizabeth* (1934); Oman, Sir Charles, *The Sixteenth Century* (1936); Pollard, A. F., *Henry VIII* (1913); Trevor Davies, R., *The Golden Century of Spain, 1501-1621* (1937); Wright, Louis B., *Middle Class Culture in Elizabethan England* (1935).

CHAPTER 6

Spain, France and the Empire

I. THE RECONSTRUCTION OF FRANCE

The development of three states—England, France, and the Empire[1]—from the close of the sixteenth century presents marked and interesting contrasts. In the first, the central power of the crown seemed securely established and by way of becoming stronger; certainly it appeared the most stable of the three in its internal structure. Yet it turned out to be the most torn by domestic strife during the following century. The constitutional story of England in this period, of utmost significance, not for England alone, but for Europe and the world as a whole, will be surveyed in a separate chapter.

For Germany, or the Empire, the sixteenth century had been one of internal turmoil where the religious issue had become intermingled with the struggle between the central imperial authority and that of local princes. The struggle was destined to continue and the disintegrating force of diversity to pursue its successful progress. The Empire had to be destroyed before rebuilding from the bottom and on a different basis could be undertaken in the Germanic world. But that was not to be until the nineteenth century.

Like the Empire, France had divisive tendencies within her, and the religious wars of the second half of the century have similarities with those of the Empire. Regionalism was still

---

[1] From the point of view of constitutional development, the English and the French are the most significant in this period; they will be treated in later chapters. The Spanish offers little that is novel. The present chapter is primarily concerned with power relationships and the international situation.

strong in France and the strife of religious difference had
served the cause of the power of the nobles. In which direction France would go, might, around 1600, appear a debatable
question. Yet it was France that was to furnish the example of
greatest stability and closest integration. This, when combined
with her resources, was to give her the place of power that
she was to achieve and long maintain in Europe.

A.   The Reign of Henry IV (1589-1610)[2]

Henry IV, the good king, was an attractive personality and,
what is more important, an able ruler. Moreover, he enjoyed
the asset of the work of national integration effected by earlier
kings, among whom Louis XI was the most outstanding. The
fruit of this work, founded as it was on the solid ground of
much common heritage, had not been wholly dissipated by the
subsequent internecine struggles. Granted good management,
it would be easier further to integrate the French nation than
permanently to disintegrate the state.

1. Henry IV's Domestic Policy. Henry IV correctly realized that what the country needed above all was internal
peace that would allow its reconstruction.

a. RELIGIOUS PEACE. The Edict of Nantes reassured the
Protestant minority but met with strong Catholic suspicion.
It had to be enforced by the king against the opposition of
several *parlements*, supreme law courts in the provinces. Religious tolerance and peace were maintained.

b. ECONOMIC DEVELOPMENT. This done, Henry turned to
the task of economic revival. The loss and ravages of prolonged
civil war had been great. In his task of reconstruction he was
ably assisted by his chief minister, a Huguenot, the Duke of
Sully. The stress was placed by him on the encouragement
of agriculture as the chief source of strength of the national
economy. The slogan of "a chicken in the pot on Sunday for
every peasant," seventeenth-century version of the "two-car
garage for every family," in homely and understandable
language aptly expressed this policy.

---

[2] Although the reign of Henry IV formally begins in 1589, it was some
years before he was in control of the country, let alone in a position to
initiate major policies.

Sully would have neglected manufacture, but the king gave free scope to another advisor, the curious character of Barthélemy de Laffemas, in this field. The silkworm, for example, was introduced in France at this time to become the basis of an important and prosperous industry. Commerce too was encouraged, and France began to intrude on the high seas where Spanish, Dutch, and English had preceded her.

At the same time, state finances were managed with care; at home, a policy of retrenchment, combined with effective collection, produced a surplus in the royal coffers, while a policy of peace abroad made possible a curtailment of the military establishment. The "Grand Design" for universal peace, though perhaps biased to serve French interest and certainly premature, is associated with Henry's name.

B.   The Interim (1610-1624)

When Henry IV was assassinated in 1610 by a religous fanatic he was widely and sincerely mourned. His passing raised a serious issue, for Marie de Medici, his widow, became regent pending the coming of age of nine year old Louis XIII (1610-1643).

The queen regent was an ambitious, but unbalanced, woman who fell under the sway of her personal favorites, Italian and others. The fragility of Henry IV's edifice appeared with a recrudescence of the intrigues of the great nobles and a threat of revival of the religious issue. The financial surplus was also soon dissipated in the granting of favors. For some fifteen years the question was open of what the course and fate of France would be.

This accumulation of difficulties led to a calling of the Estates General in 1614. The three orders—Clergy, Nobility, and Third Estate—that represented the nation had little ground in common and even greater divisions within themselves. The issue of the status of the Gallican church vis-à-vis Rome was quite as important as that of the status of the Huguenots. Little could be accomplished in the circumstances, and the Estates were dismissed in 1615. They were not to meet again for another 174 years, a fact of the utmost significance in the constitutional evolution of the French state, and of especial interest when contrasted with the role of the corresponding body in England.

Eventually, the king rebelled against the close subjection under which his mother had held him. But young Louis XIII, unlike his father, had neither strength, determination, nor clarity of purpose. His quarrel with his mother merely added a further complication to an already many-sided contest.

C. The "Reign" of Richelieu (1624-1642)

1. Richelieu's Character and Aims. Richelieu came from the small nobility of Poitou, from the class that, unlike the great nobles, was being impoverished by the economic changes of the time. Without prospects elsewhere, Richelieu had been trained for an ecclesiastical career. At twenty-one he was a bishop. The notice taken of him by Marie de Medici during the Estates of 1614 was the beginning of his fortune; for politics Richelieu was far better suited than for Holy Orders. Highly ambitious, even vain, of mediocre health but iron will, calculating and cool, all head and little heart, Richelieu fitted to a nicety the requisites of Machiavelli's Prince. He was undoubtedly a statesman of the highest caliber, of the breed to which Bismarck also belongs, and like the latter, in human or moral terms a personality of questionable attractiveness.

Not until 1624 was Richelieu firmly established in the confidence and control of the king. Even then, his path was not always smooth and he had to resort at times to the use of the ultimate and ever successful weapon, the threat of resignation. During the twenties, his policy was still hesitant and confused in appearance though his purpose was set. Apart from personal ambition, enjoyment of the use of power, this purpose was twofold: to consolidate and make supreme the power of the crown at home; to enhance the French crown to a dominant position in Europe. The first was a prerequisite to the second.

2. Richelieu's Domestic Policies

a. THE PROTESTANT QUESTION. Richelieu was a cardinal of the Roman Church and suspected of ultramontane and Spanish leanings. To many Catholics, Rome and the Jesuits were hardly less distasteful than Huguenots. But the latter enjoyed in some respects a position of privilege that might lead to their constituting a state within the state.[3] To this danger, the conditions that followed the death of Henry IV had given point. Richelieu set about breaking the political power of the Huguenots.

In order to do this, military action was needed, of which the long siege of La Rochelle in 1627-1628 was the high point. When the king entered the city, its population had been reduced from about 22,000 to some 6,000; Richelieu knew how to be ruthless. The triumph was a success against England as well, who had sought, like the Dutch, and failed, to assist the beleaguered city by sea. In fact, foreign assistance weakened the Huguenot cause in France, for there were those among them who placed national above religious allegiance—as Catholics had done in England before the Spanish threat of the Armada.[4]

To the disappointment of the more fanatical Catholics, Richelieu now gave evidence of his statesmanship by contenting himself with the political results of his victory. By the Edict of Alais (1629) Protestants were allowed in France freedom of conscience and of worship and access to public office, but were deprived of political privilege and fortified positions.

b. THE NOBLES. The power of the nobles was even more difficult to break than that of the Huguenots. Understandably, they hated Richelieu, and the story is long, picturesque, and full of plots and intrigues, especially as the king's own mother and his brother sought to hamper the Cardinal's work. But Richelieu could plot, intrigue, and spy with the best.[5] No noble head, however exalted, was sacred to him, and not a few were made to fall. The enforcement of his decree to raze all private fortifications save those that might be useful for purposes of national defense,[6] is a measure of his success, traces of which are to this day outstanding.

---

[3] Most significant in this respect was their control of some two hundred fortified towns.

[4] These are interesting examples and measures of the degree of development of "national" feeling at this time.

[5] Father Joseph, the "grey eminence," was Richelieu's right-hand man in directing much of this work. A mysterious character and an excellent subject for romantic, novelized history.

[6] This decree, incidentally, met with considerable approval among the peasantry.

c. ADMINISTRATIVE REORGANIZATION. Beyond this negative part of his task, Richelieu went on to more positive measures. The framework of the administration of the state was thoroughly reorganized. The new office of *intendant*, endowed with wide powers of police, justice, and taxation, was created. Most important, the *intendants* were usually chosen from the upper layer of the Third Estate, the competent and rising *bourgeoisie*, instead of among the great nobles.

These men were wholly dependent for their position upon the royal favor, and thus a powerful alliance was created between the crown and the vested interest of this new class of dependents. The *bourgeoisie*, at this time, found no cause to object to greater power for the crown in which it saw greater advantage for itself.[7]

For this work, Richelieu has properly been called the founder of the modern French state. The centralizing path on which he set the country has since been trodden uninterruptedly by monarchy, empire, and republic, and has made France the most highly centralized state of Europe. Richelieu had indeed succeeded in exalting the power of the crown in France. The ultimate value and consequences of his work may be questioned, but in the context of his time he undoubtedly contrived to forge a modern and effective tool. What use was made of this tool in the larger frame of Europe will best be examined in connection with the episode of the Thirty Years' War.

D. Mazarin

Richelieu died in 1642, to be followed the next year by his king. The new king, Louis XIV, was aged five, thus opening the always risky prospect of a new minority and a regency. This was the time to test the solidity of Richelieu's work.

Distrustful of his Spanish wife and of his worthless brother, Louis XIII had created a council where first place would be held by Mazarin. Mazarin was Richelieu's "legacy" to the French crown. Like Richelieu a cardinal, an Italian by birth who never could fully master French, Mazarin was destined

---

[7] What would now be called business interests were generally in favor of a strong central power and executive, which to them meant the favorable conditions of domestic stability and peace by contrast with the disorder attending the quarrels of great nobles.

to take over and carry on his predecessor's work until the king would in his own right govern. Though treading the same paths of government, Mazarin presents a thorough contrast with Richelieu. Both were able, but where the latter used force and will, Mazarin was all softness and wiles.

Many a sigh of relief was breathed in 1643, for Richelieu had had many enemies. The *Parlement* of Paris[8] annulled the late king's decree instituting the council, but Mazarin managed to reappear as chief minister. Intended by the late king to act as supervisor of the queen-regent, he filled precisely that function. Only he did it, under the revised arrangement, through the subtler device of gaining her full confidence, even affection.

1. The Fronde.[9] But Mazarin had no easy time in making good his position in the government. From Richelieu he had inherited a poor financial situation—revenues mortgaged long in advance. The search for further revenue created discontent and obstruction, the instrument of which was Paris, its people, and its *parlement*. To a degree encouraged by the contemporary English example, the *parlement* in 1648 asserted various far-reaching claims. There were barricades in Paris, but the movement was not well organized or led and was put down with relative ease when troops were brought to the capital. The "Parliamentary Fronde" is an interesting episode, but lacked the roots and the support that might have challenged royal authority in France in a manner comparable to the English.

There was also a Fronde of the nobles in which some of the greatest military names of the day—Turenne and Condé—

---

[8] The *parlements,* of which there were thirteen in France, were judicial bodies. That of Paris, of especial eminence, had come to have the right of "registering" royal decrees. From this followed that a refusal to "register," if made good, might make the Paris *parlement* a rival of the crown. The king could, by personal appearance before it (*lit de justice*), order the *parlement* to "register" his orders. Here was the making of a test of power comparable in some ways to that contemporarily taking place in England.

The example of English events had some influence in France at this time, but the French *parlement* was not a representative body and is not to be confused with the English Parliament whose origin and composition are entirely different.

[9] The name derives from a children's game played with a sling, hence expresses the nuisance value rather than seriousness of the movement.

were involved. It, too, collapsed, and by the early fifties Mazarin was fairly in control. The royal power was all the stronger for having successfully withstood this last challenge. Nobles and *parlement* had definitely and finally lost in the contest, and the monarchy could proceed toward the practice as well as the theory of absolutism unfettered.

When Mazarin died in 1661 and Louis XIV began to govern in his own name, the path was clear for him and the ground was prepared for the condition that he was to describe in his famous mot: "L'État, c'est moi."

II.   THE DISINTEGRATION OF GERMANY

The reorganized power of the French state was effectively used during the first half of the seventeenth century to enhance the position of France among the states of Europe. This meant an active foreign policy, which Richelieu and Mazarin alike pursued. The measure of their success was the displacement of Spain by France in first place of power. But the chief focus of contest was no longer in Italy, or along the Pyrenees, but rather along the expanding northeastern frontiers of France. Other powers were inevitably, and for their own ends, involved in the struggle, the chief focus and battleground of which was Germany, or the Empire.

Looked at from the point of view of the latter, the long struggle that goes under the name of the Thirty Years' War is one of the most important—and catastrophic—events of German history, pregnant with long term consequences, and in which the Franco-Spanish contest was but secondarily involved.

A.   Background and Origin of the Thirty Years' War

1. The Religious Situation. The Peace of Augsburg in 1555 had effected a compromise between the warring factions in the Empire. The principle *cujus regio ejus religio* had at the same time been a measure of the success of localism against the central power. The settlement of Augsburg proved to be but a truce, not the beginning of peace in stabilization of the religious differences. Moreover, the provisions of the settlement were not observed, chiefly in two respects. The moratorium on further secularization of ecclesiastical property (ecclesiastical reservation) was honored in the breach; especially in the south and west, in contact with lands where Calvinism had successfully taken root, that variety of Protestantism had made significant inroads.

In addition to this, the successors of Charles' brother, Ferdinand, in the Imperial dignity, Maximilian II (1564-1576), Rudolph II (1576-1612), and Matthias (1612-1619), proved to be generally weak and incompetent princes unable to arrest the disintegrating process of the Empire. The stresses that developed under the last two named Emperors were the prelude to a renewal of civil war. The immediate and narrow causes of the Thirty Years' War are religious, though the conflict was to extend much beyond this limited aspect, until the political, economic, and even international components of it were to be paramount.

The formation of rival leagues, in 1608 a union of Protestant princes led by the Calvinist Frederick, Elector Palatine; the next year a similar Catholic league of which Duke Maximilian of Bavaria was the head, was preparation for an open clash.[10]

2. The Defenestration of Prague. The specific occasion for this developed in Bohemia. In that kingdom, whose crown the Habsburgs wore, Calvinism, grafted on to the old Hussite tradition, had achieved definite success, and there was fear lest Matthias' successor, known as a staunch adherent of Rome, might tamper with Bohemian liberties. The "defenestration" of Prague in 1618, the physical ejection through a castle window of the Emperor's representatives, was followed by the proclamation of the Palatine Elector as King of Bohemia.

B.   The Thirty Years' War

1. The Bohemian Phase (1618-1625). Frederick accepted the crown though he would have to fight to make his title good. He expected a never forthcoming assistance from his English father-in-law, James I. The Emperor, now Ferdinand II, proceeded to attack Bohemia from Austria, while

---

[10] On one point both sides were in agreement. Protestant or Catholic, the princes wished further to enhance their power at the expense of the imperial.

Maximilian of Bavaria was bringing in the forces of the Catholic League.[11] Ferdinand's Spanish cousins were to operate in the Rhenish Palatinate.

The year 1620 was that of the Battle of the White Hill, famous in Bohemian annals. Tilly, the able leader of the Catholic forces, inflicted a decisive defeat on the Bohemians, henceforth thoroughly cowed, while Frederick not only failed to secure the Bohemian crown but lost his own Palatinate instead. This land was attached to Bavaria, which also gained the electoral vote. The first phase of the war closed with clear success for the Catholic cause and enhanced prestige for Habsburg arms, whether Spanish or Austrian.

2. The Danish Intervention (1625-1629). These Catholic and Habsburg successes in the Empire made for intransigeance from Ferdinand and concern from the Lutheran princes. A new turn was now given to the war by the invasion of Germany by the forces of King Christian IV of Denmark. Through his holding of Holstein the Danish king had a foothold in the Empire. Religious sympathy and economic interest prompted his action.

This asset to the Protestant cause was balanced by a Catholic gain in the person of Wallenstein. Wallenstein is a romantic figure; he was a great leader of men, an able military organizer, and remains a much controverted character. An adventurer, a *condottiere* with unlimited ambition, he put his talent in the Habsburg service, though the religious motivation would have been hard to find among his men, moved, like their leader, by the concrete and immediate desire for gain. Between Tilly and Wallenstein King Christian was conclusively beaten at Lutter in 1626, and the Protestant cause was correspondingly set back.

The result was the Peace of Lübeck (1629) whereby Denmark had to restore German bishoprics incorporated from the Catholic Church. The Edict of Restitution issued by the Emperor, also in 1629, is a measure of the Catholic success at this point. Catholic imperial commissioners were to see to the restoration to the Church of Catholic property improperly

---

[11] Spanish forces from Milan helped the Emperor, while the Protestant cause was assisted by attacks in the Austrian rear from the prince of Transylvania.

secularized since 1555. The enforcement of this decree caused both discontent and alarm among Protestants.

3. The Swedish Phase of the War (1630-1635)

a. THE RISE AND AIMS OF SWEDISH POWER. Still the conflict persisted, for Germany had now become the battleground of European rivalries. In their search for outside assistance, the Protestant princes had looked to Sweden as well as to Denmark. But rivalry between these two countries (besides Norway, Denmark held the southern tip of Sweden, and both looked to the opposite shore of the Baltic) prevented common action. The problem of the Baltic thus becomes at this time one of the first foci of international friction.

In addition to the broad factor of Swedish interest, the element of personality again looms large at this juncture. We have seen the active role played by Sweden on the Baltic scene.[12] Led by her king, Gustavus Adolphus, Sweden was now about to embark upon her seventeenth-century career which caused her for a time to play a major European role and rank in influence with greater powers. In later parlance, we should speak of a Swedish imperailsm, the aim of which was to make the Baltic a Swedish lake.

b. GUSTAVUS ADOLPHUS. The Swedish dream of conquest found an exponent in the person of Gustavus Adolphus. This grandson of Gustavus Vasa, the founder of modern Sweden, Gustavus Adolphus came to the throne in 1611, at the time when the religious issue in that country had been settled in favor of Lutheranism.

Gustavus Adolphus was one of those rare characters of which history furnishes occasional examples. Attractive in physique and personality, well tutored in the arts and letters, he turned out in addition to be one of the great military captains of all time. Some such asset was necessary to compensate for the deficiencies of Swedish resources, whether in man power or wealth.

With deliberate calculation, Gustavus Adolphus set about putting his plans into effect. The first twenty years of his reign found him involved in conflict with Russia and with

[12] See above, pp. 84, 85.

Poland. By 1629, he had forced these powers to yield much of
the southern half of the eastern shore of the Baltic. This was
also the year of the Peace of Lübeck, register of Danish
defeat, and Gustavus Adolphus now turned his attention to
the Germanic world with an eye to the enhancement of both
Swedish and Protestant prestige.

Operations began in Pomerania in 1630. The capture and
sack of Magdeburg in 1631 by Catholic forces, an episode
reminiscent of Antwerp's Spanish Fury, served to exacerbate
Lutheran feeling. Four months later Gustavus Adolphus defeated Tilly near Leipzig and started on a westward march
toward the Rhine, from which he was deflected by French influence. Turning back, and brushing past Tilly's forces, Gustavus Adolphus finally came upon the army of Wallenstein.
The battle of Lützen in the autumn of 1632 is one of history's
great military encounters: Gustavus' genius won the day, but
in the process the king met death.

The result of Lützen was therefore inconclusive. The
Swedish forces, deprived of their leader, lost their aggressive-
ness, though for a time, the Swedish Chancellor, the able
Oxenstierna, carried on the war in Germany. On the other
side, Wallenstein, defeated, suspected, and fallen into disfavor,
was ordered, or allowed to be, murdered by the Emperor in
1634. Much of the Empire was ready for a peace of exhaus-
tion, which is what the treaty signed at Prague in 1635 really
was.[13]

4. The Direct Intervention of France (1635-1648).
This settlement might have been extended into a larger and
more lasting peace had it not been for continued outside interference. It has been mentioned that Gustavus Adolphus' turn
away from the Rhine was the result of French pressure. The
reason for the effectiveness of this pressure was the fact that
France was allied with Sweden in the war.

From the standpoint of the enhancement of French power,
any weakening of the Empire was desirable. This is why
Richelieu gave subsidies to Sweden and to the Protestant
cause. However, he did not at first participate in active hostilities, being content with subsidies. But with the new turn

---

[13] This peace between the Emperor and Saxony largely undid the Edict
of Restitution, thereby allaying Protestant fears in the Empire.

of events by 1635, Richelieu decided that the time had come for direct action. The conflict was thereby prolonged for more than another decade.[14]

Direct French action in the Empire did not become important until after French power had worsted Spanish. The latter was at first successful and France herself was invaded. But after a time the tide turned. French armies overran Bavaria in 1646. Meantime negotiations had already begun as early as 1641. They were long protracted, but finally led to the signature of a number of treaties at Münster and Osnabrück. The collectivity of these agreements is known as the Peace of Westphalia.

C.   The Settlement of Westphalia

1. The Terms of the Settlement

a. POLITICAL AND TERRITORIAL PROVISIONS. In the narrower sense, the settlement of Westphalia centered on the Empire. To all intents and purposes, that institution was reduced to purely nominal existence. The fact that the princes were now free to make war and peace without restraint from the imperial authority[15] endowed the states with the attribute of sovereignty. The Habsburgs were not affected in the rule of their own possessions, the Austrian lands, Hungary, and Bohemia.

Within the Empire itself, there were significant readjustments. The state of Brandenburg acquired eastern Pomerania and several bishoprics, while Bavaria was confirmed in the possession of part of the Rhenish Palatinate. The rest of it reverted to unlucky Frederick's son. Both would henceforth have the electoral dignity.

But outsiders were also allowed to intrude. France secured Alsace, except Strasbourg; in the north, western Pomerania on the Baltic and the Bishopric of Bremen facing the North Sea went to Sweden. These territories remained in the Empire,

---

[14] On the Franco-Spanish aspect of the conflict, see below, p. 104.

[15] It might be pointed out that this amounted to the recognition of an existing condition rather than to a radical innovation. War within the Empire would now be international instead of civil. The legal sanction given to this state of affairs did, however, register a significant defeat of the centralizing forces in the Empire.

EUROPE IN 1648

— Boundary of Holy Roman Empire

SCOTLAND
Edinburgh
ENGLISH
IRELAND
MONARCHY
(Commonwealth 1649–1660) (United Kingdom 1707)
ENGLAND
London
Spanish Netherlands

United Provinces
Amsterdam
Brussels
°Paris
FRANCE
Franche
Comté
SWITZERLAND
Savoy

Navarre
Aragon
Madrid°
CASTILE
SPANISH MONARCHY
PORTUGAL
Lisbon°
Corsica
(to Genoa)
Sardinia

Stockholm
SWEDISH MONARCHY
Finland
Karelia
RUSSIA
Moscow°

DANISH MONARCHY
Copenhagen

Brandenburg
Berlin
Brandenburg Monarchy
Prussia
East

Minor German States
Saxony
Bohemia
Bavaria
Vienna°
AUSTRIAN MONARCHY
HUNGARY
Austria

Milan
Genoa
Tuscany
Papal States
Rome°
Naples°
TWO SICILIES
SPANISH MONARCHY

Venice
Venice

LITHUANIA
POLAND
Warsaw°
Kiev°
Podolia
Galicia
Moldavia
Budapest°
Hungary
Wallachia
OTTOMAN EMPIRE
Constantinople°
GREECE
Ionian Is.
(to Venice)

and their new rulers thus had a voice in its affairs, emphasizing thereby the disintegrating tendency.

Holland's independence, long established in fact, was formally recognized by Spain, and Switzerland was similarly freed of any Habsburg allegiance.

b. RELIGIOUS CLAUSES. The Thirty Years' War was begun as a religious conflict. That aspect of it was often lost sight of under the influence of political factors, as when Richelieu formed an alliance with Gustavus Adolphus to aid the Protestant princes. Yet the religious aspect may not be ignored. At Westphalia, Calvinism was granted an equal status with Lutheranism, and the year 1624 was to be the date at which the status of church property—Catholic or Protestant—was fixed. Imperial courts were to have an equal number of Catholic and Protestant judges. The religious issue may be considered liquidated from this time in the Empire, for there was no significant change in allegiance nor any recurrence of conflict on this score thereafter.

2. The Significance of the Settlement. The settlements of 1648 rank in importance with those that followed the Napoleonic wars or those that rose out of the First World War in our century. Not so much because of the territorial changes, which were not extensive, as because they mark an important turning point in the story of Europe, the emergence of the state system under which Europe has operated until our own time.

a. THE EMPIRE. The victory of the centrifugal tendency in the Empire has been mentioned. This trend had to run its full course before a process of rebuilding from the bottom would enable Germany to find her place as a unit in this state system of Europe, a process that was to take a little over two centuries. Little will be heard of Empire or Germany during this period; we have instead a Habsburg Austria, Brandenburg (soon to be Prussia), Bavaria, Saxony, and other states.

b. THE DESTRUCTION OF WAR. No less important was the fact that Germany, or the Empire, had been Europe's battleground during the Thirty Years' War. The destructiveness of that war has few parallels either before or since. No reliable statistics are available, and the report that two-thirds of the population was destroyed may seem extreme, but contemporary accounts bear ample witness to the thoroughness of destruction. Life was reduced to savagery in order to persist, over much of the land, sections of which went uncultivated, reverting to primitive brush; manners and morals, too, went primitive. Letters, the arts, and education, all those amenities that make civilization and culture, in great part disappeared under pressure of the elementary struggle for mere survival.[16] The losses, material and moral, of the episode set the Germanic world back an appreciable period of time.

III.   THE FRANCO-SPANISH STRUGGLE

While this took place in the Germanies, others had profited. Sweden seemed well launched on the way to realizing her Baltic ambitions. Seventeenth-century Sweden is one of the important states of Europe in terms of power. The same is true of Holland, the basis of whose influence was the more solid and more lasting one of commerce. But most significant of all is the rise of France.

A.   The Rise of France

France, unlike Sweden, was a large state, the largest in Europe in terms of both population and domestic resources. Good management and leadership, as distinct from the accident of military genius, would by themselves suffice to give her a place of primacy.

1. France's Spanish Policy.   It is because of these resources that her recovery was so rapid when Henry IV took the helm. After the interim of the Regency, we have seen the work of Richelieu and of Mazarin. Richelieu, in addition to his task of internal organization, was equally intent upon asserting the primacy of France in Europe. This meant a continuation, or a resumption, of the conflict, quiescent during the first quarter of the century, with the house of Habsburg, whether Spanish or Austrian.

Spain was rated the foremost power in Europe at the begin-

---

[16] The Thirty Years' War represents in this respect the climax of a long process of decline which had already been going on during most of the sixteenth century.

ning of the century, and Richelieu was bent on humbling, and possibly displacing, Spanish power. France did not renew actively her sixteenth-century struggle over Italy, but concentrated her effort and attention in the northeast. The Spanish Habsburgs, allied to their Austrian cousins, were giving them military assistance with forces stationed in the Rhenish provinces, whose task it also was to seek to undo the fact of Dutch emancipation to which Spain unrealistically refused to give formal recognition. It was thus quite natural that France and Spain should become involved in the struggle whose main battleground was Germany.

B. The Decline of Spain

For a considerable time, the performance of Spanish arms justified the renown of the Spanish name founded on the superior quality of its infantry. Although Philip IV, who came to the Spanish throne in 1621, showed in himself signs of the decadence that was increasingly to mark the Spanish dynasty, he had in the person of Count (then Duke) Olivares a worthy opponent of Richelieu. A prolonged duel went on between the two men during the twenties. Despite French and English assistance to the Dutch, the capture of Breda in 1625 seemed to hold the possibility of restoring the Spanish position in Holland.

But for all the military and cultural brilliance and prestige of Spain, the seeds of decay, long since planted, were about to bear fruit. Already in Philip II's time the country's economic policy had elements of weakness. Nothing was done to remedy this basic disability of which others were taking advantage.[17] And the rising northern star of Gustavus Adolphus was soon to make new contributions to the art of warfare.

1. The Thirty Years' War in the Franco-Spanish Conflict. With the death of her king in 1632, Sweden lost his aggressive drive, which the otherwise able Oxenstierna, ham-

---

[17] The expulsion of the Moriscos, Christians of Moorish background, in 1609 and after, was economically a loss to Spain and, like the flight of French Huguenots in 1685, was inspired by the same unprogressive outlook that had expelled the Jews from Spain in 1492.

pered besides by the policy of the erratic Queen Christina, did not long pursue. Richelieu decided at this juncture that it was time for more direct and forceful French intervention. The French phase of the Thirty Years' War begins in 1635, and the Spanish aspect of the conflict remained paramount in French eyes for all that French armies were to appear deep in Imperial territory.

Richelieu did not live to see the fruit of the policies he had patiently wrought. The initial stages of the war still seemed to confirm the Spanish military superiority. In 1636, France was invaded from the north, in 1637 from the south. But the domestic difficulties of Spain around 1640[18] began to tell on her resources. This, combined with the emergence of able French commanders, finally caused the tide to turn. The French victory of Rocroy in 1643, as much as any one event, marks this turning. Mazarin had just taken over from Richelieu and, despite the domestic opposition and difficulties that he had to contend with, was able on the whole to pursue his predecessor's foreign policy.

2. The Treaty of the Pyrenees. Amid general weariness peace was made in Westphalia, but the Franco-Spanish struggle went on. French armies, led by such men as Condé and Turenne, now generally had the better of Spanish in the field. The war moved into the Spanish Netherlands and into northern Spain. But it was another ten years before stubborn Philip IV finally bowed to the inevitable.

By the Treaty of the Pyrenees in 1659 Spain made some territorial cessions to France: Artois, and some fortified towns from the Netherlands in the north; Roussillon along the Pyrenees.[19] More important than territory, however, was the fact that this treaty may be said—especially in retrospect—to have sanctioned the downfall of Spain. France, and Europe, were about to enter the Age of Louis XIV.

---

[18] In 1640, Portugal succeeded in breaking the connection with Spain. Shortly thereafter, Philip IV also had to contend with rebellions in Naples and in Catalonia.

[19] It was also arranged that Philip IV's daughter, Maria Theresa, should marry Louis XIV. Maria Theresa was to receive a large dowry in exchange for which Louis XIV would renounce further claims on Spain. The nonpayment of this dowry was to be the basis of renewed French aggression later on.

ADDITIONAL READINGS

Ahnlund, Nils, *Gustav Adolf the Great* (1940); Clark, G. N., *The Seventeenth Century* (1947); Gardiner, S. R., *The Thirty Years' War* (1897); Hurst, Quentin, *Henry of Navarre* (1938); Jordan, G. J., *The Reunion of the Churches* (1929); Mowat, R. B., cited in Ch. 5; Ogg, David, *Europe in the Seventeenth Century* (1948); Perkins, J. B., *France under Mazarin* (2 vols., 1886); Reddaway, W. F., *History of Europe, 1610-1715* (1948); Wedgwood, C. V., *Richelieu and the French Monarchy* (1949); Wedgwood, C. V., *The Thirty Years' War* (1938).

CHAPTER 7

The English Revolutions (to 1660)

The belief has achieved wide currency in our time, in Britain as well as outside, that the British people are endowed with a special talent for the art of government. What better evidence of this than the long and admirable record of the evolution of the British state which seems to have found the secret of adapting ancient forms and institutions to the changing necessities of time, without going through the violent and often inconclusive convulsions that have beset less fortunate peoples?

A record of peaceful change, unbroken for the better part of three centuries, gives strong support to such a view. Yet, in historic terms, three centuries are fairly brief, and it is well to remember that the notion was widespread in seventeenth-century Europe that the English were a people who seemed unable to develop stable institutions. What better proof of this, at the time, than the contrast between their record and that of increasing stability and order in the affairs of other states?

When the century opened, England was a vigorous and rising nation, but hardly great as yet in terms of power. Her participation in the affairs of Europe was neither intense nor crucial, which is why little mention of it has been made hitherto, save on particular occasions. But two things were destined to happen. One is that, almost until our time, the curve of British power was to follow a steady ascendant. The other, that the pattern of the British mode of government has been emulated in ever widening circles throughout the surface of the earth. "Mother of parliaments," aptly expresses this.

The constitutional record of England is, for these reasons, one that has significance far beyond the limited sphere of purely English affairs. The seventeenth century is a critical period in this record which will now be surveyed. A brief description of the English constitution must be given first.

I. THE ENGLISH CONSTITUTION

A. Nature of the Constitution

To this day, Britain has no written constitution comparable with the document that goes under that name in the United States, for instance, and in a large number of other countries. When we speak, therefore, of the English constitution, at any point of time, this must be understood to mean the collection of laws, customs, precedents, and traditions which at that time prevail. Any constitution can always be altered, either by peaceful amendment or by violent revolution. The stress on customary practice in the case of England gives her constitution an element of imprecision as well as one of flexibility.

B. The Government

1. The Crown. At the apex of the English constitutional edifice when the reign of Queen Elizabeth closed stood the crown, which may be said to have been firmly planted in the hereditary principle by this time. The crown had great prestige and much power though the limits of it were never precisely defined. Elizabeth's own reign had done much to enhance both the prestige and the power.

2. Parliament

a. Origins of Parliament. The principle of representation, or the contractual nature of the medieval monarchy, had survived in England. Whether one trace it to Magna Carta or to older practice, Magna Carta was certainly a part of the constitution. That document, extorted from King John in 1215, asserted limitations on royal prerogative, and the practice had grown of having a parliament in England. The origin of this body may be traced back through the darkness of time, to and beyond the Norman conquest, but it is customary to speak of the body summoned by Edward I in 1295 as the "model parliament." Parliament, too, had evolved in the course of time, and by the seventeenth century had come to consist of two houses.

b. LORDS AND COMMONS. The House of Lords consisted of the high hereditary nobility and the greater prelates of the realm entitled to sit in it by virtue of their office. The House of Commons had in it representatives of the knights and burgesses in the shires and towns. The initial function of Parliament was mainly consultative and advisory, but the request that it grant new subsidies or powers of taxation could be made to imply the right of denying such request. Much of the constitutional history of England could be written in terms of the successful use by Parliament of the power of the purse. For this power could be used not only for the limited purpose of controlling expenditure itself, but also as a bargaining counter to extract from the crown ever increasing and wider powers of supervision.

In name, the king was—and is—king by the grace of God, and law is made by him "with the advice and consent" of Parliament. In practice, the story is one of steady parliamentary encroachment, until "advice and consent" might not be disregarded, hence came to supersede the royal prerogative.

C. The Situation at the Beginning of the Seventeenth Century

But in 1603, these rights were not clearly defined. The Tudors had in general been skillful in their dealings with Parliament, and they moreover were truly representative of a rising consciousness of national feeling. They were besides generally careful in their handling of money, so that no issues, either narrowly practical and specific or broadly constitutional and theoretical, were raised.

Such questions might be asked as these: had Parliament the *right* to *demand* an account of expenditure? Could it control the appointment of royal officers? How far could it control or supervise policy and administration? These would have been suitable topics for debate; no unmistakable answers could be vouchsafed to them. One aspect of the history of England while she was under Stuart rule during the seventeenth century is the providing of clear answers to questions such as the above.

I. Contrast with the rest of Europe. It is of interest to note that the sixteenth-century situation of England was not, in constitutional respects, radically different from others. France had her Estates General and her *parlements*. If anything, prior to Henry IV at least, one would have said that the English crown was stronger and rather more secure than the French. Holland successfully revolted against Spain in the sixteenth century, and spent much of the next in the throes of a struggle between the advocates of monarchical and parliamentary principles, respectively.

The Czech attempt to repudiate the Emperor and choose their own ruler, immediate cause of the Thirty Years' War, has been mentioned. But the French Estates did not meet after 1614, Bohemia was subdued by force, and the monarchical principle eventually prevailed in Holland. England alone followed a different path.[1] The issue is the simply stated one of the contest for power between the Crown and Parliament.

II. THE PRELUDE TO REVOLUTION: JAMES I (1603-1625)

When Elizabeth died in 1603, being childless, the English crown passed on to her nearest kin, James VI of Scotland, son of the same Mary Stuart executed in England in 1587. England and Scotland, neighboring states on the island of Great Britain, had a long tradition of conflict. The two countries were now united under a common crown, but they retained their separate institutions, laws, and parliaments. In both, Catholicism had been largely destroyed, but England

---

[1] Poland is the other exception to the rule that holds for the continent of Europe. Her parliament, or Diet, did indeed insist on maintaining its prerogatives at the expense of the royal power during the seventeenth and eighteenth centuries. But the Polish Diet was unable to produce a stable system of government, and Poland, unlike island Britain, was in addition surrounded by states devoted to the ideal of absolute monarchy. The result of these circumstances was the weakening of Poland and the ultimate extinction of the Polish state.

was predominantly Anglican, while Calvinism prevailed in Scotland, where the church was known as Presbyterian.

A. Character and Aims of James I

James, now the First of England, had been brought up in the Anglican faith. What is more, James, unlike his predecessor Elizabeth, took a genuine interest in matters religious and even theological.[2] His learning in that field, of better quality than his mastery of political arts, earned him from his contemporary Henry IV of France the description of "the wisest fool in Christendom."

Imbued as he was with biblical lore, James, like others after him, could find in Holy Writ ample justification for exalted views of his office. He was in his own eyes God's appointed to rule, hence responsible to no earthly agency, and master of the law of which he was the source. The power and standing of the English crown were high in 1603, but, whatever the reality, no Tudor had sought to propound theoretical views of an absolute divine right monarchy. Not so with James, whom sound logic but poor psychology impelled to seek concordance between practice and theory and to have it so recognized.

B. James I and Parliament

In addition, James was in need of funds for his extravagant tastes and schemes. Again, unlike the Tudors who had enhanced their independence by a careful husbanding of finance that minimized their need of Parliament, James found himself in need of the good will of this Parliament toward whom his attitude was cavalier. This was to look for conflict.

1. The Financial Issue. Balked by Parliament, James resorted to various devices, or subterfuges, of debatable legality in order to raise money. Parliament was further antagonized and moved to protest these measures, and beyond them the policies of the king in matters religious and foreign, as well as his general arbitrariness. Incensed at this challenge of his

[2] The standard English version of the Bible, the King James version, which he caused to be made, bears witness to this.

authority, James responded with still further arbitrariness. Uncowed, the Commons in 1621 made a "great protestation." This increased the king's anger, and both sides were standing on their respective positions when he died in 1625.

2. The Religious Quarrel. As if matters financial had not sufficed, a more narrowly religious issue began to intrude, which James' personality was highly unfit to handle.

Briefly, the issue grew out of the disintegrating force at work within the Protestant fold, which has been indicated earlier. There were some in England who felt that the breach with Rome had not gone far enough. In this they were abetted by the example of neighboring Presbyterian Scotland and the teachings of various radical Protestant preachers and theorizers. These views made progress especially among townsfolk, the commercial class, and the lower clergy. They were characterized by an intense dislike of anything reminiscent of "popery," and by emphasis on the Old Testament. The holders of them were likely to be people of determined fiber, austere in their mode of life, and intolerant of divergence. While some sought to reform the English Church from within and others turned Presbyterian, many went their individual way as Independents, often grouped together as Puritans.

These radicals had been kept in comparative check and quiet under Elizabeth. It was in keeping with James' character and general views that he should stress uniformity in the religious field as well as in the political. The religious debate at Hampton Court in 1604 evinced from him the angry declaration that he would "harry them [Dissenters] out of the land."

3. The Issue of Foreign Policy. These Dissenters and Puritans, stressing in their own lives a stern moral code, thought they perceived in James' leanings toward that most heinous of deviations, "popery." The fact that he favored a general policy of peace, and a Spanish alliance in particular,[3] seemed to confirm these suspicions, as did his failure to exert himself in behalf of his son-in-law, the Calvinist Palatine Elector and "winter king" of Bohemia. James' policy of

---

[3] He tried to arrange a marriage between his son, Charles, and the daughter of Philip III.

closer union with Scotland had little appeal in England.

The policy of peace with Spain had the further consequence of curbing the profitable English plundering of Spanish trade, and that too proved unpopular among the same group of people, for religious dissent had secured its strongest hold in the commercial middle class.

This class, moreover, from the nature of parliamentary representation, had in that body a strength out of proportion to its numbers in the population of the realm. Hurt in its material interest as well as in its moral sensibilities and religious belief by royal policy and action, it could with earnestness and righteousness use whatever weapons of opposition the constitutional armory would furnish. Despite the looming difficulties, during James' own reign matters did not exceed the point of struggle within the bounds of legality.

III. THE REVOLUTION

A.   Charles I (1625-1649)

1. Character of Charles I. James' successor, Charles, was personally neither unattractive, nor initially unpopular. The failure of the Spanish marriage scheme was pleasing to an opinion desirous of renewed war with Spain. To be sure, Charles married another Catholic princess, Henrietta Maria of France, sister of Louis XIII, and chose this occasion to give contradictory reassurances to English Protestants and to the Catholic French court. Duplicity went deep in Charles' character and augured ill for the future, especially in view of the fact that his opinions in matters of constitution and government were the same as his father's.

2. First Phase of the Conflict with Parliament. It was not long, therefore, before the struggle between Crown and Parliament, characteristic of the preceding reign, was resumed. The expenditure of subsidies granted for war with Spain, without war having been waged, was irksome and a fair cause for suspicion. Having dissolved his first Parliament, Charles did not find the new body more amenable, and it too was sent home.[4]

---

[4] Failures in foreign policy again intervened at this point. Neither the fleet sent to Cadiz nor the attempt to relieve the French Huguenots besieged by Richelieu in La Rochelle yielded any results.

Unable to resolve his financial difficulties, Charles had to call a third Parliament that would grant subsidies only when the king had signed the *Petition of Right* in 1628. No arbitrary taxation or imprisonment, no quartering of troops, and no martial law in peace time, were the royal promises. This is an illustration of the use of the power of the purse for political ends. But as Parliament would push its advantage still further, the king once more dismissed it.

3. The Period of Personal Rule. Charles would do without Parliament. This he could do in theory, since Parliament had no independent tenure and met only when called. But, in practice, there was an important condition to be fulfilled: the king must succeed in finding money for his treasury.

Subterfuges, arbitrariness, and straining of the law to produce resources must be resorted to in lieu of those taxes that Parliament alone could grant. The claim of ship money, the contention that coastal towns, later extended to inland ones, were liable to money contributions in place of furnishing ships for defense, was upheld by royal judges, but hardly enhanced loyalty to the king.[5]

a. CHARLES' RELIGIOUS POLICY. The king's religious policy had no better success than his political. Like his father again, Charles wanted conformity to the Church of England, the affairs of which he put into the hands of William Laud, archbishop of Canterbury. Laud, a high Anglican, seemed to impress an increasingly "popish" orientation on the church to the growing disgust of the Dissenters.[6]

4. The Scottish Rebellion. Worse still, or even more unwise, Charles set about enforcing religious conformity in Scotland where Anglicanism had no hold. Presbyterian Scotland rose in revolt in 1638 and this development served to reopen the constitutional struggle in England.

For the king had to convene Parliament in order to finance an army to deal with the Scottish rebellion. After a futile three

---

[5] John Hampden refused to pay ship money and took his case to court. The fact that he could do this on one hand, but that judgment went against him on the other, gives a good measure of the state of law in England at this time. Hampden achieved wide popularity for his effort.

[6] The settlement of North America, begun under James I, received a strong impulse from the emigration of Dissenters in this period.

weeks session, the Short Parliament was dissolved. But the financial need remained. Once more a Parliament came together in 1640. Technically, that body is said to have lasted for twenty years, the longest Parliament in English history, hence known as the Long Parliament. But the vicissitudes of these two decades were many. The story must now be told of the revolution in England.

B.   The Revolution Proper

1. The Long Parliament. The Scottish rebellion played into the hands of Parliament, which used the favorable situation to settle all contested constitutional points in its own favor: the right to impeach ministers,[7] the abolition of special tribunals, the elimination of financial expedients, all this was capped by the passage of a "triennial act" providing for a parliamentary session at least once in three years.

The availability of funds and some improvement in the military situation, plus divisions within Parliament on other issues, induced the king to attempt a *coup d'état*. But his attempt to arrest some members of the House of Commons merely served to anger that body and in turn brought it to the resort to illegality: it dispensed with the royal seal and proceeded to raise armed forces of its own. When the king rallied his own forces, the point of compromise seemed past and the issue had to be settled by the arbitrament of force.

2. The Civil War. Revolution and civil war were now the lot of England, split into two seemingly irreconcilable camps. The nobility and the conservative church elements (high Anglican and Catholic) supported the royal cause; the commercial class and religious dissenters followed Parliament where their strength lay. The difference in their respective accoutrement, outward symbol of their divergent views, brought into use the terms "roundhead" and "cavalier."

Parliament, under its Presbyterian leadership, formed an alliance with the Scottish rebels in 1643. After the king's defeat at Marston Moor in 1644, a compromise might yet have been achieved, but for the often witnessed tendency of revolutions, once begun, to come increasingly under the control of

---

[7] Both William Laud and the Earl of Strafford were sent to the Tower.

their more extreme proponents and of the military element.

a. THE ARMY AND ITS ROLE. Reliance on the test of force naturally tends to enhance the influence of the effective instrument of force, the army. The parliamentary army, the "New Model" army as it was called, indeed presented some unusual features. The spectacle of soldiery forswearing oaths and singing psalms instead strikes a peculiar note in military annals. But the more important reality beneath this surface was the fact that the army was imbued with high spirit, fanaticism or good morale if one prefer, in addition to which its leadership and tactics were effective. It was in fact the success of Cromwell's "Ironsides" that caused the army to be reorganized according to their model.

This army represented a tendency more extreme than that of the majority of Parliament. It would not come to terms and pursued the war until the king surrendered in 1646. Following some delay, in 1648, the army did the very thing that had precipitated civil war. This time, however, it was not a few members of Parliament, but the relatively moderate majority, that were purged. The more extreme Independent groups, some sixty members, the "Rump," could now appropriate to itself the fiction of legality. Sitting in self-appointed judgment, it passed sentence of death on the king, who was executed on January 30, 1649.

3. The Commonwealth. The revolution had run its course to the extreme of radicalism. England was henceforth to have neither king nor lords, and would be styled a Commonwealth, in fact a republic, of which a Council of State was the executive. But the Rump did not disband itself; the revolution had fallen under the control of its extreme left wing, the radical Puritans.

That stage of a revolution is apt to be characterized by an accumulation of problems which the regime handles with vigor. The present English case was no exception. In addition to the very considerable, but at least momentarily cowed, opposition in England proper, there was open rebellion in Catholic Ireland and Presbyterian Scotland, to say nothing of the commercial rivalry with Holland about to break out into open conflict.

The saving factor was the excellent army molded by Cromwell. Ireland was defeated first.[8] Scotland was next subdued, and the claimant to the throne, Prince Charles, had to seek shelter in France. The war with Holland in 1652 was more popular, for Holland was the chief commercial rival of England at this time. It followed upon the enactment of England's first Navigation Act, in 1651. This typical expression of mercantilistic practice was designed to exclude Dutch shipping from trade with England, save in the carrying of products of purely Dutch origin.

The quality of its army, the popularity of its foreign and economic policy, combined with adequate financial management, and the division of its enemies, are what enabled the Commonwealth to survive.

This sound overall management of money matters did not prevent the members of the Rump, for all their ostensible saintliness, from falling victims to the concrete and human opportunities for gain that their office provided. This was cause for transition to the next stage of the revolution, the personal dictatorship of a military leader. In 1653, Cromwell, using the inevitable biblical turn of phrase of the period, "the Lord hath done with you," sent the Rump packing and remained the sole power in Great Britain and Ireland.

4. The Protectorate or Personal Dictatorship

a. CROMWELL. Oliver Cromwell, the man who had emerged to power, was a typical member of the English squirearchy. Adhering to the Independent outlook, he was yet himself softer and less narrow than the more extreme, fanatical, and dreary exponents of the Puritanical view. Already in Parliament in 1628, he made his mark in the Long Parliament, and his unexpected military aptitude finally brought him to the summit of power. Whatever his strong religious predilections and however unusual the unwonted turn of political phrase that he used, like all masters of statecraft, Cromwell had intelligence, ability to lead and manage, and a strong sense of reality.

---

[8] The brutal treatment meted to the Irish in the aftermath of defeat was a stain on the English record, and the memory of it has poisoned to our day the relations between the two peoples.

The foreign policy of the Protectorate was one of its sources of strength, for it was a truly national policy and, on the whole, successful, reflecting as it did the growing commercial strength of England resting on seaborne trade and naval power.[9]

b. CONSTITUTIONAL DEVELOPMENT. But for the rest, the Protectorate rested on a very narrow basis of consent. Having dismissed the Rump, an appointed legislative body was created, "Barebone's Parliament," as it has been dubbed. It was a body very active and radical in disposition, but it soon surrendered its powers to Cromwell.

This failure was followed by the adoption of England's first and last written constitution, the Instrument of Government. It was this document that established the protectorate, making Cromwell Lord Protector for life. He was to be assisted by a Council of State and a unicameral triennial parliament.[10]

The new Parliament turned out to be controlled by Presbyterians and found itself at odds with Cromwell, who dismissed it in 1655. His dictatorship was thereafter not even masked, and the revolution had run its full course in restoring the very type of authority which it had initially set out to destroy.

5. The Restoration. Although Cromwell had refused the crown, when he died in 1658, his son inherited his office. But Richard Cromwell was not of his father's stamp and soon lost control of the situation. Despite the existence of extreme democratic elements, such as the Levellers, these constituted but a minute fringe of opinion. The time had not yet come for an installment of democratic practice, and the monarchical idea was still too deeply entrenched as the "normal" ordering of the state.

A section of the army intervened, restoring the Long Parliament, while General Monck arranged for the return of Prince Charles who, as Charles II, received a hearty welcome home in 1660. Technically, his reign was made to begin in 1649, date of his father's death, the intervening eleven years being

---

[9] Dunkirk was captured at one point and Jamaica taken from Spain, worsted at sea by an English fleet.

[10] The Protector could delay, but not veto, legislation. Simultaneously, Congregationalism was made the state religion. Also, Ireland was united with Great Britain in this representation.

"legally" erased from British history. The bulk of England was neither Puritan nor democratic, and her revolution left little immediate trace save for the important precedent that its very occurrence was: royal prerogative in England had been successfully challenged. The significance of this was to appear after less than three decades of restored Stuart rule.

ADDITIONAL READINGS

Bernstein, Eduard, *Cromwell and Communism: Socialism and Democracy in the Great English Revolution* (1930); Davies, Godfrey, *The Early Stuarts, 1603-1660* (1937); Firth, Sir Charles, *Oliver Cromwell and the Rule of the Puritans in England* (1925); Gooch, G. P., *Political Thought from Bacon to Halifax* (1923); Schenck, W., *The Concern for Social Justice in the Puritan Revolution* (1948); Trevelyan, G. M., *England under the Stuarts* (1947); Wedgwood, C. V., *Cromwell* (1947); Wedgwood, C. V., *Strafford, 1593-1641* (1949); Willey, Basil, *The Seventeenth Century Background* (1949); Wolfe, Don M., *Milton and the Puritan Revolution* (1948).

PART II

The State System of Europe

and the

Emancipation of Western Thought

1660 - 1789

CHAPTER 8

The Age of Louis XIV

I. THE FRANCE OF LOUIS XIV

When Mazarin, long ill, finally died in March, 1661, Louis XIV announced his intention to be henceforth his own chief minister. Twenty-three years of age, and inexperienced, the King was to make good this intention for the half century that his reign still had to run. There are very large credits as well as debits in the ledger of Louis XIV's rule, the net balance of which may be argued, but no one can gainsay that he was master of the state and that he made a profound impression upon its shape and course.

A. The King and His Advisors

If Louis XIV wanted the reality of power in his own hands, he was quite ready to assume its burdens. He worked hard at the trade of king, and the decisions which he insisted on making, whether or not they were sound, were not based on whim but on consideration and study of the matter in hand.

No one succeeded Richelieu and Mazarin in their place of power, but the King surrounded himself with advisors, inherited from Mazarin at first, who constituted a small inner cabinet or council with whose assistance important decisions were made. These advisors, men like Le Tellier and Colbert, were apt to be of relatively humble origin. In this respect, Louis XIV continued and extended the policies of Richelieu.

The Fronde, of which Louis retained the memory, was the last effort of the French nobility to assert itself. With Louis XIV the task was completed beyond retrieving of emasculating the high French nobility, who became reduced to the role of courtiers. The contrast is of significance, especially for the future, between this abdication of the nobility in France and the evolution of the same class in England. Shorn of power, but not of privilege, the French nobility reduced to purely decorative functions, would become an expensive and unnecessary parasitical burden on the body of the nation. By way of compensation, the vigorous and enterprising bourgeoisie was encouraged. Through its wealth and the positions it filled in the service of the state, this body had considerable effective power, and its sons would often enter the ranks of the nobility. To the unlimited power of the King the bourgeoisie as yet had no objection.

The task already begun of integration and centralization was not only continued but much intensified, reaching to the control of municipal organization, where its success was, however, limited. The result was order in the realm and a degree of centralized control hitherto unknown, either in France or elsewhere.

B.   Economic Policy and Development

France was a wealthy nation and by far the most populous in Europe. The King needed much money for his ambitious projects, domestic as well as foreign, and the very wasteful system of taxation was much improved.[1]

1. Colbert's Mercantilism. More fundamentally important than taxation was the development of the nation's economy. This task was entrusted to Colbert, whose duty it also was to keep the exchequer filled. Until his death in 1683 Colbert supervised and directed the economic life of the country. Tireless and little loved, an organizing genius, Colbert is the personification of the mercantilistic policy of the paternalistic state. No detail was too small for his care and attention; a mass of legislation ensued, regulating in minutest detail terms and standards of manufacture.

France was relatively backward, by comparison with Eng-

---

[1] The system of farming taxes was not abolished but its efficiency was vastly increased. It was so wasteful, at the beginning of the reign, that the cost of collection absorbed the major part of the revenue.

land and especially Holland, in matters commercial. With shrewd insight, Colbert spared no pains to attract, even "steal," skilled artisans from other countries, while large sums were invested also in state manufactures.

2. *Foreign Trade and Colonies.* Sensitive to the value of foreign trade, Colbert bent his efforts toward the creation of a merchant fleet, naval power, and the establishment of colonies.[2] If his success in these fields was limited, by reason of the other requirements of French policy and by the lack of enthusiasm for emigration of French people and capital, the bases were laid nevertheless for the vast territorial claims that France was to make overseas.

When Colbert died he left the King a highly modern and efficient tool by the standards of the time. Yet this was but a stage in a continuing story. Colbert had not succeeded in imposing the *taille* (direct land tax) on the nobility. Despite simplification of the internal tariff structure, France was still divided in this respect into three sections: the "grosses fermes," roughly the northern half of the country; the "foreign" lands, most of the south and some peripheral regions; and the "new acquisitions." Nevertheless, and to repeat, by the middle eighties, Louis XIV ruled over the most highly integrated and centralized administration in Europe. He also stood at the apogee of his reign.

C.   The Authority of the State

1. *The Authoritarian State.* There was order in the French state, which for this reason was widely considered the model of adequate government, by contrast with an England still struggling to discover a suitable domestic balance. Of real opposition there was none: the nobility had definitely surrendered, the bourgeoisie were satisfied, and the mass of the peasantry were not articulate or vocal. It should be pointed out perhaps that the burdens imposed on the country by Louis XIV's expensive foreign policy caused a national sigh

---

[2] The relative position may be judged from the fact that, around 1680, the French merchant tonnage amounted to some 80,000 tons against 100,000 for England and the Hansa, and 560,000 for Holland.

It was during this period that the bases were laid for the vast French claim to Louisiana.

of relief to accompany his demise, but this is not to be translated into active opposition. The monarchy was soundly rooted and the sigh of relief was followed by a cry of welcome for his successor: the King is dead, long live the King!

a. CENSORSHIP AND FREEDOM OF THOUGHT. Nor would there have been room for opposition in Louis XIV's domain. Such an outlook as prevailed leads to the attempted control of thought, especially in the more controversial fields of politics, religion, and morals. Censorship was active and the printed word generally suspect. This might be expected to have a deadening effect on intellectual activity. Yet such was not the case, but instead the golden age of French classicism occurs in this very period. The result may be accounted for by the fact that in such fields as art and pure literature the pressure to conform in other realms may leave the artist unaffected.

Louis XIV in fact was a great patron of the arts and of academies of art and learning. As to scientific development in the narrower sense, the Pascalian dichotomy could leave science free to operate unrestricted. Political opposition did not exist.[3]

2. The Control of Religion

a. THE GALLICAN CHURCH. The desire for uniformity and control quite naturally extended to matters religious, and the perennial issue of the respective proper powers of Church and State revived. The French clerical hierarchy was rife with nepotism and closely associated with the French state and social structure. In 1682, Louis XIV, with the reluctant assistance of Bishop Bossuet, exacted from the French episcopate a "declaration of liberties of the Gallican Church." This statement, asserting the autonomy of the royal power, and, beyond that, intruding into the sphere of the respective authorities of Pope, Council, and Bishop, contained schismatic connotations. Despite bitter controversy, there was on both sides a desire to avoid a breach, the personal relations of King and Pope re-

---

[3] Even here, it would be erroneous to conclude to a stifling of the critical spirit. There was a thriving pamphlet literature, partly clandestine, which expressed very free criticism of the king's actions and especially of his ministers. But there was no serious questioning of the fundamentals of the political system.

mained amicable, and the theoretical aspects of the issue were
not pursued.

b. REVOCATION OF THE EDICT OF NANTES. Of greater consequence was the revocation of the Edict of Nantes. Since
Richelieu, there had been no Protestant "issue" in France.
Possibly misinformed about the reality and strength of Protestantism, and ever desirous of conformity, Louis thought he
could remove a minor surviving divergence. The effort to
convert Protestants degenerated into brutal persecution. The
act of 1685, rather than induce Huguenot conversion, resulted
in a large emigration on their part to more hospitable surroundings. The loss was far greater than mere numbers
would indicate, for they were drawn from some of the most
vigorous and desirable members of the population. The loss
was wholly France's, and the gain correspondingly accrued to
Holland, Prussia, and others.[4]

3. The Deification of King and State

a. THE THEORY OF DIVINE RIGHT MONARCHY. It was the
same Bossuet (1627-1704), Bishop of Meaux, and tutor of
Louis XIV's son, who expounded the theoretical bases for the
practice of Louis' absolute methods of government.

The assertion of the divine character of kingship was not
new. Bossuet reaffirmed it and drew backing for it from Holy
Writ. The governance of men is part of divine dispensation,
and for the purpose of this government, hereditary monarchy
represents the best ordering. The King is not divine but the
sanction of his power is. He therefore partakes of the sacred
character of the priesthood, and the discharge of his function
implies the duty of absolute and unquestioning obedience by
his subjects.

The King personifies the nation, he is not responsible, his will
is law. A bad ruler—such there may be—is not removable by
human agency. Gone were any traces of the contractual
element of feudal kingship, and the doctrine of absolute divine

---

[4] Not only did France lose valuable subjects as the result of the revocation
of the Edict of Nantes, but even the purpose of the domestic enforcement of
uniformity was not accomplished. Rebellion simmered into the early years
of the eighteenth century, especially in the mountainous regions of central
France.

right monarchy stands in direct contrast to the assertion that the nation, or the people, is the repository of sovereignty.

Louis XIV's terse statement, *L'État, c'est moi* (I am the state), was no empty boast but accurate description of existing conditions. Outside of England, this theory of the state, to which the successful example of Louis XIV himself gave much support, was the normal theory of the day.

b. VERSAILLES AND THE ROI SOLEIL. As pointed out, the theory was bolstered by practice, or perhaps rather, as often with political theory, was the rationalization of this practice. Louis himself was every inch a king, and the whole tenor of his reign was calculated to give tangible outward evidence of the prestige and power that were his and France's.

The best single manifestation of this magnificence was the imposing pile which he erected at Versailles, in the midst of former wilderness. Versailles—henceforth the seat of court and government—palace and gardens, was laid in truly grandiose style, and in good taste, expressing the quality of harmonious, if formal, order characteristic of the classical age of France. It was fitting background for the glory of the *Grand Monarque*.

4. The Leadership of France in Europe. Spain had been definitely displaced, and France's position of primacy acknowledged abroad. The aspects of this primacy were two: the more lasting and creditable one of culture; the less attractive one of power.

As to the former, the royal patronage of art is reminiscent of the practice of Renaissance Popes and Medici. The results were not of as high order as in Italy in the domain of the plastic and pictorial arts, but in letters they were outstanding, and highly creditable in architecture. Perhaps most significant is the quantity of influential books written in France when compared with the output of other countries at this time. Also, these books were now for the most part written in French rather than classic Latin. The bases were being laid for the eighteenth-century standing of the French language.

II.   THE FOREIGN POLICY OF LOUIS XIV

But Louis XIV was not content with cultural prestige. In

cruder forms he wanted to assert and use his power. His ambition did not extend to Napoleonic visions of dominating a united Europe under his direct rule, but he was bent on further humbling his rivals and extending the boundaries of his domain.

To these ends, military power was needed. France had already able generals, such as Turenne and Condé, when Louis assumed personal control. While Colbert provided the funds, much care was lavished on reorganizing the army. In this task, Louis had the services of an organizer of the first rank, his war minister Louvois.[5] The name of Vauban ranks high in the annals of military engineering. With these assets, and the resources of France, Louis XIV was able to pursue an aggressive policy of expansion which inevitably meant armed conflict with his neighbors. In view of France's central position and importance at this time, the foreign policy of Louis XIV is a convenient focus for a survey of the international situation of Europe, save in the east, during this period.

A.   The War of Devolution

The beginning was relatively modest, directed at the Spanish Netherlands alone. Philip IV of Spain died in 1665 and was succeeded by the incompetent and weak Charles II. Using the fact that his wife, Maria Theresa, was Philip IV's elder daughter, Louis entered in her behalf a claim to the Netherlands on the flimsy pretext that the private Netherlandish law of inheritance should apply to the country as a whole.

The success of French arms was made easier by a diplomacy which had contrived to immobilize other potential opponents.[6] The whole Spanish Netherlands would have been conquered but for a composition of the Anglo-Dutch quarrel which resulted in their joint opposition, in which Sweden also joined, to French expansion. Rather than face the coalition, Louis made peace, and the treaty of Aix-la-Chapelle in 1668 gave him a small but valuable area, including Lille.

---

[5] Louvois, made a marquis, was Le Tellier's son, and succeeded his father. at the war office.

[6] Also, Holland and England who were among these, were at war with each other at this time.

ACQUISITIONS OF
LOUIS XIV and LOUIS XV

Acquisitions of Louis XIV
Acquisitions of Louis XV

SCALE OF MILES

0   50   100   150   200

B. The Dutch War

Louis' resentment was mainly directed against the Dutch, whom he held primarily responsible for the frustration of his plans. Moreover, the rising commercial power of France provided the same economic reasons for war that had caused the Anglo-Dutch conflicts.

1. The Condition of Holland. In addition, the domestic condition of Holland seemed to make the time propitious for attack. For twenty years the country had been rent by strife between two opposing factions: the Stadholder, of the Orange house, led the conservative, centralizing, monarchical party against which stood the urban, bourgeois, decentralizing, and generally more liberal tendency led by the Grand Pensionary, John De Witt at this time. The latter group had been in control, but the Orange opposition was gathering strength as William III of Orange was about to come of age.

2. The War. Again, Louis made diplomatic preparations which succeeded at first in isolating Holland. French money bought off Sweden and England.[7] As the war opened in 1672, the Dutch, threatened with disaster, rose against De Witt, who was murdered, and rallied around William III, who became Stadholder and assumed leadership of the resistance. The partial flooding of the country was resorted to.

But the contest was uneven and the Dutch would have made concessions. Louis' intransigeance served to extend the war. The Emperor, the Brandenburg Elector, and Spain joined against France. Faced with this coalition, French arms were still successful, but the intervention of England—Charles II's hand was forced by Parliament—induced Louis to accept a new compromise. The treaty of Nimwegen in 1678 registered the fact that Spain, rather than Holland, which went unscathed, was to furnish the compensations. France acquired more Netherlandish border fortresses and the province of Franche Comté.

---

[7] Charles II in England, desirous of freeing himself from dependence upon Parliament, concluded in 1670 the treaty of Dover with Louis XIV. In exchange for a pension from the latter he promised neutrality in the forthcoming war.

C. The Apogee of Louis XIV's Reign

The next ten years were years of peace, relative peace at least. They constitute the apogee of Louis XIV's reign, when the splendor of the sun king was not yet dimmed by the drain of vaster and more costly military adventures.

1. "Natural Boundaries" Versus the Balance of Power. Louis' ambition was not satisfied and the aim of his policy was taking clearer shape, which was to extend the frontiers of France to the Rhine. The theoretical justification of "natural boundaries," those of ancient Gaul, was advanced to cloak the cruder desire for additional territory.

For a time it was a devious policy of gnawing. Combining the terms of Westphalia which spoke of cessions "with their dependencies," with an industrious foraging through ancient feudal charters, the imperial town of Strasbourg in Alsace was claimed along with others. Its resistance, like that of Luxembourg, was easily overcome and the protests of Emperor and Spanish king ignored. The Chambers of Reunion, the special courts established by Louis XIV to search titles of sovereignty, were doing efficient, if high-handed, work.

There was inevitable concern over the growing power of the French king and the arbitrary use of this power. To the theoretical bases of his claim to "natural boundaries," an answer now appeared, the balance of power theory, basically the assertion that all states had an equal right to existence and that none should grow so strong as to endanger the life and possessions of others.

D. The War of the League of Augsburg

1. The League of Augsburg. More concretely, this meant a coalition, which was formed as early as 1686 under the leadership of Emperor Leopold, mainly for the protection of the Empire. The League of Augsburg initially included, besides the Emperor and various German princes, Sweden and Spain. Undeterred, Louis XIV sent armies into the Palatinate in 1688 to make good a claim he had advanced. The Palatinate was thoroughly devastated, but unforeseen developments at this point broadened the struggle, to which they gave a new turn.

The restored Stuarts in England, Charles II, then his brother James II, had pursued a policy favorable to Louis XIV, whose personal power and methods they admired and would have imitated. This policy was not popular in England, where it was felt that French commercial rivalry had superseded Dutch. The effort to adhere to it was one aspect of the attempt at personal rule which, for other reasons as well, mainly domestic, brought the Stuarts to grief in England. In 1688 there took place in that country the so-called Glorious Revolution, the effect of which was to bring to the English throne as co-rulers James' daughter Mary and her husband, none other than William III of Orange, Louis' archenemy.[8]

2. The War. The result of the English upset was that England and Holland now joined the coalition and that the war was extended overseas.[9] The war was long, lasting eight years, but inconclusive. France was able to hold her own against the coalition, but not to secure victory. The treaty of Ryswick, in 1697, registered the stalemate. The one real gain for France was a clear title to all Alsace. But against this Louis' other claims had to be yielded. Lorraine, occupied since the Dutch war, had to be evacuated; the Dutch obtained a favorable commercial treaty and were allowed to garrison the border fortresses of the Spanish Netherlands, while Louis XIV also recognized William as ruler of England.

Despite the lack of French success, the fact that it had taken such a coalition to contain French power was in itself a measure of that power. But Louis was not humbled; rather, with the passing of the years, he gave evidence of the usual effects of arbitrariness unchecked.

E.   The Spanish Succession

Peace again was of brief duration, for complications in another quarter opened for Louis the possibility of realizing

---

[8] For the domestic and constitutional developments in England, see below, pp. 135ff.

[9] The overseas or imperial aspects of the Anglo-French struggle, which opened with this war and continued through a number of others and is sometimes described as the second Hundred Years' War, had relatively little effect in Europe. They are important for other reasons, and it will be convenient to treat this imperial conflict in a separate chapter.

schemes of vaster import than the mere "natural frontier" of the Rhine.

1. The Spanish Question. By 1697 it was apparent that the end could not be far off for the sorry figure that was Charles II, king of Spain. Charles had neither children nor brothers; his nearest male kin was Emperor Leopold I. Spain, for all her decline, still was rated a major power, and the Spanish possessions were vast. To have the Spanish inheritance revert to the Austrian Habsburgs would revive visions of the Empire of Charles V. Louis XIV's France, far stronger than the sixteenth-century realm of the Valois, could hardly be expected to let this come to pass.

From the point of view of the Spanish dynasty, the first consideration was to avoid a division of its possessions. Emperor Leopold was married to one of Charles II's sisters; Louis XIV to another, whose dowry moreover Spain had never paid. Might not Louis XIV, his lands contiguous to Spain and with his power, better insure the integrity of the Spanish domain?

From the point of view of Europe as a whole, the adjunction of Spain and all that went with her to either France or Austria would have meant a major upset in the balance of power.[10] The issue of the Spanish succession was the major concern of the diplomacy of Europe during the closing years of the seventeenth century. Various partition schemes were considered between the Emperor, Louis XIV, and William III. But when Charles died in 1700 it appeared that French diplomacy had scored, for his last will (there had been others) turned his possessions over to Louis' grandson, Philip of Anjou, with the proviso that their integrity must be preserved.

Knowing the consequences of acceptance, Louis had a momentary hesitation. But finally he hailed his grandson first Bourbon king of Spain. Louis did not wait, but anticipated the outbreak of inevitable hostilities by evicting the Dutch garrisons from the barrier fortresses. France and Spain were

---

[10] The economic aspects of the issue were no less important, especially for the leading commercial countries, England and Holland. The prospect of a fusion of the Spanish and French empires could not but be highly unpalatable to them.

to be ranged against a grand alliance consisting of England, Holland, the Emperor, and some German princes.[11]

2. The War of the Spanish Succession. The war was long, lasting just over a decade, and was fought on a large scale and in many places, in Europe as well as overseas. It was truly a European, not to say a world, war.[12] France had by now lost her best generals, and the better military leadership was on the side of the allies, among whom Prince Eugene of Savoy and the Duke of Marlborough distinguished themselves. A measure of the seriousness of the conflict may be gathered from the fact that it was one of the relatively rare occasions when the English thought it necessary to contribute a substantial land effort on the continent.

A series of lost battles drove the French within their own frontiers. But the threat of invasion produced a renewed effort on the part of both Louis XIV and of his people, who, in the circumstances, responded to his appeal. The military situation was in part redressed, and this in combination with the usual bane of coalitions, divergences among the allies,[13] laid the bases for a peace of compromise which was registered in the treaty of Utrecht in 1713.

3. The Peace of Utrecht. The result of this treaty was a division of the Spanish inheritance, somewhat along the lines of the prewar partition agreements. Louis' grandson retained the Spanish crown, as Philip V, founder of the Bourbon line of Spain. But the peace stipulated a ban on any future union of the French and Spanish crowns. Even so, this major Bourbon gain was balanced by compensations to the Austrian Habsburgs, whose influence henceforth would supersede the

---

[11] These were the Electors of Brandenburg, Hanover, and the Palatinate. Bavaria, on the other hand, joined France. Portugal, after a while, joined the coalition, and Savoy, initially with France, changed sides.

[12] Eastern Europe was also involved in major hostilities, the Great Northern War occurring at the same time as that of the Spanish Succession. The two wars went on parallel and did not become part of one generalized conflict. For that reason, the eastern issues will be dealt with in a separate chapter.

[13] Domestic English politics resulted in the disgrace of Marlborough and in a decreased interest in the prosecution of the war. Also, the fact that Archduke Charles, the candidate of the allies for the Spanish crown, became Emperor in 1711, destroyed much of the balance of power motivation.

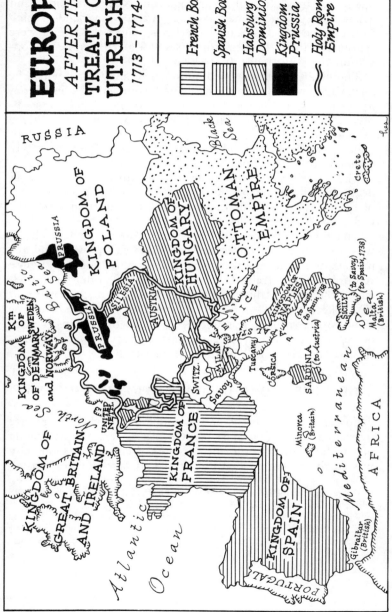

EUROPE
AFTER THE
TREATY OF
UTRECHT
1713 - 1714

French Bourbons
Spanish Bourbons
Habsburg Dominions
Kingdom of Prussia
Holy Roman Empire

RUSSIA

Black Sea

Crete

KINGDOM OF POLAND

PRUSSIA

KINGDOM OF HUNGARY

OTTOMAN EMPIRE

Km of Baltic Sea

KINGDOM OF DENMARK and NORWAY

SWEDEN

PRUSSIA

SILESIA

AUSTRIA

VENICE

Sea

SICILY (to Savoy) (to Spain, 1738)

Malta (British)

KINGDOM OF GREAT BRITAIN AND IRELAND

North Sea

UNITED NETH.

SWITZ.

MILAN

Savoy

PAPAL STATES

Tuscany (to Austria)

KINGDOM OF NAPLES (to Austria; to Spain, 1738)

CORSICA

SARDINIA (to Austria)

Atlantic Ocean

KINGDOM OF FRANCE

Minorca (Britain)

Mediterranean

AFRICA

KINGDOM OF SPAIN

PORTUGAL

Gibraltar (British)

Spanish in Italy through their acquiring Naples, Sardinia, and Milan. They also superseded Spain in the Netherlands, which thus became the Austrian Netherlands, where the Dutch were reinstated in the "barrier" fortresses and given a trade monopoly on the River Scheldt.

The Spanish empire was untouched and went with the Spanish crown, but England secured commercial concessions in Spain proper,[14] in the colonies (the *Asiento*), and a monopoly of the slave trade. Her other colonial gains were at the expense of France.

Both Brandenburg and Savoy were confirmed in their newly acquired royal dignity.[15]

The Bourbon dynastic gain was confirmation of Spain's decline. Still important, she was by way of becoming a pawn of the power politics of Europe: from the Austrian wake, she had passed into the French.

The power of Louis XIV's France, though held in check, was great and recognized as such. But this power, and the military use of it, had meant hardship for the country, whose resources were strained. On his deathbed, Louis acknowledged the error of his conquering ways. His successor, Louis XV, like his great grandfather, was also aged five when he came to the throne. His uncle, the Duke of Orleans, was to be regent. The legacy to eighteenth-century France of Louis XIV's long reign will be considered later.

III.   THE GLORIOUS REVOLUTION IN ENGLAND

For all the discontent and grumbling produced in France by the administration of Louis XIV, there was no questioning of the form of government; absolute divine right monarchy was so firmly entrenched that it would take the mismanage-

---

[14] She also retained control of the strategically valuable base of Gibraltar, which she had seized in 1704, but yielded Minorca.

[15] In 1720, Savoy exchanged with Austria Sicily for Sardinia. It is at this time that the Emperor recognized Savoy as a kingdom, having similarly recognized Brandenburg, henceforth Prussia, during the War of the Spanish Succession.

ment of the better part of a century before the system would encompass its own ruin.

A.   The Restoration in England

Just before Louis XIV assumed personal control in France, Charles II, in 1660, had regained the throne of England. The English revolutionaries, the Independents, had enjoyed too narrow a basis of support to have been able to implant a durable system of government. In 1660, it was widely felt that "the government is, and ought to be, by King, Lords, and Commons." This meant at once a recognition of the legitimacy of the Stuart ruler, which in turn might be translated as recognition of the divine sanction of royal authority, or as a reassertion of limitation on the royal prerogative. All that could be said was that the experiment of Commonwealth and Protectorate had been rejected as a failure, but the issue which had begun to disturb the English body politic with the first James and had come to a head under Charles I was not settled. The answer to the question of the proper distribution of power under the British constitution was not to be given its initial form for another twenty-eight years.

1. Charles II (1660-1685). Some things were clear. The bulk of the forces which had supported Parliament during the forties, if they had rejected the Independent dictatorship, had not become converted to Bossuet's views of the monarchy. Even among those who had fought for the king, and whose victory his return represented, the landed aristocracy and the established Church of England, there were few followers of Bossuet.

But Bossuet's doctrine was precisely the one that appealed to restored Charles II. Long resident in France, cousin of the French king, he had strong leanings towards both divine right absolutism and catholicism. Charles II, however, was in his character and person very different from his earnest grandfather. His charm was great, and this asset he used with intelligence to dissemble his real aims. He had sufficient tact and skill to be able to live out his reign despite the mounting opposition he aroused.

Charles was fortunate in the financial arrangements of the beginning of his reign; a revenue of well over £1,000,000 might have sufficed for tastes less extravagant than his own.[16] A suspicious Parliament of 1665-1667 entered the novel claim to make specified grants and to demand an accounting of their expenditure. There were in this the makings of a revival of the quarrel which had plagued the first two Stuarts. Charles thought he had found a partial answer in the treaty of Dover of 1670 with Louis XIV.[17]

2. The Policies of Charles II

a. THE RELIGIOUS QUESTION. For all his skill and masterful dissembling, Charles was set on enforcing policies of his own. He could for a time capitalize on the revulsion against the extremes of Puritanism and Independency to reinstate the Church of England. During the first five years of his rule, a series of acts imposed various disabilities on Dissenters.[18]

b. THE KING AND PARLIAMENT. But Charles went far beyond this in his sympathies for Catholicism, on which path he had little following. His "declaration of indulgence" in 1672, a claim to the right to suspend the operation of existing law, brought the issue back to the constitutional ground on which it had been fought twenty years earlier. The fear of Catholic influence, greater perhaps than it need have been, was widespread, and the answer of the Commons to the royal claim was the Exclusion Act of 1679, barring from the succession Charles' brother and heir, James.[19]

The debate waxed intense over the Exclusion Act, which was eventually defeated by the Lords. This result was due to the fact that there was among them a sufficiently strong faction who, while not inclined to Catholicism, felt that there

---

[16] As is often the case after the austerity of revolution, the Restoration was a period of relaxation and laxity for which the court was a model.

One source of the king's revenue was the annual grant by Parliament of £100,000 in compensation for the abolition of certain feudal dues. The final abandonment of the last vestige of feudal theory in England was an expression of economic progress and of the rising importance of capitalist interests.

[17] See above, note 7.

[18] These were the Corporation Act (1661), the Act of Uniformity (1662), the Conventicle Act (1664), the Five Mile Act (1665).

[19] Prince James had openly become a Catholic in 1672.

was even greater danger in the implied parliamentary claim to superiority over the Crown. These became known as Tories and their opponents Whigs, henceforth the names of the parties, or factions, contending for the mastery of British politics.

3. *James II (1685-1688)*. There matters rested for a time, and when Charles died in 1685, becoming an avowed Catholic *in extremis*, he was duly succeeded by his brother James. James represented the union of belief in both Catholicism and absolutism. His arbitrariness, his efforts to make use of further declarations of indulgence, weakened the strength of Tories opposed to tampering with the Crown. By way of compensation was the fact, however, that James' heirs, his daughters Mary and Anne, were both Protestant.

B.   The Glorious Revolution

But the birth, in 1688, of a son to James brought dismay, for with it came the prospect of the permanency of Catholicism on the British throne. When, upon the invitation of parliamentary leaders, William III of Orange, husband of James' elder daughter, Mary, landed in England, his progress was unopposed. James fled to France, last of the Stuart kings.[20]

1. *The Bill of Rights*. The successful, and bloodless, revolutionary act was promptly translated into the law of England. The Bill of Rights of 1689 stipulated that henceforth the bearer of the Crown must be a member of the Church of England. The act went on to prescribe limitations of the royal prerogative, and to specify the rights of subjects of the king. Of great importance was the shrewd use of the power of the purse. Parliament would henceforth make military appropriations (Mutiny Act) on a yearly basis only.[21]

2. *Significance of the Glorious Revolution*. Revolutions

---

[20] There was support for James in Scotland and in Ireland, but it was successfully suppressed.

[21] In 1689 also, the religious issue was dealt with, granting toleration to Dissenters, but tightening the restrictions on Catholics.

The issue of the succession to the Crown was finally settled by the Act of Settlement in 1701, as the result of which, following the reign of Anne, Mary's sister, the present Hanoverian dynasty came to England.

have come and gone and they have often been disappointingly
sterile in their outcome. The very mildness of the Glorious
Revolution may have been one of the reasons for the far-
reaching permanence of its effects. It was the last revolution in
Britain, whose constitution has since offered the unique example
of steady evolution to the point where one may feel that any
further change may be encompassed by the British system
without ever the need of further revolution.

a. THE LIMITED OR CONSTITUTIONAL MONARCHY. The central point of the change that took place in 1688 is the assertion
of the authority of Parliament above that of the Crown. The
coinage and official acts of the realm may still bear the rubric
"King by the grace of God"; the less exalted reality was that
the king was such by the will of Parliament. Since the crystal-
lization of the system of constitutional or limited monarchy
occurred during the following century, this may be an appropriate place to trace the sequence of that story.

The monarchy was limited by the fact that the crown had
wholly lost the power of the purse. The king could not make
laws, and, after a time, could not prevent the making of them
either. The veto, never officially abolished, was last used by
Queen Anne. The rights of subjects against arbitrary power
were safeguarded by the law, of which the Habeas Corpus
Act of 1679 is the single most apt expression. Deprived of an
army, since Parliament controlled the funds, the king could
not in fact wage war, nor could he retain ministers in office
unless they enjoyed the confidence of Parliament. Some of
these practices came gradually to be accepted as traditions
rather than written laws; their power is no less.

b. PARLIAMENT. What was this Parliament? The Lords
held place by right of birth or office, or by ennoblement. As
to the Commons, they represented in 1688 and for a long
time thereafter a very limited ruling class, a narrow oligarchy
of landed and commercial wealth. But the principle of representation was all-important.

John Locke (1632-1704), the apologist of the Glorious
Revolution, could theorize in his *Treatise on Government*
about the people's rights. Who were the people? If "active
citizens," to use a later nomenclature, were few, the content
of the term was elastic; it could be and was to be steadily

enlarged, transforming eventually without violent shocks the seventeenth- and eighteenth-century oligarchy into a twentieth-century democracy.

3. The Eighteenth-Century Constitutional Development. But the supremacy of Parliament, whatever its content and composition, was the supremely important meaning of 1688. Certain favorable, and purely adventitious, circumstances helped to confirm this parliamentary supremacy. When William of Orange came to England, he was co-ruler with his wife, Mary. William was relatively unconcerned with the domestic British scene, being more interested in such things as the coalition against Louis XIV, in which both Holland and England were engaged. Parliament he accepted without demur, and found he could govern most smoothly if he chose ministers of whatever party was dominant in that body.

a. THE HANOVERIAN DYNASTY. Anne, Mary's sister, who succeeded William for twelve years (1702-1714), was somewhat more conscious of the royal prerogative; but when she died the Act of Settlement brought to the English throne George I of Hanover.[22] George I (1714-1727) and his son George II (1727-1760) both knew little of England. They were essentially foreigners sitting upon a throne whither unforeseen accident had brought them,[23] and were content to leave in charge of affairs the ministers, Robert Walpole and the elder Pitt, who enjoyed the confidence of Parliament.

b. THE CABINET SYSTEM. In this fashion the Cabinet system took root and shape in the political landscape of Britain. The term has already been used in the time of Charles II when it rather described the king's privy council, but it now came to mean that group of men, headed by the Prime Minister, the leader of the majority party in the House of Commons, who carried on the task of government. The practice, like much of British constitutional practice, was not sanctioned by legisla-

---

[22] In order to preserve the union of England and Scotland which had resulted from the accession of the Stuart dynasty to the English throne, an Act of Union was passed in 1707.

[23] There was some support for a Stuart restoration, mainly in Scotland. James II himself, in 1715, and his grandson, "Bonnie Prince Charlie," the Young Pretender, in 1745, made abortive attempts to regain the throne.

tive enactment, but merely grew in the favorable climate of
the Hanoverian rule.

c. GEORGE III. George III (1760-1820) was the first of that
house who may be called authentically British, and consequently took a greater interest in the politics of what he considered his own country. His efforts to reassert more power[24]
were neither very successful nor pursued in great earnest. By
the second half of the eighteenth century the British parliamentary system had taken final shape. It could be left to time
to effect further transformation of its practice through the
simple device of modifying the content of that elastic concept
of Locke's, "the people."[25]

---

[24] George III sought to govern with the aid of the "King's friends," mainly
Tories. From 1770 to 1782, as a result in part of electoral manipulations, the
Tory Lord North was his prime minister. This, it will be remembered,
was a period less than successful in British imperial management, witnessing as it did the loss of the American colonies.

[25] As to the basis of representation, going back to the time of Charles
II, it had become a century later full of preposterous abuses, of which the
"rotten boroughs" were the most glaring illustration. Not until the great
Reform Bill of 1832 was this situation righted.

ADDITIONAL READINGS

Ashley, Maurice, *Louis XIV and the Greatness of France* (1948); Bryant,
Arthur, *King Charles II* (1940); Clark, G. N., *The Later Stuarts, 1660-
1714* (1934); Clark, G. N., cited in Ch. 6, Cole, Charles W., *Colbert and
a Century of French Mercantilism* (2 vols., 1939); Gooch, G. P., *English
Democratic Ideas in the Seventeenth Century* (ed. J. Laski, 1927); Mowat,
R. B., cited in Ch. 5; Ogg, David, *England in the Reign of Charles II* (2
vols., 1934); Ogg, David, cited in Ch. 6; Perkins, J. B., *France under
Louis XIV* (2 vols., 1897); Petrie, Sir Charles, *Louis XIV* (1940);
Rayner, Robert M., *European History, 1648-1789* (1949).

CHAPTER 9

The Transformation of Austria and the Rise of Prussia

I. THE SITUATION BEFORE 1740

A. The Habsburg Domain and Its Transformation

1. The Empire after Westphalia. The settlement of Westphalia is an important landmark in the story of the Holy Roman Empire. Territorially, the complete severance of Holland and Switzerland was little more than formalizing an already accomplished fact. France secured Alsace and Sweden secured Pomerania, but these lands remained within the Imperial bounds. Rather more important than these changes was the virtual autonomy granted the component units of the Empire, which transformed it into a loose federation of some three hundred parts. There was still an Emperor, as usual elected and normally a Habsburg; there was a Diet also, meeting in Ratisbon. But all this had little more than nominal reality.

The territory of the Empire was overwhelmingly Germanic, save for Bohemia and the Spanish Netherlands. But it lagged far behind the western nations in the degree of its national development. The reasons for this are several interlocking facts. Commercially and economically, the Empire had been well developed into the sixteenth century, and its bankers had shared in the opening up of New World resources. But the digression into politico-religious struggles, of which the Thirty Years' War was the climax, had caused much retrogression. There is debate about the extent of physical loss caused

by that episode, but no question that it was very great. The
war was a death blow to the once potent Hanseatic League,
whose heirs were now the traders of Holland, France, and
England. The peasantry had fallen to an unusually low estate.
From the war, the Empire as a whole emerged impoverished,
religiously divided between Catholicism, Lutheranism, and
Calvinism, and politically atomized.

2. The Habsburg Domain Proper. After 1648 the significance of the Imperial dignity may be considered purely
honorific. What power the Habsburgs commanded derived
from their own resources. These were considerable. There
was the solid block which had grown out of the expansion of
the original East Mark (Oestmark = Austria) west and south
into the Alps, roughly modern Austria. In addition, the
crowns of Bohemia and of Hungary belonged to the Habsburgs.

This constituted a huge solid block of territory, usually
referred to as the Austrian empire, from the fact that the
Habsburg capital Vienna was the center of its administration.
Despite much looseness in the structure, it was by itself ample
to give the Austrian house great power status in Europe.

a. THE STRUGGLE WITH THE TURKS. Some of this territory
still had to be reconquered after 1648. The Habsburgs, foremost Germanic power in any event, and related to the Spanish
house, were naturally involved in the disputes of which France
was the center.[1] But the menace to the east of them, from
the Ottoman Turks, was even more important. The Habsburgs
were the bulwark of Europe against their advance.

The Hungarian situation had been stabilized during the sixteenth century, after the Turkish failure before Vienna, on
the basis of a tripartite division: roughly a third under Turkish
rule, a similar portion under the Habsburgs, and a nearly
autonomous Transylvania.[2] The Habsburg share had to pay
tribute to the Sultan, from which it was not freed until the

---

[1] See the preceding chapter for the wars of Louis XIV.

[2] Protestantism, mainly in the Calvinist form, made considerable headway
in Hungary. The Prince of Transylvania was a Protestant. The counter
Reformation achieved marked, though not complete, success in Hungary and
incidentally helped the re-establishment of Habsburg control.

turn of the century, after the "Long War" with the Turks (1593-1606).

This Ottoman pressure, at the back door of Europe, must ever be borne in mind when one thinks of the balance and relationships of the whole, the Habsburgs being the point of contact with both the East and West. Internal troubles of their own had prevented the Turks from taking advantage of the difficulties that beset the Emperor during the Thirty Years' War.

The very year that closed the settlement of Westphalia marked the accession of a new Sultan, Mohammed IV (1648-1687), who sought to resume the earlier aggressive policy of the Turks. Hungary was wholly overrun in 1682, and the following year Vienna besieged for the second time by the Turks. In 1683, as in 1529, Vienna successfully withstood the siege.[3]

The war was long drawn out,[4] but its conclusion, the treaty of Carlowitz in 1699, saw the Turks surrender the territory north of the Danube. This treaty, of great consequence in eastern European annals, registered the irrevocable passing of Ottoman power into the stage of steady decline that was to characterize it for the next two hundred years.[5] At least momentarily rid of the Turkish danger, the Habsburgs could concentrate their attention and efforts on the issue of the Spanish succession.

3. Emperor Charles VI (1711-1740). Soon after he came into the Habsburg inheritance, the treaty of Utrecht effected an important change in the domain of Emperor Charles VI. The Austrian Habsburg house had now predominant influence

[3] This war has sometimes been referred to as the "last crusade" from the fact that the Emperor received much assistance from other Christian rulers. Vienna was in large part saved by the timely intervention of a Polish army led by John Sobieski, and even Louis XIV, the Habsburg's archenemy, offered assistance.

Venice, also threatened by the Turks, was involved in this and other wars. Though no longer the power that she once had been, she still had considerable importance, especially at sea.

[4] This was the time of the war of the League of Augsburg, in which the contribution of Austria was naturally impeded by the Turkish war.

[5] The results of Carlowitz were confirmed and extended by the total liberation of Hungary in another war terminated by the treaty of Passarowitz in 1718.

in Italy and had acquired the former Spànish Netherlands. The latter were a dubious asset, being so far removed from the main center of Habsburg power.

The example of centralized and integrated Louis XIV's France, enhanced by the evidence of French power, was not lost on other European rulers. Charles VI attacked the problem of centralization, but even in the compact block of territory made up of Austria, Bohemia, and Hungary, his success was impeded by the wide disparity of the peoples.

a. THE ISSUE OF SUCCESSION. In addition, the same issue of succession came to plague the Austrian house as had troubled the Spanish. Aware of the fate of the Spanish domain, in which fate he himself had had a hand, Charles was primarily concerned with the preservation of the integrity of his own lands. To this end he issued a Pragmatic Sanction, for which he first secured the assent of his various possessions.

His failure of male heirs gave added point to his precautions, and he labored assiduously to obtain similar agreement of foreign powers. In exchange for various concessions, his efforts were crowned with success. When he died in 1740 he left his daughter Maria Theresa an impressive collection of documents that guaranteed her title. But the same year 1740 saw Frederick II mount the Prussian throne. His comment, if cynical, was apt, that Charles would have better served his daughter's interest by leaving her a good army instead of paper charters. Prussia was about to embark on her role of Austria's nemesis.

4. The Minor German States. The dust of states, some three hundred, in the Empire, their history, politics, and rivalries constitute a burden on both memory and attention. Nevertheless, some of these units, though of secondary rank, were of sufficient size and power to warrant at least mention. Within the Germanic world especially, their weight could be at times significant.

a. BAVARIA. Like Austria, Bavaria was Catholic. It was her ruler, Maximilian I, who had headed the Catholic League of the Thirty Years' War, and at Westphalia Bavaria received part of the Palatinate and the electoral dignity. The bond of common religion did not prevent Bavarian suspicion of intended Austrian encroachment. In the war of the Spanish

Succession, Bavaria had been allied to France as she was later on to be to Prussia, when that state became Austria's chief competitor.

b. SAXONY. Situated in the very center of the Germanic world, Saxony might have been a candidate for the role that came to be Brandenburg's. But the leadership of the Protestant world which had been hers in the time of Luther, whose main protector the Saxon Elector had been, was surrendered to Brandenburg when Saxony allied herself with Austria against the Hohenzollerns. During the eighteenth century, while Saxony remained Protestant, her ruler became Catholic. This he did with an eye to the Polish throne, an ambition that was realized, but with most unfortunate consequences for Saxony as well as for Poland.[6]

c. HANOVER. Hanover, too, became an electorate after the war of the Spanish succession. The chief significance of this state stretching from Brandenburg to the North Sea, lay in the fact that it was the cradle of the dynasty that ascended the British throne in 1714. The personal union gave Britain a peculiar stake and interest in the Germanic world.

But far the most important of the Germanic states whose steady ascent gave it a role of European, and eventually even of world, dimensions was Brandenburg, or Prussia, whose course must now be traced.

B. The Rise of Prussia

1. The State of Brandenburg. During the course of the long—and still continuing—struggle between Teuton and Slav, the march *(Mark)* of Brandenburg had been established as an outpost of Germandom, astride the Elbe. Gradually, the outpost expanded in the flat, unbroken country to, and beyond, the Oder River. To this territory came in 1415, by way of the Nürenberg burgravate, the family of Hohenzollern, originating from a small south German hilltop castle, while the electoral dignity was conferred upon it by the Emperor. This association was destined to last until 1918.

Though uneven, the curve of Brandenburgian fortunes is

[6] See Chapter 10.

a steadily rising one through the centuries. The first Hohen-zollern Élector already set the pattern for many of his succes-sors by the assertion and consolidation of an enlightened paternalistic despotism. During the first phase of the Reforma-tion, though Saxony played a more outstanding role of leader-ship, the Brandenburg Élector became Lutheran and profited by the current practice of seizing ecclesiastical property. But it was in the seventeenth century that the fortunes of Hohen-zollern Brandenburg really began to prosper.

On the eve of the Thirty Years' War, in 1614, the Duchy of Cleves on the lower Rhine was acquired by inheritance. In the same manner the Duchy of Prussia was acquired in 1618.[7] The Hohenzollerns had begun the process of gnawing their way across Germany from the Rhine to the Vistula.

Brandenburg suffered during the Thirty Years' War from being one of the battlegrounds for rival Swedish and Imperial armies, but was fortunate in the change of her rulers as that conflict was drawing to a close.

2. The Great Elector (1640-1688)

a. FOREIGN POLICY. In 1640, Frederick William, known to history as the Great Elector, came to the rule of Brandenburg. His first task was to extricate himself from the Thirty Years' War. This he did with such success that at Westphalia Bran-denburg received the four valuable secularized bishoprics of Cammin, Halberstadt, Minden, and Magdeburg, as well as the eastern half of the Duchy of Pomerania.[8]

Frederick William could use diplomacy as well as force. Intruding in a conflict that was primarily between Poland and Sweden, he emerged from the "First Northern War" (1655-1660) with a clear title to East Prussia. He intervened similarly in the Dutch wars of Louis XIV which brought in Sweden as

---

[7] The religious-military order of the Teutonic Knights had christianized by conquest the lands around the southeast Baltic, to which it brought at the same time a Germanic ruling class. The Grand Master of the order, a Hohenzollern, espoused Lutheranism and made Prussia a hereditary Duchy in the sixteenth century. Before this, in 1466, the western part of Prussia had become incorporated into Poland, and East Prussia alone went to the Bran-denburg Elector in 1618. In his new capacity, he was vassal of the Polish King.

[8] The rest went to Sweden.

AT THE DEATH OF
THE GREAT ELECTOR

②
1614 ~ 1688

Farther Pomerania
1648

Ravensberg - *1614*

Cleves
1614

Berlin

East Prussia - *1618*

Mark *1614*

Magdeburg - *1648*

THE CONQUEST OF
SILESIA

③
1688 ~ 1748

1744

1720

Berlin

Silesia - *1745*

PARTITIONS OF
POLAND

1748 ~ 1807

West Prussia
1772

Berlin

Temporary Gains
1793/95 ~ 1807

GROWTH OF PRUSSIA, 1417~1918

200 MILES

a French ally. He was frustrated of the fruits of victory, but the defeat of Ferbellin in 1675, which he inflicted upon Sweden, put his state to the forefront of military powers in the Baltic region.[9] His efforts toward Silesia had no significant results.

b. DOMESTIC REORGANIZATION. But the cares of foreign policy did not distract the Great Elector from the domestic scene, where his accomplishments were even more important. His views of the proper ordering of the state were similar to those of his contemporary Louis XIV; his task in some respects resembles that of Richelieu. In his case, he succeeded in breaking the power of the diets, foci of local resistance, in his territorially scattered domains, which he endowed with a uniform and centralized administration.

The Great Elector was fully awake to the value of economic development, for which he strove in his relatively poorly endowed lands. When misguided Louis XIV revoked the Edict of Nantes, some twenty thousand French Huguenots were made welcome in Brandenburg. They gave Berlin its real start as an important center. When he died in 1688, after a reign of almost half a century, Frederick William had deserved well from his state, whose recovery he had nursed and whose power he had organized and enlarged.

3. The Beginnings of Prussia (1688-1740). The Great Elector seemed to have exhausted for a time the energy of his line. His successor, Frederick III (1688-1713), had little strength. Nevertheless, the major contest of the Spanish Succession that took place in his time, gave him the opportunity of securing imperial sanction for the assumption of the royal title. Henceforth, Prussia displaces Brandenburg in the nomenclature of states.[10]

a. FREDERICK WILLIAM I (1713-1740). The next Prussian king, Frederick William I, ranks among the curiosities of his-

---

[9] A parallel might be drawn between the contemporary rise of France at Spain's expense and that of Brandenburg on the smaller northeastern European stage.

[10] Brandenburg being an imperial fief, while East Prussia was outside the Empire, the coronation took place in Königsberg and the title assumed was that of King *in* Prussia. The reason for the "in" was to forestall Polish objections, West Prussia being Polish.

tory. Like his grandfather, he possessed great energy, much of which flowed, however, into trivial channels. Idleness anywhere he abhorred and would pursue in petty ways. But he had large enough vision also to realize the value of a body of civil servants of high integrity and competence. The tradition of the Prussian civil service has remained one of the great assets of that state.

But the army was his first and last love, on which, though otherwise parsimonious, he would lavish expense and care. Doubling its size to some 80,000 men,[11] staffed by officers not allowed to buy their commissions as was the normal practice of the time, he made it into the most precise and efficient fighting machine of the day. His eccentric craze for tall soldiers, six-footers whom he sedulously recruited for his Potsdam guard, contributed to the amusement of Europe. The tool that he had forged was little used by him, but, taking advantage of Sweden's misfortune in the Great Northern War[12] at the beginning of the century, he managed to secure nearly all Swedish Pomerania, thereby gaining for Prussia the valuable port of Stettin and the mouth of the Oder. Prussia no longer had cause to fear Sweden.

b. THE CROWN PRINCE FREDERICK. Just as the Great Elector and his son had been at odds, so likewise Frederick William I was not happy in his own son and heir, Frederick. The crown prince was not only fond of his flute, but of the softer amenities of life in general; arts and the intellect had for him more attraction than the more uncouth life of soldiering and the dull routine of administration. The king was brutal with his son; when the latter sought refuge in escape, he was caused to witness the execution of his best friend, after which the crown prince himself was imprisoned. Young Frederick surrendered. He applied himself to the trade of soldier-king; gifted as he was he learned it well. His taste for art he never lost, but he had taken the measure of the ways of life and of statecraft.

When he mounted the throne in 1740, in the same year as

---

[11] Such an army, ranking in size with those of much larger states like France and Austria, may be regarded as an overinvestment in military power, justifying sharp-witted Frederick II's characterization of war as Prussia's national industry.

[12] See Chapter 10.

Maria Theresa in Austria, he was fully prepared to put into practice the harsh learned lessons of his young experience.

II. THE AUSTRO-PRUSSIAN CONFLICT

Prussia was a much smaller entity than the "empire" of Austria, whether in population, territory, or resources. But, as Frederick himself was to put it, the very paucity of Prussia's resources caused her to make war her "national industry."

In purely military terms, Prussia's establishment was on a par with that of the great powers; its technical quality was better than theirs. Also, Frederick has come to be ranked among the great military commanders of all time. Prussia was ready to embark on the path of challenging Austria for primacy in the Germanic world, or central Europe. The contest about to begin was to last more than a hundred years. In its first stage it was the focus of European diplomacy in the middle of the eighteenth century.

A. The Issue of the Austrian Succession

1. The Rival Coalitions. Smiling cynically at Maria Theresa's collection of paper guarantees, Frederick entered into an alliance with Bavaria and France. The basis of this coalition was the French desire for the Austrian Netherlands, the prospect of the imperial title for the Bavarian Elector, and the Austrian province of Silesia for Prussia.[13] But the war was not to be confined to these states. Britain, always in favor of the balance of power, opposed to French expansion in the Netherlands,[14] at odds with Spain since 1739,[15] decided to support Maria Theresa, while Spain joined France in the hope of regaining some of her lost position in Italy. In addition, Saxony and Sardinia joined the opponents of Austria, while Holland, fearful of French encroachment, was on the other side. The conflict thus involved the major part of Europe.

2. The War of the Austrian Succession. Frederick was

---

[13] The acquisition of Silesia would double Prussia's population and make her, next to Austria, the leading German state.

[14] She had, moreover, obtained economic advantages in the Netherlands as the price of her recognition of Charles VI's Pragmatic Sanction.

[15] This conflict, of imperial and economic origin, went by the name of the War of Jenkins' Ear.

initially successful in Silesia, which he had secured by 1742. But Maria Theresa, rallying her peoples, achieved in turn successes against the Bavarians and the French. Frederick reentered the war; in 1745, the cession of Silesia was again confirmed, whereupon he withdrew from the contest.[16] The war lasted on, inconclusively, for three years, and was closed by the treaty of Aix-la-Chapelle in 1748. Silesia was definitely confirmed to Frederick, and Francis of Lorraine, Maria Theresa's husband, became Emperor.

Despite its duration, the war had caused relatively little havoc, justifying the reputation for mildness of eighteenth-century warfare. It will be noted that there were really two wholly distinct conflicts: the Austro-Prussian in central Europe, and the Anglo-French, mainly imperial.[17] The traditional Bourbon-Habsburg rivalry caused them to merge. From the standpoint of the former, the war of the Austrian Succession was but a preliminary skirmish.

B. The Seven Years' War

1. The Diplomatic Revolution. Either conflict had more concrete reality than the Bourbon-Habsburg difference, more a matter of tradition than of acute divergence by this time. Maria Theresa, unreconciled to the outcome of the war, made preparations for a revanche.

At home, she set about the task of reconstruction and reform, creating in Vienna a more centralized administration for her diverse possessions. Diplomatically, she was assisted in her preparations by the able Count Kaunitz. The cooperation of Saxony and of the Russian Tsarina Elizabeth was easily obtained. But to change the traditional French enmity into alliance was considered so radical a departure from established alignments that the reversal has been called the Diplomatic Revolution.[18] The counterpart of this, by automatic play of

---

[16] Meanwhile Saxony had made peace and Sardinia had gone over to the Austrian side.

[17] The Anglo-French conflict is dealt with separately in Chapter 11.

[18] Louis XV was at first reluctant, and Kaunitz had to enlist the assistance of his current mistress, Madame de Pompadour. Frederick's caustic tongue, which he had used in the cases of both Pompadour and Tsarina, played a role in these matters. But there was deeper reality to the Diplomatic Revolution than the injured feelings of ladies.

power balance one might say, was an Anglo-Prussian alliance.

2. The War in Europe. Hostilities between Britain and France had actually opened before their outbreak on the continent, where the conflict did not begin until two years later, in 1756.

a. FREDERICK'S CONDUCT OF THE WAR. Frederick capitalized on the advantage of seizing the initiative, overrunning Saxony, but his enemies were far superior in numbers and he had to withdraw from Bohemia into his own lands. Russian, Swedish, Austrian, and French armies were converging upon him, but Frederick's generalship proved equal to the task, and he was able to meet and defeat separately, the French at Rossbach and the Austrians at Leuthen in 1757. These brilliant victories gave him a respite, but not peace.

The scanty resources of Prussia had been strained by the effort, though some English assistance was forthcoming. Frederick had to face the Austrians and the Russians in 1758 and 1759, and dark days were ahead for him. The accession of George III in England meant a weakening of English support, and he had cause to despair. For a brief time, even Berlin was in Russian hands. It is Frederick's generalship in these campaigns as much as the fortitude of his character that have earned him the qualification of Great.

b. THE PEACE OF HUBERTUSBURG. When all seemed lost, an unexpected accident saved him. In January, 1762, his sworn enemy the Tsarina died. Her successor, mad Peter III, was Frederick's admirer; not only did he come to terms, but he would turn his former enemy's ally.[19] France for some time had not been active in the war in Europe, concentrating on the English phase of the conflict,[20] and Frederick could come to terms with Austria. The treaty of Hubertusburg, in 1763, ended the war in Europe. Prussia was merely confirmed in the possession of Silesia, but she had made good the claim to great power standing in military terms.

---

[19] Peter was superseded by Catherine in 1762, but she adopted toward Prussia a policy of benevolent neutrality.

[20] In 1761, as a result of the so-called Family Compact, Spain came into the war, but her intervention was too late to retrieve Bourbon fortunes, and she merely shared in France's defeat.

C. The Prussian State of Frederick II

1. Foreign Affairs: Poland and Bavaria. Frederick reigned in Prussia for almost another quarter of a century. It was a period of peace, unbroken save for his participation in the first partition of Poland in 1772, together with Austria and Russia. Prussia's share was the smallest, consisting of West Prussia, but highly valuable since it established territorial continuity between Brandenburg and East Prussia.

When the issue of Bavarian succession was used by Austria in 1778 to seek to enlarge her possessions, Frederick's threat of war sufficed to block the Austrian scheme. Prussia's claim to leadership in the Germanic world could no longer be dismissed.

2. Frederick, the Enlightened Despot. Frederick was absolute master of his state. In this respect, his views of constitutional theory differed little from those of Louis XIV, but the contrast is enlightening between Louis' phrase, "I am the state," and Frederick's variant, "I am the first servant of the state." The practice may have differed little, but Frederick, living in the age of the Enlightenment, was an enlightened despot.

a. HIS DOMESTIC POLICIES. Frederick was indeed a faithful and devoted servant of the state. Prussia was small; power and war might for her prove a sound investment, but the most must be made of what she had. A good administration and army she already possessed, but economic matters were no less worthy of the ruler's care. Frederick did much to foster both agriculture and manufacture, adhering in this respect to the prevailing mercantilistic practice of the age. He continued to emphasize the strong paternalistic tradition characteristic of the Prussian state.

b. HIS CHARACTER. In his own tastes and person, Frederick was appreciative of culture. He founded the Prussian Academy of Science whither foreigners were invited. The nationalism of our day was unknown to the eighteenth century. Frederick might defeat the French in battle, but France was the cultural center of the day, and Frederick preferred the use of French to his own native German. He called Voltaire to his court in order to perfect his practice, and it is perhaps not surprising that two such personalities should, after a while, have clashed. The flute that had worried his father continued to be his solace.

The enlightened outlook of the age he fully shared. From the beginning of his reign he introduced a policy of broad religious toleration; judicial procedure he reformed: the abolition of torture was a radical step for the time.

D. The Austrian Domain

1. Maria Theresa. Frederick's Austrian contemporary was not enlightened, in the eighteenth-century sense of the term; she was a good mother and Catholic. But she was also a conscientious and benevolent ruler, having at heart the welfare of her lands and her peoples.

2. Joseph II. Maria Theresa's son, Joseph, assumed the imperial title upon the death of her husband, Francis I, in 1765, and succeeded her in the Habsburg domain when she in turn died in 1780. Joseph II was enlightened with a vengeance, and offers a good example of the shortcomings of the doctrinaire approach in government. His ten year reign was a period of turmoil, when much of the old order was disturbed without leaving lasting traces of his reforms.

Thoroughly steeped in the French Enlightenment, unreasonably dedicated to rationality, if traditions and customs ran counter to the dictates of reason, they must be brought in line with these dictates. Serfs must be free, the administration of his domains centralized, the Church controlled and purged of superstitious practices, education spread, industry developed, his subjects coerced into being happy. From them, however, his abstractly admirable program evinced more bewilderment than gratitude. Well-intentioned Joseph was unqualifiedly a failure.[21]

---

[21] Enlightened, or benevolent, despotism was the order of the day and found adherents in other European states as well. Charles III of Naples (1738-1759), then of Spain (1759-1788); Joseph I of Portugal (1750-1777), and his famous minister Pombal; the rulers of Sweden, of Sardinia, of Tuscany, during the second part of the eighteenth century, all fit the same description.

ADDITIONAL READINGS

Atkinson, C. T., *Germany, 1715-1815* (1908); Bruford, Walter H., *Germany in the Eighteenth Century; the Social Background of the Literary Revival* (1935); Fay, Sidney B., *The Rise of Brandenburg-Prussia to 1786* (1937); Frischauer, Paul, *The Imperial Crown: the Story of the Rise and Fall of the Holy Roman and Austrian Empires* (1939); Gershoy, Leo, *From Despotism to Revolution, 1763-1789* (1944); Gooch, G. P., *Frederick the Great: the Ruler, the Writer, the Man* (1947); Marczali, Henrik, *Hungary in the Eighteenth Century* (1910); Marriott, J. A. R., and Robertson, C. G., *The Evolution of Prussia* (1946); Maurice, C. E., *The Life of Frederick William: the Great Elector of Brandenburg* (1926); Schwarz, Henry F., *The Imperial Privy Council in the Seventeenth Century* (1943); Sorel, Albert, *Europe under the Old Regime* (1947); Temperley, H. W. V., *Frederick the Great and Kaiser Joseph* (1915); Valentin, Veit, *The German People, Their History and Civilization from the Holy Roman Empire to the Third Reich* (1946).

(*Note.* In addition to the limited aspect of purely Germanic, or central European, affairs, this chapter provides a good focus for the study of continental relations and diplomacy in general.)

CHAPTER 10

Rearrangements
in Eastern Europe

As the seventeenth century was drawing to a close, three great states, empires they might be called, stood out in eastern Europe as important powers: Sweden had made the Baltic her own lake; Poland, or Poland-Lithuania, stretched through the Ukraine nearly to the Black Sea, the shores of which were wholly under the control of the Ottoman power.

Another century had radically altered this picture and the consequent relationship of power. Sweden was purely Swedish,[1] Poland no longer existed as an independent state, and the Ottoman Empire, though still very large, was definitely in retreat and decay, about to become the ever dying "sick man of Europe." In place of these we find a newcomer, Russia, now an important factor in the affairs of Europe; a Prussia, still small, but ranking in power with the great; and a transformed Habsburg domain, born of the ruins of the Holy Roman Empire. The Habsburg transformation and the rise of Prussia have been traced in the preceding chapter. We must now turn to the story of the other states that have just been mentioned.

I.   THE EMERGENCE OF RUSSIA

A.   Russia to 1689

In the whole of the modern story of Europe so far related, mention has hardly been made of Russia. That is for the

---

[1] Save for Finland, retained until 1809.

simple reason that Russia, or Muscovy, lay essentially beyond the confines of the various developments characteristic of what was Europe. But since Russia was destined to become an increasingly important factor in the affairs of this Europe, a brief glance must be cast over her past and nature. Some basic factors and influences stand out.

1. The Russian Land. That of geography should perhaps come first, the vast enormity of the formless plain that covers virtually the whole of what came to be known as European Russia.[2] Even the line of the Ural Mountains, or rather hills, supposedly separating Europe from Asia, is largely an artificial piece of geographic nomenclature. The same flatland extends throughout Eurasia from the North Sea to the Pacific, from Kamchatka to the Zuyder Zee.

2. Byzantine and Asiatic Influences. East of Germany, the people in this plain are Slavic, but various influences have shaped them.[3] They became Christians, like the rest of Europe, but for the Russians, their Christianity came from Constantinople. As the eastern Roman empire finally went down before the conquering Turks, the church in Russia secured emancipation from the jurisdiction of the Greek Patriarch of Constantinople. This took place in 1582.[4]

The Russian plain had been the scene of the activity, military and economic, of Northmen from whom its very name derives (Rus, Red). Later, conquering Asiatic hordes had overrun the land. The Mongols just reached the Adriatic, but their power in the Russian land became established. The process of emancipation from their rule was taking place at the opening of the modern age in Europe. Muscovy, the little

---

[2] The extension of this plain across all Poland and northern Germany constitutes one of the fundamental facts of the European landscape and history.

[3] This refers primarily to European Russia. Russia in Asia, Siberia, was very sparsely settled by native Asiatic peoples, and settlement into it from European Russia introduced a large Slavic element into Siberia as well. Conversely, the earlier Asiatic conquest of Russia has left traces in the population of the European part of the country.

[4] It was in 1582 that the Gregorian calendar was introduced in the west. The eastern Church did not adopt it, hence the growing discrepancy in dating between eastern and western Europe. It is only in our own time that eastern Europe has adopted the Gregorian calendar.

state around Moscow, was leader in this movement of liberation, and her ruler came to assume the title of Tsar of Russia.[5]
In one respect, the entire story of Russia to the present day
might be told as that of the gradual expansion of the initial
Duchy of Muscovy.

3. *Muscovy and its Growth.* The line of Muscovite rulers,
among whom stand out two Ivans, the Great and the Terrible,
labored to increase their power and that of their state. This
line died out at the close of the sixteenth century and there
ensued the "troublous times"; Poles were in Moscow and
Swedes in Novgorod. Finally, there emerged in control a
new line, the Romanovs, whose founder, Michael, came to
the throne in 1613 and whose dynasty was to endure just three
centuries.

a. WESTERN OBSTACLES. The Russian state was backward
and so regarded by the rest of Europe, with whom its contacts
were relatively scant.[6] Poland, for instance, was far more
advanced and civilized, the true outpost of western civilization.
Poland, moreover, as the result of the Lithuanian union,
stretched over much of what has come to be known as the
Ukraine.[7] In the Ukraine were Cossacks, hardy and independent frontiersmen, but they found themselves caught between the Russian and the Polish pressures. The settlement of
Andrussovo in 1667 is an important landmark in the story of
Russo-Polish relations, for it put a definitive stop to Poland's
eastern expansion, which was set back at the line of the
Dnieper, while Smolensk was also lost to it.

The first half of the seventeenth century saw Sweden firmly
planted around the Baltic, hence blocking the Russian push in
that direction. In the south, the Turks had taken over from
the Tartars the region around the Black Sea.

b. EASTWARD EXPANSION. During the seventeenth century
also, there was considerable expansion toward the east, settle-

---

[5] The title Tsar (Caesar) implied a claim to the inheritance of Rome,
the new Rome being of course Constantinople.

[6] There was a certain amount of trade, as witnessed by the organization
of the English Muscovy Company, for example.

[7] It is perhaps not proper to speak of the Ukraine until the nineteenth
century, but the name may be used for convenience in describing a region.

ment as much as, if not more than, conquest. The push was rapid across Siberia, and toward the end of the century the broad Pacific had been reached.[8] The issue is often debated whether Russia is mainly Asiatic or Western. Sitting astride the Eurasian land mass, it may be said that she had been shaking off for some time the shackles of Asiatic dominance and was about to initiate her first serious western orientation. This task is associated with the name of Peter, called the Great.

B.   Peter the Great

1. Peter's Character. The epithet was earned because of intelligence and strength combined. Peter early understood the superiority of western ways which he set about, with single-mindedness of purpose, to learn and emulate. He visited this west himself in 1697-1698, and the story of his sojourn as carpenter in a Dutch shipyard is apt expression of one facet of his character.

There were others. Physically huge and powerful, he was an uncouth and sensual barbarian who knew not the ways of restraint. One would have difficulty visualizing his contemporary Louis XIV personally wielding the executioner's sword, or having his own son executed. Two things stand out in Peter's reign: the character he impressed upon the Russian state; and its expansion.

2. The Russian State. The advantages of centralized control seemed demonstrated in the west. Autocracy and arbitrariness may be related to, but are not necessarily synonymous with, powerful centralization.

a. THE REVOLT OF THE STRELTSI. It was while on his western journey, between Vienna and Venice, that news came to Peter of the revolt of the *Streltsi*.[9] Hurrying home, he suppressed the revolt with utmost ruthlessness: thousands were killed in an orgy of blood wherein the Tsar in person shared. This gave him the opportunity to rebuild an army that would be thoroughly his own. This army was henceforth to be a

---

[8] This expansion did not stop there, for, crossing the Behring Strait in the early eighteenth century, it continued along the American coast, down to California.

[9] The *Streltsi* were a national militia wherein the forces of conservation found expression, hence they were inimical to Peter's ideas.

prime tool for domestic reform as well as for foreign conquest. Concurrently, administration was reorganized, the country being divided into provinces, or "governments."

b. PETER'S AUTOCRACY. Having destroyed the *Streltsi*, the nobility of the boyars was ignored by simply not calling it into assembly. Instead, many new nobles were created, but the revolutionizing of Russian society did not reach the lower mass of serfs. Nothing must stand in the way of the Tsar's absolute authority. The church also was brought in line; the Moscow Patriarch was shorn of his authority, which was vested in a Holy Synod, appointed by the Tsar and headed by a layman. The Russian Church became thereafter an obedient tool of the state.

c. FORCED WESTERNIZATION. In every way, to minutest detail of personal garb and fashion, Peter strove to break down the hold of old Russian ways and to introduce western modes in their place.[10] Some of this may seem humorous, but it was all part of a single purpose and plan. Peter wanted to make Russia modern, to bring her into the western stream, in order to make her a power in Europe. Fond of the sea and understanding its significance for purposes of contact with the outside world, his policy may be summed up in his own phrase, securing a window on the sea.

For landlocked Russia this meant conflict with two of her neighbors, the Ottoman Empire, which held the shores of the Black Sea, and Sweden in control of the Baltic coasts.[11] As early as 1695, taking advantage of an Austro-Turkish conflict, Peter secured control of the Black Sea port of Azov. But this initial success was short-lived; Azov had to be relinquished and Peter's effort and success were destined to be directed toward Sweden.

---

[10] The picturesque tale of Peter going among his nobles with a pair of shears with which he trimmed their patriarchal beards is well known. Such changes, seemingly superficial, are symbolic and a measure of the intense speed of reform. In our time, the wearing of the fez was similarly forbidden in Kemalist Turkey.

[11] It is an interesting fact of geography, of the utmost significance in the history of modern Russia, that this largest of states on earth can have no good access to the world's open waters. Even the Black Sea and the Baltic are landlocked bodies of water.

II. RUSSIA ENTERS THE EUROPEAN STAGE

A. The End of Sweden's Power

1. The Seventeenth-Century Heyday of Swedish Power.
For a time, roughly through the seventeenth century, Sweden ranked with the great powers of Europe. But, unlike Prussia's, Sweden's career of power was short-lived. It, too, rested on an overinvestment in military power, for the more solid resources of Sweden proper, population or wealth in all its forms, were too scant to support lasting power. Her military strength, once broken, could not be revived.[12]

From the time of her emergence to separate status, Sweden had kept encroaching around the Baltic. Estonia was acquired in 1561. But it was Gustavus Adolphus who made her an important power. By the time the peace of Westphalia was made, Sweden had obtained control of the important German base of Bremen and of western Pomerania, in addition to Livonia (modern Latvia) and the eastern part of the Gulf of Finland. The peace of Oliva in 1660 confirmed the failure of Prussian, Polish, and Danish efforts to curb the power of Sweden. Had her domestic affairs been better ordered she might have pursued her career of empire. Charles XI (1660-1697) was an able ruler but his work was not continued after him.

2. The Great Northern War

a. THE COALITION AGAINST SWEDEN. His successor was a mere youth, Charles XII. Shortly after the latter's accession, Tsar Peter returning from his western journey contrived an alliance between himself, Poland-Saxony, and Denmark (Brandenburg withdrew at the last moment), whose purpose it was

---

[12] The success of Prussia by contrast was due to the fact that she was able gradually to incorporate new territories, which in turn gave sounder foundation to the basis of her military strength, and also to the fact that her kings, while militarily minded, were fully alive to the importance of administrative and economic development. This stands in marked contrast with the more exclusively military interest of some of Sweden's rulers. Sweden was also hampered, unlike Prussia, by the lack of homogeneity of her acquisitions.

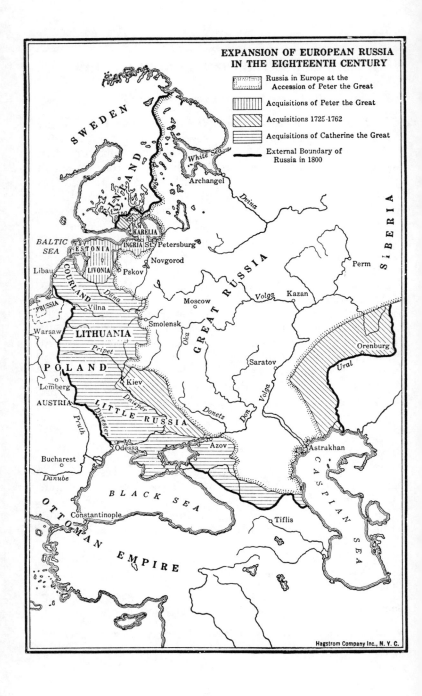

EXPANSION OF EUROPEAN RUSSIA
IN THE EIGHTEENTH CENTURY

Russia in Europe at the
Accession of Peter the Great

Acquisitions of Peter the Great

Acquisitions 1725-1762

Acquisitions of Catherine the Great

External Boundary of
Russia in 1800

SWEDEN

FINLAND

White Sea

Archangel

Dvina

SIBERIA

BALTIC
SEA

KARELIA

INGRIA St. Petersburg

ESTONIA

Novgorod

Perm

Libau

LIVONIA

Pskov

GREAT RUSSIA

COURLAND

Dûna

PRUSSIA

Vilna

Moscow

Volga

Kazan

Warsaw

Smolensk

LITHUANIA

Oka

Orenburg

Pripet

POLAND

Saratov

Ural

Lemberg

Kiev

Volga

AUSTRIA

LITTLE RUSSIA

Dnieper

Donetz

Don

Pruth

Dniester

Bucharest

Odessa

Azov

Astrakhan

Danube

BLACK SEA

CASPIAN SEA

OTTOMAN EMPIRE

Constantinople

Tiflis

Hagstrom Company Inc., N. Y. C.

to reduce Sweden to Scandinavia proper plus Finland, while dividing the rest of her Baltic possessions.[13]

b. CHARLES XII's INITIAL CAMPAIGN. But the allies had taken the wrong measure of the young Swedish king. One of history's curious characters, this impetuous "madman of the north," enjoyed talents of limited scope, but of a high order in the military field. Taking advantage of the geographically scattered position of his enemies, Charles XII in 1700 moved against the Danes, whom he defeated and forced to withdraw.

With surprising rapidity, he turned from Denmark to Russia. At Narva, in 1700 again, a vastly superior (in numbers) Russian force was thoroughly defeated by his equally superior (in quality) Swedish army. Tsar Peter, however, did not abandon the struggle—vast space has ever been Russia's asset—and Charles now showed the deficiencies of his political judgment and the handicap of mere stubbornness.

Augustus, Elector of Saxony and King of Poland, he considered his chief enemy, and against him he turned. Military success he achieved as usual, but he became inextricably involved in the large Polish land and in the confused intricacies of Polish politics.

c. THE END OF CHARLES XII. The war went on. Peter had meanwhile reorganized his army and secured a foothold at the bottom of the Gulf of Finland. Charles would move on to Moscow. But when his army, after the rigors of a Russian winter, met the Russians at Poltava in 1709, the result was a Russian victory. Charles fled to Turkey, where he remained five years, during which time that country joined the war.[14] Finally forced to leave, when he returned to Sweden the situation had deteriorated past retrieving. Appropriately, he met death on the field of battle, in 1718, in Norway. The outcome of his career of adventure was that the Swedish nobility asserted greater power at the expense of the crown and that

---

[13] The western powers and Austria were primarily concerned at this time with the issue of the Spanish Succession, and Peter failed to interest them in the affairs of northeastern Europe. As a consequence, the two wars went on simultaneously, but did not become connected.

[14] Russia was thoroughly defeated in the war with Turkey, which as a result regained Azov in 1711.

the Swedish star had definitely and permanently set in the firmament of power.

3. The Treaties of Stockholm and Nystadt. The treaties of Stockholm in 1719-1720 eliminated Sweden from the Germanic world. Stralsund alone she retained, the rest of her possessions being shared by Prussia (Pomerania, Stettin, and the mouth of the Oder), Hanover (Bremen and the mouths of the Elbe and Weser), and Denmark (Holstein). The chief gainer, however, was Russia. The treaty of Nystadt in 1721 gave her full access to the Baltic with the acquisition of Carelia, Ingria, Estonia, and Livonia.

4. Tsar Peter's Success . St. Petersburg. The reign of Peter the Great had thus witnessed the downfall of Sweden and the launching of Russia on her western inspired career. His "window on the sea" was the concrete manifestation of his achievement and of the new orientation of Russia.

To emphasize the change even more clearly, as early as 1700, Peter had begun the foundation of St. Petersburg on the banks of the Neva River. The laying of the new city was in itself a triumph over nature. Like Louis XIV's Versailles in France, this was henceforth the seat of Russia's government; by contrast with Byzantine Moscow and its Kremlin, the face of St. Petersburg was western.

Peter's son and heir was a disappointment to his father, as young Frederick of Prussia had been to his. It is to a degree a measure of Peter's character and Russian ways that the fate of the Tsarevitch was death under torture.

B. The Vicissitudes of Eighteenth-Century Poland

It has been pointed out that, during the seventeenth century, Russia had on her borders three states, each one of which, in terms of power, was rather stronger than herself. Sweden was the first with whom accounts were settled; the story of the Ottoman Empire lingers into the twentieth century. But the most radical fate of all was to be that of Poland, destined to complete destruction during the eighteenth century.[15]

---

[15] These changes meant profound alteration, if not destruction, of the existing European balance of power. It is worth noting that French policy had generally leaned on alliances with Sweden, Poland, and Turkey.

1. Poland to 1697. In Polish history, the sixteenth century is usually regarded as a golden age accompanied by the flowering of both power and culture. Polish influence tended to become dominant in the vast state of Poland-Lithuania cemented in 1569 by the Union of Lublin, following an earlier personal union of the lands.

a. <u>DOMESTIC DISABILITIES OF POLAND.</u> But the next century was one of relative decline. The reasons for this were partly foreign, the wars in which Poland was involved. But even more, perhaps, they were domestic. One was the failure to enact constitutional reform that was needed.

The Polish nobility was numerous, some of it quite poor, but highly jealous of its rights. Within itself, this nobility, the *szlachta*, was strongly democratic, yet its assumption of exclusive identification with the Polish nation was narrow. To the significance of commercial endeavor it was blind and to the practice of it inimical. The famous *liberum veto*,[16] though not as disastrous as strict adherence to its principle might indicate, was none the less a barrier to the functioning of effective government.

The Polish Crown. Lacking the asset of a western bourgeoisie, Poland also failed to develop a strong central executive. The elective principle of her monarchy was retained; it was an invitation to the prosperity of factions, "confederations" as they were often styled, and, even more, to foreign interference. After the Jagellonian dynasty had ended with Sigismund II in 1572, Poland had a variety of kings, some native, some of foreign extraction. The great Sobieski (1674-1696), who for a time restored Polish prestige, thus was followed upon the throne in 1697 by Augustus II, Elector of Saxony. The Saxon-Polish connection was not to prove a fortunate experiment.

2. Poland to 1763

a. AUGUSTUS OF SAXONY AND STANISLAS LESZCZINSKI. The accession of the Saxon Elector to the Polish throne in 1697 had itself been in part the result of foreign interference, and

---

[16] Essentially, the principle of unanimity in the Diet.

opposition to it was strong in Poland. The country was involved in the Great Northern War, and Charles XII actively
interfered in her domestic politics, procuring the substitution
of Stanislas Leszczinski in place of Augustus in 1704. But,
following the Swedish reverse at Poltava, Augustus once more
was king.[17] Despite opposition, he retained his throne until
1733, when the issue of his succession was cause for war.

b. THE WAR OF THE POLISH SUCCESSION. This war, despite
its name, was fought primarily by outside powers, and much
of it in desultory fashion. The Poles, weary of foreigners,
brought in once more Stanislas Leszczinski. His chief outside
support was France,[18] and the war was fought mainly by
France and Spain ranged against an Austro-Russian combination.[19] It was fought and settled in the west, and France
yielded to Russian insistence—a Russian army advanced to
Warsaw—acquiescing in the election of Augustus III of Saxony
as king.[20]

c. AUGUSTUS III. The reign of Augustus III was inglorious.
The central European scene was dominated by Frederick II
of Prussia and his conflict with the House of Habsburg, in
which Poland did not participate directly, although Augustus'
Saxony did. The issue of internal reform was inconclusively
debated in Poland, whose course was generally dominated by
combined Russo-Prussian influence.[21]

When Augustus III died, this influence, by a curious reversal,
procured the election to the throne of Stanislas Poniatowski,
a Pole, cultured but lacking strength, a man moreover who
had been Catherine's lover and who remained personally loyal
to her—an odd position for a would-be patriotic king of

---

[17] It is of interest, and a measure of power relationships in eastern Europe,
that the peace of 1711 between Russia and Turkey contained a Russian
promise of noninterference in Polish affairs. This promise, however, was
not honored, and Turkey was subsequently unable to enforce its fulfillment.

[18] Leszczinski was Louis XV's father-in-law.

[19] Sweden and Turkey failed to play an effective part in containing
Russia, as France had expected that they would.

[20] Leszczinski was compensated with the Duchy of Lorraine which, upon
his death, was to revert to France.

[21] Russia's participation in the Seven Years War against Prussia was an
exceptional deviation in this tendency.

Poland. The reign of Empress Catherine II of Russia will make a better focus for the remainder of this story.

C.   Catherine the Great of Russia

The interval, 1725 to 1762, between the death of Peter I and the accession of Catherine II to the throne of Russia saw that position filled by rulers of little distinction, or worse. Peter's work was not undone, however, nor the direction he had impelled on Russia reversed, and when Catherine began her reign she may be said to have taken up where he had left off.

1. Catherine's Character and Policies. Herself a German princess, the wife of Tsar Peter III, her intelligence enabled her quickly to take the measure of her new and at first bewilderingly unfamiliar surroundings. Her husband's accession to the throne in 1762 was "conveniently" followed by his demise within a year; Catherine remained sole mistress of Russia till 1796.

Western in her own background, she adopted, outwardly at least, the religion of her new country. She combined the brutal ruthlessness of her Russian predecessor Peter with the cynicism of her German contemporary Frederick. For the success of her policies in terms of Russian power, as well as for the excesses of her private life, she may deserve the appellation Great.

At home, Catherine showed little interest in the welfare of the Russian people, better left in their benighted ignorance, surest guarantee of the tranquillity of her own position; though she was not unappreciative of such things, for instance, as the value of technical improvements in English agriculture. Enlightened ideas she knew, and a superficial veneer of them she adopted. French became the language of polite Russian society; with Voltaire she corresponded, and Diderot she invited to Russia. One must keep up with civilized Europe, for the sake of appearances, if for no other reason. But Catherine's main interest and greatest achievement lay in the realm of foreign policy.

2. The Partitions of Poland. Of the three great states along Russia's borders, Peter had definitely disposed of Sweden.

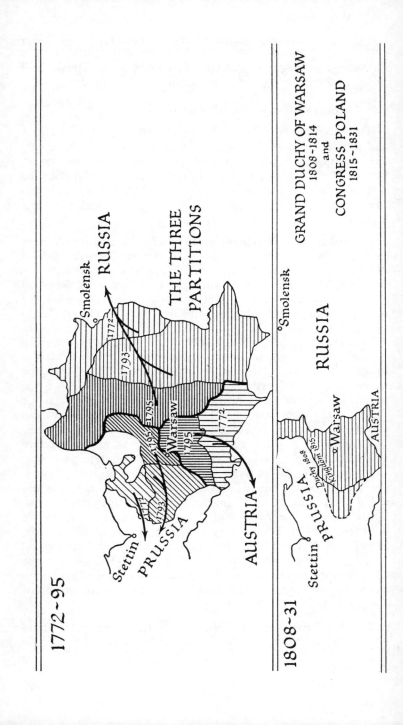

1772-95

Smolensk

1772
1793
1795

RUSSIA

THE THREE
PARTITIONS

Stettin
1772
1793
1795
Warsaw
1795
1772

PRUSSIA

AUSTRIA

1808-31

Smolensk

Stettin
PRUSSIA
Duchy 1808
Kingdom 1815
Warsaw

RUSSIA

AUSTRIA

GRAND DUCHY OF WARSAW
1808-1814
and
CONGRESS POLAND
1815-1831

On the remaining two Catherine focused her attention.

The election of Poniatowski to the Polish throne in 1764 meant continued Russian influence in Poland. Prussia had also supported him as the price for Russian alliance, which continued to operate, as far as Poland was concerned, to the effect of preventing the reform of an anarchic constitution.

a. THE FIRST PARTITION, 1772. Russia had entertained designs of absorbing all Poland, but the realization of the strength of united Polish opposition, plus other embroilments,[22] made Catherine responsive to Frederick's suggestion of partition. Between these two at first, then with Austria, agreement was reached in 1772, as the result of which Austria secured Galicia, Prussia obtained West Prussia,[23] and Russia took the section east of the Düna and Dnieper Rivers. The rest of Europe remained deaf to the appeals of Poniatowski, and Russian bayonets induced ratification of the arrangement by the Polish Diet.

b. THE SECOND AND THIRD PARTITIONS. There was alarm in Poland, where many saw at last the writing on the wall. But all attempts at union and reform were thwarted by the interference of her neighbors. The task begun by them in 1772 was not completed for some time. Catherine lived on to see the effect of enlightened ideas in France, which embarked on her career of revolution in 1789. The international embroilments growing out of the French upheaval seemed a propitious occasion to attend to Polish matters. Russia and Prussia in 1793, these two and Austria in 1795, completed the task of total elimination of Poland from the map of Europe.[24]

This destruction of a large European state has been called one of the major crimes in history. Certainly, it was a callous violation of the implicit rules that governed the relations of

---

[22] Russia was at war with Turkey from 1768 to 1774.

[23] Thorn and Danzig remained Polish for the time, but Danzig was of little use to Poland, since she was cut off from the sea.

[24] At the eleventh hour, serious reforms were enacted in Poland. The famous Four Year Diet enacted in 1791 a new constitution, quite comparable in terms of modernity to the French charter of the same year. This constitution, among other things, established a hereditary monarchy and substituted majority rule for the *liberum veto*. Also, unlike the French, the Polish constitution was not accompanied by revolution. But the very fact that the constitutional transformation had taken place without Russian consent was cause for Russian intervention, leading to the partition of 1793.

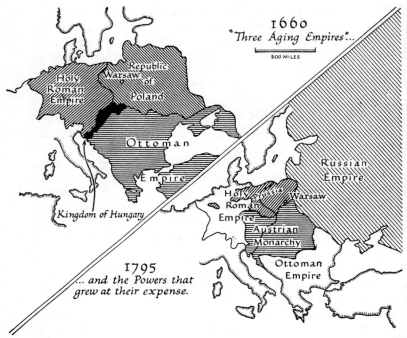

The old Polish Republic became defunct in 1795, the Holy Roman Empire in 1806, the Ottoman Empire not until 1923. Their successors in central-eastern Europe, the Russian, Austrian and Prussian monarchies, established themselves as great powers in the seventeenth and eighteenth centuries, and perished in 1918 in the First World War.

the European community of states, to say nothing of the violence that it did to the national feelings of the Polish people.

3. The Retreat of the Ottoman Empire. Polish affairs did not detract from Catherine's attention to the Ottoman problem. After the treaty of Carlowitz in 1699, the Ottoman Empire could at best hold its own for a while. Traditionally, the Habsburgs and Venice had filled the role of Europe's bulwark against the Turkish threat.

The threat was now reversed, and the process of Ottoman retreat had begun. For a time, Austria and Russia, separated by Polish and Turkish territory, could cooperate in the offensive directed against the Ottoman domain. Once their successes had brought them into contiguity, their rivalry over the further division of spoils was to become increasingly acute, one of the chief components of the Near Eastern Question.

a. CATHERINE'S FIRST WAR AGAINST TURKEY. The first Russo-Turkish clash during Catherine's reign took place in 1768, as the result of Russian territorial violation of Turkey in connection with intervention in Polish affairs.

Russian arms were successful against those of a decadent Turkey, and the treaty of Kutchuk Kainarji, which closed the war in 1774, is a landmark in Russian foreign policy as well as in Ottoman history. Not only did Russia secure access to the Black Sea,[25] but, of equal importance for the future, she obtained the right to interfere in internal Ottoman affairs. This she gained through the Turkish promise of administrative reforms in the Danubian Principalities of Moldavia and Wallachia, and through the grant to Russia of the protection of Orthodox Christians in the Ottoman Empire.[26]

b. FURTHER TURKISH RETREAT. Joseph II of Austria went to war with Turkey in 1786. Belgrade was taken, but had to be retroceded. Russia, also involved, in 1788 fared better. The process of Ottoman decay had, if anything, gathered momentum during the interval since Kutchuk Kainarji. The treaty of Jassy in 1792 established the Russo-Turkish frontier along the Dniester River. When Catherine died in 1796, the western borders of Russia had been brought to a line running from Libau to Odessa. Russia was definitely, not only a European power, but one of the great powers of Europe.

---

[25] Azov was ceded outright to Russia, and the Khanate of Crimea became independent. This was a step toward its annexation by Russia in 1783.

[26] During the war, Russia had encouraged the Greek desire for independence, and a Russian fleet had sailed from the Baltic to the Aegean, where it engaged in successful action against the Turkish fleet.

As an aftermath of the war Austria demanded and obtained the cession of Bukowina.

ADDITIONAL READINGS

Anderson, R. C., *Naval Wars in the Baltic, 1522-1850* (1910); Bain, R. N., *Slavonic Europe: a Political History of Poland and Russia from 1147 to 1796* (1908); Halecki, Oscar, cited in Ch. 5; Kerner, R. J., *The Urge to the Sea: the Course of Russian History* (1942); Konovalov, S., *Russo-Polish Relations: an Historical Survey* (1945); Laskowski, O., *Jan III Sobieski, 1629-1696* (1941); Lord, Robert H., *The Second Partition of Poland* (1915); Reddaway, W. F. et al, *The Cambridge History of Poland* (1941), vol. 2; Schuyler, Eugene, *Peter the Great* (2 vols., 1884); Sorel, Albert, *The Eastern Question in the Eighteenth Century* (1898); Sumner, B. H., *Peter the Great and the Ottoman Empire* (1949).

CHAPTER 11

Competition for Empire

I. THE SITUATION UP TO 1689

A. The Nature of European Expansion

1. The Motivations. The outburst of European expansion beyond the limits of the continent of Europe and its surrounding islands that began toward the end of the fifteenth century, and the early fruits of that expansion, have been surveyed in an earlier chapter. As much as any single thing, the fact that from that time, Europe explored, conquered, settled, and in a variety of ways increasingly set the pattern for the future development of the world, constitutes one of the major themes of the history of four hundred years.

The sheer desire for knowledge along with the lust for gold, the wish to save the heathen and to reap the rewards of trade, were all mingled in this endeavor. Much exploring was done by missionaries, in the settled Far East and in the empty spaces of the New World, but gold and trade were the incentives that led to the more permanent results, and to the greater conflicts.

2. The Spanish, the Portuguese, and the Dutch. Spain and Portugal enjoyed a virtual monopoly in the initial stages of this development. In 1494, the whole planet was allotted between them by the Pope. The Dutch were next in the race for empire, establishing their own mainly at the expense of the Portuguese. Reaping the benefits of trade and banking, of which activity, grafted on their earlier European experience, Rotterdam became the capital of Europe.[1]

---

[1] The Dutch rise to empire was involved with the religious issue of the time and the successful fight for independence from Spain.

3. The French and the English. The French and the English were late in entering the imperial competition. Their sixteenth-century activity was small compared with that of the Spanish or Portuguese, but the English especially gained much valuable maritime experience in their raiding of Spanish ships. The distinction between piracy and trade was not then the clearer thing of later days. The episode of the Spanish Armada in 1588 may be said to have established the basis of the future sea power of England.

By the turn of the century, there was recovery that was to prove lasting in France, and in both countries commerce was an activity of increasing importance. The English East India Company was chartered in 1600, a measure of the interest in the Far Eastern trade and of the manner in which the process of expansion was operating. Chartered companies with wide powers, rather than governments themselves and directly, were the agents of Europe's expansion. The role of governments was none the less important, for besides the granting of charters and concessions, they took much interest in terms of trade. The numerous acts of mercantilistic legislation typify the seventeenth-century view of the state's interest in the national trade.[2]

a. THE SEVENTEENTH-CENTURY SETTLEMENT OF NORTH AMERICA. The advent of the Stuarts in England coincided with the initiation of the English development in America. From slow and painful beginnings, a steady stream of emigration settled along the Atlantic Coast from present Maine to Georgia. Simultaneously, the French were penetrating the St. Lawrence valley and claiming the lands on both sides of the Gulf of St. Lawrence. Following their exploration of the Mississippi, similar claims were advanced to that river's basin, the vast Louisiana Territory. Both French and English also began some lodgments in Caribbean islands.

4. The Rivalries and Conflicts. But these colonies of settlement were of slow growth at first, and more important was the trade with the more settled East. The middle of the century witnessed a bitter commercial struggle between the English and the Dutch, against whom England's first Naviga-

---

[2] See Chapter 3.

tion Act in 1651 was primarily directed.[3] The Dutch had a near monopoly of the Eastern trade, and their explorers ranged the Pacific and Indian Oceans.[4] The rivalry directed against Spain[5] by Dutch and English was superseded by an Anglo-Dutch conflict.

a. THE ANGLO-DUTCH WARS. The points of contact and conflict were numerous: slave trade of Africa, Atlantic fisheries, North American settlements, but above all trade. The Dutch East India Company had shut off its English rivals from the Spice Islands trade.[6] The rivalry was national and operated independently of the vicissitudes of politics at home. It was during the Commonwealth in England that the first Anglo-Dutch war (1652-1654) was fought. The Dutch were fully equal, if not superior, to the English on the sea, but the treaty of Westminster registered a limited English gain—a trading post in the Spice Islands.[7]

b. BEGINNINGS OF THE ANGLO-FRENCH CONFLICT. Again in 1665-1667, there was war, as the result of which the Dutch were evicted from the North American mainland.[8] The restored Stuarts leaned on French support for purposes of their domestic policy, and the third Anglo-Dutch war (1672-1674) merged with the French attack on Holland.[9] But by this time the situation was already changing. The abrupt reversal in England that brought William of Orange to that country's throne occurred at a time when it had begun to appear in England that the "natural" and more serious enemy was France rather than Holland. William was Louis XIV's arch-enemy, but mainly for reasons of continental European politics. However, this fitted to a nicety the English desire for divided

---

[3] The Dutch were also active in the New World, where they established themselves in New Amsterdam and in some West Indian islands.

[4] Tasman circumnavigated Australia, and the Cape of Good Hope was settled in the middle of the seventeenth century.

[5] Spain and Portugal being joined from 1580 to 1640, attacks were directed equally against both.

[6] The famous "massacre of Amboyna" in 1623 is one of the outstanding episodes in the Anglo-Dutch contest in the Far East.

[7] The Dutch were also faced with trouble in Brazil, which Portugal regained from them in 1662.

[8] New Amsterdam, renamed New York, was captured in 1664.

[9] See above, p. 128.

power on the continent and for the humbling of what was becoming their chief imperial rival.

The war of the League of Augsburg in Europe has been surveyed. From another point of view that war was also the opening of a major imperial contest that found England and France ranged against each other in what has been called the Second Hundred Years' War.[10]

II.   THE ANGLO-FRENCH CONFLICT

A.   The Situation in 1689

1. Differences Between France and England.   The conflict may in brief be said to have grown out of the marked and successful seventeenth-century economic growth of the two countries which came to be the two chief economic powers of the time. Their policies in many ways were similar, Colbert being a model exponent of the mercantilistic view and practice to which the Commonwealth adhered.

But if the mercantilistic view flourished in England as well as in France, the whole authoritarian and centralizing tendency of the French state allowed less scope to individual endeavor. English Dissenters went to the English colonies; as late as 1685, French Huguenots were lost to France and went, not to French settlements across the seas, but rather to Prussia and to Holland.[11]

2. The Theaters of Conflict.   As the long struggle was about to open, English and French confronted each other in the New World and in Asia.[12]   Both also had establishments in some West Indian islands. These were small but derived great significance from the importance of the sugar trade.

a. THE NORTH AMERICAN MAINLAND.   The mainland of the

---

[10] The first Hundred Years' War was the conflict waged during the fourteenth and fifteenth centuries, growing out of the Norman conquest and subsequent dynastic entanglements, and the issue of which was basically whether or not England should control territory on the continent proper, an issue eventually settled in the negative.

[11] Some indeed found their way overseas, to the American colonies for example, or, by way of Holland, to South Africa.

[12] In Africa, the French had posts in Senegal and Madagascar, the British in Gambia and the Gold Coast. But the African rivalry was secondary at this time.

North American continent, outside the regions under Spanish control and a thin coastal edge of English settlements, was largely wilderness which supported a sparse population of Indian tribes, the stage of development of whose culture was primitive. Such a relative vacuum could not indefinitely persist in the face of expanding, aggressive economies and cultures.

Throughout the seventeenth century a steady stream of settlers had flowed from England, until it had pre-empted the entire length of coast from present Maine to Georgia. Fishing, trade, and tobacco plantations were the bases of life of the North American settlements.[13] By 1689, a solid block of territory between the ocean and the Alleghenies had been settled or organized, though royal charters spoke of grants "from sea to sea."

The French settlers were relatively few, but French claims were vast. Moving up the St. Lawrence valley, through the Great Lakes, La Salle in 1682 had ridden down the Mississippi River. As Louisiana, named for the reigning king, claim was laid to the entire basin of the mighty stream. If settlers were few, explorers, missionaries, *coureurs des bois*, ranged far and wide.

Land, furs, sugar, coveted by both French and English, were ample grounds for competition. English expansion beyond the Alleghenies was hemmed in on all sides by French claims and a growing line of military outposts.

b. INDIA. On the opposite side of the planet, India, unlike North America, was populous and possessed of ancient culture and wealth. The huge subcontinent was under the rule of Moslem conquerors. But the rule of the Great Mogul was loose, and the entry of Europeans, to whom India meant trade, was an easy matter. From the beginning of the seventeenth century the English had intruded on this Portuguese preserve. By 1689, they had establishments at Bombay, Madras, and Calcutta.

The French came somewhat later, after the *Compagnie des Indes* had been reorganized in 1664, and established them-

[13] There was also a settlement in Newfoundland, and the Hudson Bay Company, mainly interested in the fur trade of the north, had been chartered in 1670.

selves in Chandernagor and Pondicherry, near Calcutta and Madras, respectively. These various outposts of trade, small in themselves, were wedges of future penetration on a greater scale.

3. Position of the Rivals. India and North America were the main scenes of the Anglo-French conflict that opened in 1689. Each side had some assets. France was much the larger, more populous, and richer country; but against this stood the crucial fact that her attention must inevitably give priority to matters continental and to land power, to the detriment of matters imperial and to sea power.

The English economic and financial structure also had some advantages over the French. In North America, English settlers were far more numerous than French. But, to make up for this, in America as in India, the French had generally better success than the English in their dealings with the native peoples and powers.

B.   The First Three Wars

1. The War of the League of Augsburg. The European War of the League of Augsburg was, overseas, a first and inconclusive skirmish.[14] Port Royal in Acadia fell to New England colonists, whose rear was raided by Count Frontenac's Indian allies. The treaty of Ryswick (1697) restored the *status quo ante.*

2. The War of the Spanish Succession. Next came the War of the Spanish Succession, Queen Anne's War in America, the results of which, while of some consequence imperially, were still inconclusive. English and Dutch sea power mastered in more decisive fashion French and Spanish. Again Port Royal fell, though Montreal and Quebec successfully resisted. The treaty of Utrecht (1713) confirmed Britain in clear possession of Acadia—henceforth New Scotland—Newfoundland, and Hudson Bay, as well as West Indian St. Kitts. From Spain, Britain exacted the important economic advantages written into the *Asiento.*[15]

---

[14] This was known in America as King William's War.

[15] This gave Britain the monopoly of the slave trade for Spanish America —4800 slaves a year for thirty years—and the right to send one trading ship a year to Porto Bello.

3. The War of the Austrian Succession. This arrangement was almost an invitation to abuses. Abused it was, and in 1739 Anglo-Spanish hostilities, the War of Jenkins' Ear, were resumed. They merged into the European War of the Austrian Succession. France and Britain again collided in North America (King George's War, 1744-1748) and also in India this time. Once more, the treaty of Aix-la-Chapelle was an inconclusive truce whereby all conquests were restored.

C. The Definitive Triumph of Britain

1. French Preparations for Future Conflict. Even before the last mentioned war, the French had been both vigorous and active in consolidating their imperial power. Louisbourg on Cape Breton island, and a whole line of westward stretching military posts (Niagara, Detroit, Sault Ste. Marie), as well as settlements in the south (Mobile, New Orleans), were established. In India, the able and enterprising Dupleix achieved considerable success in training and using native forces and in participating in the rivalries of native powers.

2. The Seven Years' War. This growing French activity was prelude to the final act. It opened in 1754, preceding the Seven Years' War, which was its counterpart in Europe.

a. THE WAR IN NORTH AMERICA. In North America the specific occasion for conflict was the issue of control of the Ohio Valley. Success attended the French in the initial phase of the French and Indian Wars, as this phase of the conflict is known in North America, and the prospect of English fortunes seemed low in the year 1756,[16] which brought the able Montcalm to the command of the French forces.

But the arrival to power of the Elder Pitt in England induced that country to renewed efforts, which soon bore fruit. The tide turned with the capture in 1758 of Louisbourg and of the French forts Duquesne (subsequently Fort Pitt, hence Pittsburgh) and Ticonderoga. The war moved into the St. Lawrence valley, where Wolfe snatched victory from seeming

---

[16] In Europe, the war was going badly for Frederick of Prussia, Britain's ally, while the British themselves were defeated in the Mediterranean and lost Minorca.

failure with the capture of Quebec in 1759.[17] The fall of Montreal in the next year, and French maritime defeats, could not be retrieved by the belated intervention of Spain, which was thereby merely involved in a common defeat.

b. THE WAR IN INDIA. The course of the war in India paralleled the American phase. Interference in native politics, specifically Dupleix's success in installing his candidate in the Carnatic, was the occasion for hostilities. Dupleix found at last his match in Robert Clive, initially a clerk in the employ of the British Company, who found warfare and politics more suited to his talents. After ousting Dupleix's protégé from the Carnatic, he interfered in Bengal, where he similarly procured the success of the British candidate. By 1761 British dominance was established on the east coast of India.[18]

c. THE TREATY OF PARIS. The outcome of hostilities was clear and the treaty of Paris restored peace in 1763. Its terms were harsh where France was concerned, for they were tantamount to her elimination as an imperial power. In India, she retained some trading posts destined to future insignificance. Of her American possessions, nothing was left on the mainland.[19] Some Caribbean islands, Guiana, some fishing rights, and two minute islands off Newfoundland were all that remained of an empire that had rivaled the British. It would take more than a century before France would become again the second imperial power.

3. American Independence. To this highly important result, a footnote should be added. The very removal of the French danger from the North American continent also removed from the British colonies the need for British protection. The American declaration of independence followed by thirteen years the treaty of Paris, and in their war of independence French assistance played a vital role in the success of the thirteen colonies. The British setback that the recognition of American independence constituted was a negative

---

[17] Quebec was defended by Montcalm. Both he and Wolfe were killed during this battle.

[18] Dupleix had meantime fallen in disgrace and been recalled to France.

[19] Territory east of the Mississippi was ceded to England; the western section of Louisiana went to Spain, from whom Britain took Florida.

French success, for France herself regained no colonies by the treaty of Versailles of 1783.[20]

III. CONTINUED GROWTH OF BRITAIN AND THE EMPIRE AFTER 1763

A. Britain's Imperial Primacy

Freed as she was from the competition of her chief rival, France, Britain went on to consolidate and expand her imperial position. Other empires, Dutch, Portuguese, and Spanish, continued to exist, but no serious threat was contained in them. In addition to, or in connection with, this newly acquired British position of imperial primacy, went definite primacy in naval power. British imperial and naval primacy were to last unchallenged into the twentieth century.

1. Britain in Asia. In India, Clive continued his work, but it was with the advent of his successor, Warren Hastings, in 1772, that the Regulating Act of the following year created the unifying office of Governor General for all the Indian possessions, and laid the bases of organized growth and development. The East India Company was still the agent of British activity in India, but its officials had to be confirmed by the King.

Infiltrating in Indian politics, posing as protector of the ever more impotent Great Mogul, Britain's power steadily spread and became paramount. At the end of the century, two distinguished governors, Lord Cornwallis (1786-1793) of American fame, and the Marquis of Wellesley (1798-1805), added luster to the British record in India.

The Company was also active beyond the confines of India. By 1795, control had been acquired of the important passage between the Indian Ocean and the Far Eastern seas, location

---

[20] Only Tobago and Senegal were restored. Spain, however, having also joined in the war, regained Florida.

In the light of future developments, American independence may be regarded as an event of enormous importance. At the time, however, and from the standpoint of European developments, it appeared as of relatively minor consequence.

of future Singapore, and the foundations laid for the future British Straits Settlements.[21]

2. Exploration. Much exploration went on, British and other, during the eighteenth century. The name of Captain Cook stands out among explorers of this period. Australia was known before him, but he, ranging across the wide Pacific, laid the bases for the British claim to that continent. Used for the transportation of convicts at first, the settlement and development of Australia, as of New Zealand, belong essentially to the next century.

B.   Economic Changes in Eighteenth-Century Britain

1. Commercial Development. This imperial progress of Britain went on parallel with significant changes in the economy of the British islands themselves. Trade grew, and the political organization of eighteenth-century Britain favored this growth.

The tendency away from the accepted mercantilistic theory became increasingly marked, and took the form of relaxation in the practice of its enforcement. If the law was not formally altered, the terms "free trade" and *laissez faire* were entering the economic thought of the latter part of the century.[22] The year 1776 saw, not only the American Declaration of Independence, but also the publication of Adam Smith's *Wealth of Nations*, future bible of the new economic outlook.

2. The Agricultural Revolution. Important as was commerce, agriculture was not neglected in eighteenth-century England. On the contrary, it made such progress as to warrant the use of the phrase "agricultural revolution." The general economic expansion of the period, more narrowly the near doubling of the population during the course of the century, was the incentive.

The work was done by experimentally-minded landowners

---

[21] Malacca was acquired from the Dutch in 1795, as well as Ceylon. The French revolutionary and Napoleonic wars served also as pretext for the acquisition of the Dutch possession of the Cape of Good Hope.

[22] The battle for free trade was not formally won until well into the nineteenth century. These ideas were by no means exclusively or even primarily English, as the existence of the Physiocrats in France and the very expression *laissez faire* indicate.

possessed of capital, gentlemen farmers such as Jethro Tull and the picturesque "Turnip" Townshend. Land productivity was much increased, and in general the technical quality of its management put English agriculture in advance of others.

3. Beginnings of the Industrial Revolution. But even more important, especially for the future, than the agricultural improvement was the so-called Industrial Revolution. The large scale use of mechanical power in manufacturing processes depended for its success on the combination of a number of circumstances.

The presence in England in near proximity of coal and iron, basic materials of industry to this day, available capital in the hands of an enterprising mercantile class, and certain technological developments or inventions, made England the first home of industry, the effects of which began to be substantial during the last third of the century. The advantages of this prior development and its various consequences, economic, political, and social, were to be well-nigh incalculable. The seeds of it were planted at this time; the story itself belongs in a later chapter.

ADDITIONAL READINGS

Buffington, A. H., *The Second Hundred Years' War, 1689-1815* (1929); Dorn, Walter L., *Competition for Empire, 1740-1763* (1940); Hyma, Albert, *The Dutch in the Far East* (1942); Mackinder, Halford J., *Britain and the British Seas* (1914); Mahan, Alfred Thayer, *The Influence of Sea Power on History, 1660-1783* (1906); Schuyler, Robert L., *The Fall of the Old Colonial System* (1945); Seeley, Sir John R., *The Expansion of England* (1895); Willcox, William B., *Star of Empire: a Study of Britain as a World Power, 1485-1945* (1950); Williams, Basil, *The Whig Supremacy, 1714-1760* (1939); Williamson, J. A., *The Ocean in English History* (1941); Wrong, G. M., *The Rise and Fall of New France* (2 vols., 1928).
See also some of the titles under Chapter 3.

CHAPTER 12

The Enlightenment

I. THE AGE OF REASON

A. War, Politics, and Ideas

Change in the realm of thought, the prevalent *Zeitgeist*, is, or at least appears to be, more elusive and gradual than that connected with the more manifestly obvious upheavals of wars and revolutions. The date 1648, for instance, associated with the great international settlement of Westphalia, occasion for a far reaching readjustment of the European state system, or that of 1660, which brings to mind Louis XIV, the English Restoration, Franco-Spanish power relationship, changes around the Baltic, are reasonably natural chronological breaking points in Europe's story.

It might be pointed out that the year 1642 was marked by Galileo's death and Newton's birth. Highly suitable for centenary commemoration, it would be an act of symbolic and imaginative license to give that date the same importance in the history of ideas as the above-mentioned ones in the record of political change.

It would be fair enough to say that the second half of the seventeenth century, roughly the period of Louis XIV's personal and active rule, witnessed the culmination of the political development for which the bases had been laid before, especially in France, as well as the fruition of seeds the planting of which may be associated with the names of Galileo and Descartes. The two developments are indeed related by more than the mere accident of contemporaneity. "Ancients" and "moderns" might pursue what is in fact a perennial and everlasting debate; there is no question that the classical ideal of order based on reason made a deep imprint on the age. Its manifestations may be seen in the ordering of the state as well as in the manners, the buildings, even the gardens of Versailles.

B. The Newtonian Synthesis

It is fitting that the greatest triumph of man's use of the rational faculty should lie in the domain of science. The ground for this had been prepared, and the increasing recognition of the importance of the scientific endeavor may be seen in the nearly simultaneous foundation of the Royal Society (1660) in England and of the French Academy of Sciences (1666).[1]

1. The Law of Universal Gravitation

a. THE CONCEPT OF NATURAL LAW. Among his many inquiries, Galileo had investigated the laws of motion in general, and those of falling bodies in particular. Such an investigation in itself postulates the major and fundamental assumption—now commonplace but at first revolutionary—that the world of matter is subject to the rule of law, to which may be added the further assumption that the human rational faculty is capable of apprehending such law.

b. NEWTON'S ACCOMPLISHMENT. Young Newton early showed an interest in the sort of inquiry that had attracted Galileo. These investigations greatly depend for their success on mathematical tools. The Cartesian synthesis of geometric and algebraic concepts was one such. Newton himself propounded the Theory of Fluxions, or calculus.[2] This alone, powerful and ingenious concept that made use of the notion of changing quantity (infinitesimals), would warrant him high place in the annals of mathematical science. But Newton's thought went deeper, revealing the insight characteristic of genius.

---

[1] The French Academy, of purely literary purpose, had been founded by Richelieu in 1635. This body has no English counterpart.

[2] The credit for the discovery of the calculus goes independently to the German philosopher Leibnitz, whose symbolism was in fact less clumsy than Newton's.

The famous story of the falling apple aptly illustrates the
point. To broaden the concept of falling bodies, of weight,
into that of the general attraction of matter, and then to form-
ulate the law of that attraction, so that falling stone, projected
cannon ball, and planet, are seen to behave according to one
and the same principle, that of universal gravitation, is unquestionably one of the great achievements of the human mind.

It is only the widespread, but foolish, notion that mathematics is necessarily abstruse that prevents many from per-
ceiving the elegance and beauty that reside in the small piece
of symbolism, $F \sim \frac{m \cdot m'}{d^2}$.[3] Here is in indeed the music—the
simple ordered harmony—of the celestial spheres. Newton's
result was reached mainly with the use of pencil and paper,
with little experimentation of his own; he relied upon the
results of observations made by others, giving all the more
impressive a demonstration of the power of human reason.

2. The New Climate of Thought. This is not the place to
retail the achievements of other scientific work of the period.
Newton himself dealt with other subjects as well—the theory
of light, for instance—but the discovery of the law of universal
gravitation has been selected as illustration because of its in-
trinsic importance and because it served as perfect focus for
a change in the intellectual climate, the consequences of which
may well be described as incalculable.

The significance of this change, which went far beyond the
technical scientific discovery that it was, took time to reveal
itself. The most important part of Newton's work was done
while he was young, that is, well before the beginning of the
eighteenth century. Though his scientific interest continued
through his long life, much of his time was spent at the Mint
and, revealingly, in now forgotten biblical disquisitions. But
whether he would or no, and largely thanks to him, the turn
from the seventeenth to the eighteenth century is well described in the title of a recent work, *The Crisis of European
Thought, 1680-1715.*[4]

---

[3] In ordinary language: the force of attraction of any two pieces of
matter is directly proportional to the product of their masses, and inversely
proportional to the square of their distances.

[4] *La Crise de la conscience européenne,* by Paul Hazard (1935).

II. THE AGE OF THE ENLIGHTENMENT

A. The Progress of Science in the Eighteenth Century

In the limited and technical sense, quite apart from philosophical or other implications, the Newtonian synthesis was a remarkable enough achievement. It represented at once the closing of one chapter and the opening of a new in the attempt of man to understand the universe around him.

1. Mechanical Science. Progress was steady and substantial in the field of mathematics. Newton's universe was a machine, the secret of which had yielded to man's probing. Astronomy, too, both observational and as celestial mechanics, made great progress, culminating in Laplace's masterpiece, the *Mécanique céleste*, dating from the turn from the eighteenth to the nineteenth century. The mathematical formulation of mechanical explanation is the most typical, brilliant, and characteristic achievement of eighteenth-century science.

2. Natural Science. Natural science has no comparable accomplishment to offer, being still at the preliminary stage of organizing and classifying nomenclature. The name of Swedish Linnaeus stands out in the botanical aspect of this development, which was much aided by the information brought back to Europe by exploring expeditions. These expeditions were numerous, the English with such men as Captain Cook leading the way, though by no means monopolizing this activity, which centered to a large extent in the still relatively unknown Pacific. Thus was geographical knowledge increased and improved, but also knowledge increased and speculation fostered about the earth, its evolution, as well as about its fauna, its flora, and the diversity of representatives of the human species. Buffon is another of the outstanding names in this development.

3. Social Science and the Literary Disciplines. Interest in man, whether his individual functioning, his behavior as social animal, or in the record of his past, was not only widespread, but this study was influenced by the example of success in the exact sciences. John Locke, Newton's somewhat older contemporary, was not political scientist only, but philosopher and psychologist as well. To the problem of knowledge, epistemology, he devoted attention, and propounded the sensationalist view. It was natural that the eighteenth century, in view of its other accomplishments and interests, should display curiosity about the origin and nature of ideas, and the relation to their formation of experiment and sensation, sifted and ordered by the rational faculty in the process of producing knowledge.

One may now begin to speak of the social sciences. History as a discipline is ancient, but it, too, felt the scientific influence. If Gibbon's views of Christian Rome are not wholly above prejudice, his great work[5] represents none the less a new standard of scholarship. Vico and Voltaire were concerned with philosophical aspects of the subject,[6] and the collation and organization of source materials received a fresh impulse, especially among the Benedictine Order.[7] If history can never hope to be science, this was at least an attempt at approximating the scientific ideal in its case.

B.   Rationalism and The Enlightenment

1. Faith in Reason. But what is most significant is the sum total of this activity, all of which was deeply colored by the Newtonian synthesis. The World Machine was now explained for all to see and understand, much as a clockmaker can explain the functioning of his clock. The clock simile is indeed the most common at this time.

There was every reason to be impressed by this triumph of human reason, and it should be no cause for surprise that the rational faculty in man should have been exalted and the tendency yielded to, to extrapolate into the hope, wish, or faith, that in time all would yield to the exercise of human reason.

Such belief rests on underlying assumptions, which may or may not be warranted. It is more human than rational to

---

[5] *History of the Decline and Fall of the Roman Empire* (1776-1788).

[6] Vico's views were expressed in his *Principi d'una scienza nuova,* while Voltaire's *Essai sur les moeurs* presented a wholly secular interpretation of world history, including the development of religions.

[7] The congregation of St. Maur in France was particularly active in this work. Muratori in Italy, a priest but not a Benedictine, earned the title of "father of Italian history" for his researches and compilation of sources.

proceed by analogy, and the potential fallacy of this stands clearly exposed in retrospect, but the impact must be stressed again of the combined novelty and magnitude of the accomplishment.

2. Deism and the Philosophes

a. RELIGION AND THE ENLIGHTENMENT. A problem arises at this point. The Cartesian-Pascalian dichotomy between reason and faith no longer suffices. Yet the divinity is not rejected, but rather the argument is used that there could be no clock without clockmaker. But this is precisely the point, for the deity is thereby removed to the position of creator of the universe and its laws; God is mathematician, hence essentially and primarily reason. The ingenuity of His creation may command admiration and respect, but hardly love. And surely, it would be beneath His dignity to tamper arbitrarily with the operation of His own creation. Prayer is futile, and miracles represent but foolish belief in man's importance.

With this vague and generalized deism some, especially the more radical Protestant sects, might find easy accommodation. But organized and institutionalized religion, most of all the Roman variety, could hardly be expected to divest itself of so much that was essential to its functioning.

The enlightened exponents of the new looked upon the priestly caste as impostors, exploiting for their own advantage the naive innocence of the many, to the "enlightenment" of whom they were professionally and inevitably opposed. "*Écrasez l'infâme!*" was Voltaire's retort; crush the infamous thing, meaning superstition and prejudice. But since the Church fostered these things, the line of demarcation became hard to draw. Anticlericalism has always been a more flourishing tendency in Catholic than in Protestant countries.

b. THE GREAT ENCYCLOPEDIA. A group of men, especially in France, came to be known as *philosophes*, who generally adhered to such views. They were not necessarily philosophers in the narrow and technical sense of the word,[8] but rather in

---

[8] *Philosophe* is the French for philosopher. It is convenient to use the French word in English, as consecrated by usage, to distinguish and refer to this particular eighteenth-century group of men. Among them were scientists, but the literary tendency dominates.

the etymological—lovers of wisdom—a wisdom which to them was synonymous with enlightened acceptance of the new. Orthodoxy, often associated with intolerance, they would oppose, but otherwise they were humane and tolerant. To the enlightenment of other men they would gladly contribute, and this desire presided over the birth of that ambitious undertaking, the *Grande Encyclopédie*.

Encyclopedias there had been before, but this was something new in that category of work. Not only was the great encyclopedia to be the repository of the latest information available; it was to be itself an instrument of enlightenment, an agency through which to fight obscurantism. Many titles would serve as headings under which propaganda rather than pure scholarship could have free rein. For all this, in part because of this, the *Grande Encyclopédie* is one of the great monuments of the eighteenth century.

c. THE PLACE OF FRANCE IN THE MOVEMENT. This work and the center of the whole movement were French, and French as a language had by this time in large measure superseded Latin as the common medium of cultured exchange. But the fact must be emphasized that there were no nationalistic (as we understand the word today) overtones in this development.

The *philosophes*, whether French or other, may have conversed and corresponded in French, and in large numbers congregated in Paris, but their outlook was humanistic. Man and mankind were their concern. It merely happened that France was the place where a more advanced development of culture had occurred,[9] hence the country that could lead the way for all. It was fitting, all the same, that French Voltaire should represent the essence and himself be the incarnation of the movement.

3. Voltaire. Born in 1694, in comfortable bourgeois circumstances, Voltaire came of age in the twilight of the Great

---

[9] The relation is interesting to consider between cultural influence and power. Louis XIV's France fought much of Europe, but after him, though still the strongest European power, in terms of resources and potential at least, France's power declined. The eighteenth-century military record, from Louis XIV to the Revolution, is at best mixed. But this in no way reflected on the standing of French culture which reached its widest influence during this very period.

Monarch's reign. Of the freer age of the Regency and of Louis XV, he was to be epitome and standard bearer. To all phases of the intellectual activity of his time he was alive. Even science was young enough for the educated layman to be a commoner breed than is possible in our day of vastly wider knowledge. Apart from dabbling in physical experiment, Voltaire was the great popular exponent of the Newtonian synthesis and world machine. Himself no original mind like Newton, his influence in some respects was greater. This influence was due to the merit of literary style: if simple clarity of thought and expression has been associated with the French language, none better than Voltaire exemplifies the point.

Voltaire was above all a literary man. He wrote verse, plays, and history, but it is as popularizer of ideas that his fame was established. He fought with vigor, using sarcastic wit in the service of his belief, for tolerance, and above all for intellectual freedom.[10] His own career well epitomized the century: he ran afoul of the arbitrariness of the French state and the discriminations of French society, for a brief time knew the Bastille, then profitable exile in England. But he was also pensioner of this same state and, in old age, a man of European fame, he settled on his Ferney estate, conveniently close to the Swiss border in case of need. His visit to Paris toward the end of his life was a triumphal journey.

4. *The Organization of Society.* Voltaire is often credited, and with justice, with being one of the precursors of the French Revolution. Yet he himself was anything but an egalitarian revolutionary. In justice he believed, and in the free expression of ideas; but of the capabilities of the masses of men to order their own governance he had no high opinion. His ideal was aristocratic, though intellect rather than birth would be the proper basis of distinction. Enlightened despotism, a Frederick II, was his ideal of government.

a. THE GOVERNMENT OF EIGHTEENTH-CENTURY FRANCE. The government of eighteenth-century France was no enlightened despotism, however. Despotic in form it was, though hardly oppressive in practice, as the case of Voltaire himself goes to

---

[10] "I do not believe a word that you say, but I shall fight to the death for your right to say it," is the often quoted terse form of this belief.

prove. Despotism tempered by corruption, with the stress on "tempered" and on "corruption" better describes it. In any event, an unsatisfactory condition, especially by canons of rational intelligence. What there was of enlightened Europe, and of enlightened France, looked elsewhere for political models. Aside from the enduring admiration of antiquity, England, nearer in place and time, attracted the attention and praise of progressive *philosophes*.

b. THE ENGLISH MODEL. The government of eighteenth-century Britain was rather different in practice from what it has subsequently come to be. What, by present day standards, would be considered gross and corrupt abuse was then accepted practice. Nevertheless, the Glorious Revolution, dignified in its theory by the Lockean apology, had unquestionably introduced into the British government a novel and fruitful principle, diametrically opposed to that of divine sanction for rule.

Voltaire's exile took him to England during the twenties of the century. There he observed the Newtonian influence[11] and the form of government, or at least his conception of the form of that government. Both he admired, and with both he proceeded to make his own country widely acquainted. The effects of his *Elements of the Philosophy of Newton* (1738) have been mentioned; his *Philosophical Letters on the English* (1733) conveyed his admiration for the English system. The implications of the Lockean doctrine need not be cause for dissension at this stage. Locke, Voltaire, and many a British Whig, then and long after, would agree that "the people" meant the qualified, the educated, and the competent, and them alone.

c. MONTESQUIEU. Of greater substance as political thinker, less universal than Voltaire in his activity, was Montesquieu. He too found fault with the unchecked absolutism of Louis XIV, thinking that the feudal nobility had served a useful role before its power had been broken. Student of Roman institutions and history, his name has mainly become associated with the great doctrine of the division of power in government, the system of checks and balances of which the

---

[11] The hold of the Cartesian influence in France was an obstacle to the introduction of the Newtonian views; hence all the greater importance attaching to Voltaire's work of popularization.

young American republic soon to be born was to see the most thoroughgoing and lasting application.[12]

d. OMENS OF POLITICAL AND ECONOMIC CHANGE. To a considerable extent, Voltaire's desired freedom of thought was realized in practice in the France of his day. Censorship did exist, but it was either very lax, or else works by it unsanctioned would be printed in Holland, whence they would easily find their way across the border. Civilized France, nobility of birth and talent, would meet in the salons presided over by great ladies of the day. These salons were important factors in the exchange and spread of new ideas.

It was part of the prevailing sophistication, decay perhaps of an existing order, that its beneficiaries should condone attacks upon it while there were few that rose in its defense. Louis XV's quip, *"après moi le déluge"* (let the flood come after me), is adequate expression of both intelligent appraisal and cynical callousness.

For the most part, Voltaire, Montesquieu, *philosophes*, and encyclopedists were serious minded reformers. Among some of them one finds an early awareness of what was destined to become of such overwhelming importance, "economics," a word coined partly in derision at this time. England offered the most marked example of economic change in the eighteenth century, when the agricultural revolution took place, to be shortly followed by the industrial.

The term "industrial revolution" is a late invention. But there was much awareness and discussion of changing conditions of trade. The Physiocrats in France thought that a more liberal economic policy on the part of the state, *laissez faire*, would both enhance the national wealth and help solve the increasingly acute fiscal problem that faced the country. English Adam Smith is the accepted prophet of the doctrine, and it was in England rather than France that changes in manufacturing methods were first to occur on a substantial scale. The effects of the industrial revolution hardly belong, however, to the pre-French revolutionary period but rather to the post-Napoleonic story.

5. The Phenomenon of Rousseau. Voltaire has been

[12] Montesquieu's chief work is the *Spirit of Laws* (1748).

cited as the most representative impersonation of the Enlightenment. It might be argued whether or not his contemporary Rousseau should be included under the same rubric. But no record of the story of eighteenth-century thought would be complete without him, for his influence has been very considerable.

a. ROUSSEAU'S CHARACTER. Rousseau's background was Calvinist Geneva, his early circumstances were not prosperous, and his personality and career furnish as good an example as history provides of perfect maladjustment. Pathological he may be called, though not trespassing the bounds of sanity; his is a perfect case for modern psychological analysis—his frank *Confessions* would furnish much material for this—the results of which would, however, be irrelevant to this story, for his ideas, whatever their filiation and source, are what matters.

b. ROUSSEAU'S SOCIAL THOUGHT AND ROMANTICISM. Rousseau reflects much of his time, but also stands out in marked contrast with it. Though for different reasons, he too reacted against the practice of his day and joined the critics of the existing status. Far more thoroughgoing and radical than Voltaire, he saw in society itself—eighteenth-century artificial, sophisticated, French society was an extreme example—the source of evil among men.

"Man is born good, it is society depraves him," went his thesis.[13] Not over troubled by consistency, he also went on to elaborate a contractual theory of society. Fanciful and unfounded in any fact as the theory may have been, the *Social Contract* is an important work in the story of political theory, for, hypothesis or fact, from it can be made to derive a whole set of social relationships and a foundation for the state. The general will, the rights of the majority, are political myths that owe much to the Rousseauean analysis.[14]

---

[13] That an essay defending such a thesis should receive an official prize is a measure of the liberalism prevailing in practice in France.

[14] It should be emphasized that there is much inconsistency in the totality of Rousseau's social analysis, as will appear from a comparison of the thesis of the *Social Contact* with that expounded earlier in the *Origin of Inequality among Men,* for instance. Also, the *Social Contract* attracted far less attention in its own day than other works of Rousseau, such as *Émile* or the *Nouvelle Héloïse.*

Along with this went further fancy. The concept of the "noble savage" was generally popular in the eighteenth century.[15] It fitted to a nicety into Rousseau's cantankerous dissatisfaction with the society around him. Instinct, natural feelings, and emotions were sounder guides to conduct than the constructions of the rational faculty. The state of nature was to be exalted. The success of this novel approach, annexed though it was by what was most artificial in eighteenth-century society—vide Marie Antoinette's games at milkmaid imitation—none the less represented a serious reaction against the excess of artificiality in the civilized life of the day. If the dominant note of the eighteenth century is cold, clear reason, the beginnings of the Romantic movement, especially in Germany and England, also belong to it.[16] And so likewise does Rousseau as his novel, the *Nouvelle Héloïse*, well illustrates.

c. ROUSSEAU'S VIEWS ON EDUCATION. Much of this was fancy, as remote from reality as the most artificial aspects of urbane court behavior. But some of it, also, struck a remarkably modern note. *Émile* is a treatise on education which has had considerable influence on the course of that activity, and one would have to grant that much of it is simple hard good sense. It was characteristic of the man that, devising the ideal education, he should dispose of his own progeny at the foundlings.

C. The Civilized Eighteenth Century

1. Optimism and Progress. Any age, in its totality, will offer a wide variety of expression; yet it is fair to speak at times of a dominant note in the *Zeitgeist*. By contrast with the sixteenth century, seething with violent dissent in the

---

[15] This idea, derived from the beginning, but highly imperfect, knowledge of primitive civilizations, was, among other things, a convenient stick with which to belabor existing institutions at home. Montesquieu's *Persian Letters* belong in this same tradition of criticism.

[16] It is a notable fact that the level of artistic production of the eighteenth century represents a decline from the high point of the Renaissance, if one allows for the outstanding and marked exception of music. Whether this phenomenon is to be connected with the dominant stress on reason, characteristic of the eighteenth-century *Zeitgeist,* rather than on the imaginative and emotive faculties would make an interesting point for discussion.

effort to find new bearings in place of the destroyed medieval synthesis, the eighteenth century had found the intellectual security of a novel faith, the faith in reason.

Confidence and optimism were natural by-products of this faith. Not the later confidence brought to man by the effective subjugation of the forces of nature and the utilization of its resources, for technology and applied science do not loom large for almost another century, but the confidence born of the proved capability of intellectual understanding. Understanding and reason, when applied to man in the mass, would produce the good society.

The eighteenth century was civilized, tolerant, and increasingly humane. Even penology was being humanized under the proddings of enlightened reformers[17] and equally enlightened despots. The optimistic belief in progress logically thrived in this climate.[18] Typical *philosophe* that he was, Condorcet would not let his having run afoul of the Revolution becloud his confidence; before committing suicide in 1793 he penned the *Outline of the Progress of the Human Mind*.

2. Cosmopolitanism. As pointed out before, the eighteenth century knew none of our bigoted nationalism, instead of which an urbane cosmopolitanism prevailed. Rulers and states could compete and fight wars; that was their nature, but eighteenth-century men had reached a high point of humaneness, and a minimum of ideological intransigeance pervades their behavior.

Our modern national allegiances would have seemed small and narrow: no stigma attached to French Voltaire congratulating Prussian Frederick for his defeat of the French king; the French government was merely civilized, not run by traitors, when it instructed its navy not to interfere with the activities of English Captain Cook while France was at war with England. Captain Cook was after all doing important work of lasting value, he was enlarging the boundaries of knowledge.

---

[17] Beccaria's book, *Dei delitti e delle pene* (1764), achieved considerable notice and popularity.

[18] The fact should be stressed that the accepted view was that of a static condition, or alternately of cycles in history. The concept of progress is a novel one, antithesis of either, and logically related to the unprecedented phenomenon of modern scientific development.

III. THE AMERICAN REVOLUTION

A. Criticism of Existing Conditions in Europe

The tolerant free play of the intellect, wherever the results might lead, usually betokens either of two conditions of society: one of strength, when institutions are so firmly rooted that, feeling impervious to attack or criticism, they can afford the safe magnanimity of tolerance; else one of weakness, when decadence has sapped the vigor of belief in the rightness of the existing order, which therefore cannot bear defense or is not worth a probably futile effort at such.

The civilized eighteenth century gave full scope to the corrosive exercise of the intellectual faculty. In what was in many respects the most advanced of all countries, there was least effort to effect timely change. The French Revolution is so large an event as to call for separate treatment. Before this event shook Europe to her very foundations, the New World was the scene of a smaller upheaval.

B. The Rebellion of the American Colonies

If one may say that the seeds of twentieth-century America go back to the eighteenth, to read back into that time the present world position and significance of the United States would be a prime example of manhandled history. In its contemporary context, the American Revolution was a relatively minor ripple, an interesting example, within the British complex, of the fact that mercantilistic practice was outmoded; example also of hesitancy in both diplomacy and war, of carelessness and divided counsels in Britain; across the ocean, a doubtful issue, far from commanding universal or even overwhelming assent, made in large part successful by the adventitious intrusion of intra-European rivalries.

Were this all, the episode would hardly warrant mention in this story. What makes it of interest and significance, without unduly magnifying its contemporary importance, is its relation to the developments that have been traced in this chapter. Eighteenth-century America, even apart from her colonial status, quite naturally followed Europe in her cultural progress. The revolution caused the emergence to leadership in the new state of an unusual and remarkable constellation of men. As illustrations, Franklin and Jefferson might be chosen of individuals steeped in the climate of the Enlightenment.

1. The American Constitution. Allowing that the young Republic enjoyed over older Europe the advantages of a society inevitably less burdened by the weight of an ancient social structure, the American Declaration of Independence and the subsequently drawn constitution were novel and startling departures in the field of governmental practice. Locke and Montesquieu had joined hands in the guarantee of individual rights and freedoms, made stronger by the deliberate fragmentation of power.

As to the phrase, "the right to the pursuit of happiness," its appearance in usually so staid a document as a state paper might indeed raise the question whether unfathomable naïveté had seized the seat of government, or whether truly a new society was being born. In 1776, when one-sidedly proclaimed to independence, or in 1783, when formally recognized by Britain, America did not command power that was worth reckoning; but this fact gives the ideas that prevailed over her birth to distinct nationhood all the more interest and meaning.

ADDITIONAL READINGS

Becker, Carl, *The Heavenly City of the Eighteenth Century Philosophers* (1932); Brailsford, H. N., *Voltaire* (1935); Bury, John B., *The Idea of Progress: an Enquiry into its Origin and Growth* (1932); Butterfield, Herbert, *The Origins of Modern Science, 1300-1800* (1949); Cobban, Alfred, *Rousseau and the Modern State* (1934); Collingwood, R. G., *The Idea of Nature* (1945); Dampier, Sir William C. D., *A History of Science and Its Relations with Philosophy and Religion* (1949); Dunning, William A., *A History of Political Theories from Luther to Montesquieu* (1905); Frankel, Charles, *The Faith of Reason: the Idea of Progress in the French Enlightenment* (1941); Mornet, Daniel, *French Thought in the Eighteenth Century* (1929); Sullivan, John N., *Isaac Newton, 1642-1727* (1938); Taylor, F. Sherwood, *The March of Mind* (1939); Whitehead, A. N., *Science and the Modern World* (1925); Willey, Basil, *The Eighteenth Century Background* (1940); Wolf, Abraham, *A History of Science, Technology and Philosophy in the Eighteenth Century* (1952).
See also some of the titles under Chapter 2.

PART III

The Era of the French Revolution

and the

Napoleonic Episode

1789 - 1815

CHAPTER 13

The French Revolution

I. BACKGROUND AND CAUSES OF THE REVOLUTION

A. The Condition of France

1. The Place in History of the French Revolution. If one look at some of the modern surveys of history, collections like the *Cambridge Modern History*, or the more recent *Peuples et civilisations*, for instance, it will be found that one volume out of roughly a dozen is given over to the ten year span of the episode of the French Revolution. This is a measure of the importance that history has come to attach to that upheaval, which marks indeed for most of Europe, and much besides, the opening of what may be called our own age, an age characterized by the dominance of such forces as go under the labels of democracy, liberalism, industry, and nationalism.

What appear as sharp breaks in the course of history, sudden eruptions, are deceivingly such, for, allowing for the accidental role of circumstance and personality, they have roots whose depth is commensurate with their own magnitude. Our own time has witnessed a political disturbance of comparable dimensions, a fact that lends added interest to the earlier. But from the start it is essential to observe an important difference between the two events. The Russian Revolution of our day took place in what was at the time the most backward among the important states of Europe; France in 1789 represented in most respects the most advanced development of European culture.

2. Influence of the English Model of Government. To this last statement an important qualification is needed. The

French Revolution, other than for the fact of war, had little effect in Britain. If the trend away from absolutism toward some form of popular control of government be regarded as the "normal" or "inevitable" course of history during the past two or three centuries, then England was politically in advance of the rest of Europe.[1]

After her seventeenth-century turmoil, from 1688, England had solved the problem—as may be seen in retrospect—of adaptation to unlimited change within the framework of a flexible constitution. By the end of the eighteenth century, Britain was a limited monarchy in that the power of the crown was subject to definite restrictions as the result of prerogatives vested in a Parliament that represented the British people. A limited representation, to be sure, hence tantamount to the rule of a powerful oligarchy; one which, however, had shown the ability and willingness to recruit fresh blood from the ranks of lower classes. The British government, as we have seen, was regarded as a model worthy of imitation by Voltaire and his enlightened compeers.

3. Peculiarities of the French Situation. On the continent, things were otherwise. As one moved toward the east a powerful aristocracy was still found, but even there the principle of absolutism was generally accepted, as it was in France.

France had her aristocracy, but much of it had been emasculated as a class with a social function by the perhaps too successful work of the seventeenth-century monarchy.[2] One consequence of this was a generally more advanced condition in France—by comparison with countries farther east—of the Third Estate generally. But it was also a condition of greater unbalance. For the French nobility enjoyed privileges for which no compensating function or service was performed.[3] Some of the same conditions applied to the clergy, whose upper

---

[1] Somewhat the same may be said of such a continental state as Holland, which was too small, however, to play a role of leadership on the whole European stage.

[2] The contrast between the French and English aristocracies, their recruitment, and their role in the state, explains much of the divergent domestic courses of England and France.

[3] This does not apply to the small nobility resident on the land, but to the nobility resident at Versailles.

strata, almost exclusively of noble origin, were both worldly
and wealthy. Actually, neither clergy nor nobility represented
overwhelming numbers, some 1 per cent of the population in
a country of 24,000,000.[4]

a. CONDITIONS OF THE PEASANTS. A picture often used to be
drawn of the miserable condition of the French people in their
mass and of the shocking abuses under which they labored,
which finally drove them to the revolt of exasperation. The
individual items of the picture may have been correct, but
the sum total largely false. The description of the conditions
of life of the French peasant, his brutishness, the dues and
obligations that were his, the arrogance of hunting nobles with
which he had to put up, are true enough facts; but they have
little meaning save in the context, either of earlier native, or
else of other contemporary, practice. To compare them with
twentieth-century conditions can only mislead and distort.
With the exception of England, the lot of the French peasant
was the best in Europe.

b. THE BOURGEOISIE. But if the peasantry constituted the
vastly overwhelming bulk of the Third Estate in terms of
numbers, the much smaller segment that was the bourgeoisie
was something else again. This section contained ability and
wealth; the new ideas of the age, the whole Enlightenment,
were particularly its own; it was highly articulate and conscious
of the shortcomings of the existing system. It was not so much
that the French state was worse or more backward than others,
but rather that the factor of relative obsolescence of its institutions, just because it was more advanced than most, stood
out in sharper relief.

One more thing may be pointed out about France. For all
the cosmopolitanism that existed, the French nation was by this
time highly developed in consciousness, and the French state
represented the greatest degree extant of integration and had
the most highly developed bureaucracy.

B.   Immediate Causes of the Revolution

The generalization that revolution occurred in France just
because that country was more advanced and richer may be

---

[4] The French clergy was actually less numerous and no more highly
endowed than that of the Church of England.

warranted. How and why this occurred deserves, nevertheless, closer consideration.

The long reign of Louis XV (1715-1774) witnessed considerable progress and expansion of an economic nature, but no corresponding political change. What was at the beginning of the century an effective machine of government had toward its end become obsolescent. Louis XV judged the situation with clarity and accuracy, but was content to enjoy its benefits while he lasted, reigning in the decadent glow of nonenforced absolute rule.

1. Louis XVI. His successor, Louis XVI, was of a different stamp. He was heir to a difficult situation, yet one not past retrieving. Of reform there was need, but a strong ruler alone might have enacted it. Louis XVI was an honest and well-meaning man, of very limited intellect and little strength of character. Toying with locks and caring for his family were occupations better suited to his capabilities than the rule of a great state in crisis.

2. The Financial Situation. Most briefly and concretely, the crisis was financial in nature. The unsupervised expenses of an irresponsible ruler and his court, combined with the system of taxation and tax collection that obtained brought growing deficits to the French exchequer. In theory, the situation could easily be righted, for the resources of France were the greatest of any European state; the problem was one of management, not of means.[5] The known extent of these resources made in fact possible considerable borrowing, but this, failing fiscal reform, merely served to postpone and aggravate the gathering crisis.

a. Effects of the War with England. In these circumstances France elected to renew the war with England when it appeared that the cause of the revolting American colonies might, with some help, succeed. The calculation proved correct, but also costly. If it was not exactly the straw that broke the camel's back, by 1783, the French financial situation was definitely serious. This is the most definite and concrete connection between the American and the French revolutions,

---

[5] This is clearly shown by the soundness of French finance during the Napoleonic period.

rather more important and real at the time than the ideological weight of example.

b. FAILURE OF ATTEMPTED SOLUTIONS. Various ministers, Turgot, Necker, and others, had come and gone in an attempt to restore the fiscal situation; the attempt was bound to be futile in the failure of far-reaching reforms. A last effort in 1787 and 1788, the essence of which was voluntary consent of the nobility to some taxation, was wrecked by its refusal.[6] The further attempt to coerce the *parlements*, especially that of Paris, led to their passive resistance, and to a virtual paralysis of the governmental machine. In desperation, and as a last resort, it was decided to call the Estates General of the realm. The call was issued by the King on July 5, 1788.

3. The Call for the Estates General and the Elections. The Estates General was an ancient institution of the French kingdom, but its last meeting had been in 1614. The intervening period is as long as that which has elapsed from the American declaration of independence to the present time, a span of 175 years, during which the government of France had developed into the absolutism that it was.

a. THE ISSUE OF THE SIZE OF REPRESENTATION. Many questions therefore, procedural and others, were raised by the King's act and he invited advice from his subjects. The ten months that precede the meeting of the Estates are of crucial importance. The call had the support of both nobility and Third Estate, and particularly of the articulate, politically minded, section of the latter, the bourgeoisie.

But at this point agreement ended. As a class, the nobility had in mind a program of genuine reforms that would curtail the arbitrary power of the Crown; the Estates were henceforth to share in ruling. But the Estates, or Orders, were three; they should remain separate, thus amounting to a tricameral parliament. The decision of the Paris *parlement* in September, confirming this arrangement, incensed the Third

---

[6] This is an oversimplification of the complexities of the situation in 1787-1788, when the *parlements* played an important role. The year 1788 saw what may be called the first, and at the same time the last, "budget" of the *ancien régime*. It showed an estimated 503,000,000 francs of revenue against 619,000,000 of expense, more than half of which was earmarked for debt service.

Estate, whose answer was supplied by Abbé Siéyès' pamphlet, *What is the Third Estate?* published in February, 1789. Proceeding to answer his own question, Siéyès said "Nothing"; but, he went on, "What should it be?—Everything." Weak as usual, the king hedged and offered compensation by deciding that the membership of the Third Estate should be double that of the other Orders.

b. THE CAHIERS. The winter of 1788-1789 was a curious period. It was unusually severe and economic conditions were bad; there was hardship in Paris, while the operation of government was virtually at a standstill throughout the country. But there was also much and active discussion, which resulted in the famous *cahiers*. These contained statements of grievances and important though limited suggestions for reform. We are unusually well informed on the state of opinion in France at this crucial time, because of the extent and freedom of discussion and of the fullness of its record. Understandably, it was the literate and articulate bourgeois, local lawyers and such, who generally took the leadership and penned the *cahiers* of the Third Estate, not the peasants whose views, however, were not wholly muted.

c. THE FAILURE OF THE CROWN. The absolute French monarchy had built itself on the ruins of the noble class, in which task the bourgeoisie had assisted it. But the nobility, though curbed, still had importance, potentially at least. The bourgeoisie on its side was no longer content with its place.

The possibility of an alliance between enlightened nobles and bourgeois was not wholly excluded, and might have produced a result not dissimilar from that which has prevailed in England.[7] But no strong leadership emerged at this point. The Crown, which in this crucial hour might have saved the day, had it used its still very great prestige to effect a not impossible mediation and conciliation, failed the country through the weakness of its well-meaning but incompetent bearer. The stage was set for the great struggle about to begin, and which,

---

[7] The chief contestants in the struggle for power were the nobility and the Third Estate. The First Estate, the clergy, had no position of its own, but was rather divided in its sympathies in accordance with the origin— noble or Third Estate, bishops and curés—of its members.

in some respects still unresolved, to this day troubles the
French nation.

II. THE FIRST PHASE OF THE REVOLUTION:
THE CONSTITUTIONAL MONARCHY

A. The National Constituent Assembly

1. The Meeting of the Estates General. The Estates General came together in May, 1789. Ostensibly, their task was
definite, and limited to solving the financial problem, but the
larger constitutional issue was, by implication at least, paramount in all minds.

a. THE TENNIS COURT OATH. A specific procedural issue
intruded at once. How should the Estates organize themselves
and vote: by Order, as a tricameral body; or by head, as one
body with a vote for each individual member?[8] When the
Third Estate found its meeting hall barred, its members gathered in a neighboring tennis court where, on June 20, they
took the since famous oath not to disband until the country
had been endowed with a new constitution. This had little
to do with finance, and was clearly a revolutionary act. Of
particular significance was the fact that, to all intents and
purposes, the King was in alliance with, or prisoner of, his
nobility, and so considered by the commoners.

Their challenge went essentially unanswered, and thus they
won the first round of the battle, for the King, loath to use
force as he might have, yielded to the determination of the
Third Estate.[9] The National Assembly, as it was henceforth
styled, representative of the French nation, had come into
existence. The King still reigned, but sovereignty was in the
hands of the people's delegates.

2. Enter Paris. The generally, if momentarily, poor economic condition of the country has been mentioned. Poor

---

[8] The arrangements of the preceding autumn implied or assumed, but
did not specifically state, that voting should be by Order.

[9] There was a period of hesitation when the tide was turned by the
adherence to the position of the Third Estate of a large section of the
First (the lower clergy) and even of some members of the nobility.

The gathering of troops gave ground to the suspicion that force might
be resorted to.

crops, bread scarcity, high prices, increased beggary and brigandage, together with the virtual breakdown of an administration brought to a standstill by expectation of certain but unknown change, all went to create that country-wide restlessness known as the *grande peur* (the great fear) of 1789. Paris was a large city by the standards of the time, the largest of the continent, and therefore contained the inevitable proportion of proletariat—and of mob.

a. THE FALL OF THE BASTILLE. While in the country peasants were taking the law into their own hands, refusing to abide by ancient, but about to be changed, custom, a Paris demonstration marched on the Bastille prison on July 14.

The place was by this time more symbolic than real evidence of the arbitrary power of the King. The situation, as such situations will, turned ugly, and after the governor had surrendered he was killed. His head, and that of the mayor of Paris, stuck on pikes, were paraded by the triumphant mob. The symbolic significance of the act has prevailed, and July 14 is the national holiday of republican France.

b. THE ABOLITION OF FEUDALISM. Again the king acquiesced, in the formation of a national guard[10] and of a new municipal government for Paris. The consequences of this were to be far-reaching on the whole subsequent course of the revolution. In Versailles, less than a month later, the newly formed National Assembly, during the famous "night of August 4," proceeded to sweep away the rights and privileges of feudal origin.[11]

c. THE DECLARATION OF THE RIGHTS OF MAN. Three weeks later, on August 26, another famous document was issued. The Declaration of the Rights of Man and Citizen, broadly reminiscent of earlier British and American assertions of individual rights, was thereafter, in France and outside, the charter of the revolutionary struggle for freedom. *Liberté, égalité, fraternité*, is the slogan of the French Revolution.

d. THE MARCH ON VERSAILLES. Great changes had been effected in less than two months in the ancient structure of the

---

[10] Lafayette received command of this guard.

[11] Compensation, initially provided for, was eliminated in the later, more radical, phase of the revolution.

French monarchy. But much detailed work of organization remained to be done before the new state would be ready to function, and there appeared at once an issue that divided the Assembly, the question of the royal veto, of the extent in other words, of the power of the executive.[12]

Once more Paris intervened when a dubious mob took the road to Versailles. Potential tragedy was averted, partly by Lafayette, whose National Guard went along with the mob. When it set out again for Paris, the weird cortège had in its midst the royal coach bearing king, queen, and dauphin, to be henceforth residents of the Tuileries.

More important perhaps, the National Assembly also went to Paris. The somewhat ludicrous, if picturesque, aspects of the Paris-bound procession should be ignored in favor of more significant reality. King and Assembly were now hostages of the city where the radical element had its greatest stronghold. Not for some time, but eventually, the consequences of this "imprisonment" in Paris were to appear.

B.   The Work of the Constituent Assembly

1. The Constitution of 1791. For a time the revolutionary fever seemed spent, and the Assembly proceeded with its appointed task of constitution drafting. This took about two years: by September, 1791 France was endowed with such a document. It did not serve the country long, but the fact of its novelty, if no other, would suffice to give it importance. The work of the Assembly must be briefly summarized.

a. THE FRANCHISE. In keeping with the initial Declaration of the Rights of Man, in turn reflection of the prevailing background and climate of the Enlightenment, the underlying principles of the new order were to be two: freedom and equality. Freedom to do that which would not injure others; as to equality, one might be tempted to recall the quip: "all men are equal, but some are more equal than others."

This found expression mainly in the distinction between "active" and "passive" citizens, and in the high property quali-

---

[12] Some favored a division of power with a strong royal veto. The more radical, or "patriot," party, suspicious of the King and of the nobility, some of whom had already emigrated, favored no more than a suspensive veto.

fications for the franchise. Locke's "people," as pointed out in other connections, is an elastic concept. In fairness, it may be pointed out that the twentieth-century assumption that the fact of having reached a certain chronological point in life implies competence to pass judgment on matters political, while it may be a useful fiction, is certainly a fiction. Apart from the generally accepted view of the time, the restriction on the franchise reflected the composition of the Assembly, consisting of able, well-intentioned, and high-minded—unusually high-minded as such bodies go—bourgeois who set high store on property, its rights, and its protection.

b. THE LIMITED MONARCHY. As to the government, France would be a constitutional or limited monarchy with a unicameral legislature representing the nation, henceforth the source and repository of sovereignty. The king, still possessed of important powers, was nevertheless severely restricted; his power of veto was not more than suspensive.[13] There was no separate coequal judiciary branch of the government as in the American Constitution. Thus, from the start, France set the example, which has been widely followed, of the overwhelming concentration of power in the legislative branch.

c. ADMINISTRATIVE REORGANIZATION. The administration of the country was thoroughly reorganized. With deliberate intent, that seemed to Burke sheer mania for destruction, and in order to emphasize the break between the old and the new, the old provinces were replaced by eighty-three wholly new, and arbitrarily drawn, administrative divisions, or *départements*. The result of this was intentional decentralization on the one hand, the central power having little control over the local, and on the other uniformity of organization. This last aspect alone was destined to survive.

2. Religion and Finance. Money has ever played a crucial role in the affairs of men and states. It was an issue of fiscality that provided the initial impulse for the French Revolution in the calling of the Estates General. This body, become a National Constituent Assembly, had done anything but attend

---

[13] His attempted flight from the country, intercepted at Varennes, in June, 1791, naturally cast suspicion upon him and tended to justify those who saw him as the ally and chief agent of the old aristocracy.

to the finances of the state. Yet that issue, too, remained and must be faced. When at last it was, the results were far-reaching and perhaps unexpected.

a. THE ASSIGNATS AND THE CIVIL CONSTITUTION OF THE CLERGY. The solution, in brief, was to seize the substantial property belonging to the Church, against which security *assignats*, or paper money, were issued. Seizure of church property by the state was no complete novelty, in France or elsewhere, but things went far beyond this point. The state would now provide for the clergy, under the civil constitution of 1790. There was no intention at first to attack religion, but rather to regard the Church in France as a subordinate institution of the state. It is this last aspect, rather than specific provisions, that precipitated the break.

b. THE BREAK BETWEEN THE REVOLUTION AND THE CHURCH. Negotiation might have bridged the gap, but intransigeance and poor diplomacy caused the Pope to go beyond the limited issue to a general condemnation of the principles of the Revolution. The answer was a complete break with Rome, the requirement of an oath of allegiance, refused by most of the clergy, and the appointment of a duplicate set of subservient, or "juring," clergy.

The mass of the French nation was Catholic. This turn of affairs bewildered it, and the clergy, which had played so important a part in giving the revolution its successful start, now in its overwhelming bulk turned against it. It carried with it considerable support, especially among sections of the peasantry.[14] The unpremeditated turn of the religious issue to a degree distorted the whole course of the revolution.

3. Résumé: France in 1791. The work of the National Assembly was formally complete with the acceptance on September 14, 1791 of the constitution by the King. On the thirtieth, the Assembly disbanded to make room for its successor, the first regularly elected body to govern the country under the new dispensation. If the new body, the Legislative Assembly, lasted barely one year, that was due in large part to conditions already in existence at the time of its birth.

---

[14] The position on this issue of the supporters of the *ancien régime* did not matter, since they were enemies of the Revolution in any event.

a. THE COUNTRY DIVIDED. When the constitution had finally been completed, it seemed that the millennium had not quite been achieved. Apart from what may be called the court party, irreconcilable supporters of the *ancien régime*, the very large degree of unanimity which had supported the early stages of the revolution had evidently vanished. The real beneficiaries of the change were, for one thing, too few. Peasants and proletariat both had cause to be disappointed, to say nothing of sections of the bourgeoisie itself. The weapon of *égalité* was to be turned against those who had first appealed to it, then limited its application. Radical groups were becoming vocal.

The economic and administrative changes that were instituted disturbed many existing interests and customs. Guilds and *compagnonnages* [15] were abolished, partly in deference to an early application of the *laissez faire* view of economic relationships. The disposition of church property led to much speculation. This was an inflationary period, and much was heard about hoarders, manipulators, and *nouveaux riches*.

All of this might be called birth pangs of a new order which would, after a time, find its new basis of stability. Whether or not it would or might have is, however, futile speculation, for events on a larger scale were about to overtake the revolution.

C. The Legislative Assembly, 1791-1792

1. Europe and the Revolution

a. HOPES AND FEARS OUTSIDE OF FRANCE. Such important changes as had taken place in the greatest of European powers, in the country moreover to which Europe was accustomed to look for leadership in ideas, could not leave the continent unmoved. Just what the meaning of the revolution was, was not at first too clear, but such essentials as popular instead of divine right sovereignty soon emerged. As might be expected, all Europe was soon split into two camps, the leanings of which ever since have tended to be labeled liberal and conservative, forces of movement or change versus forces of preservation, either hoping for or fearing continued leadership from France.

---

[15] These were journeymen's associations that may be regarded as an early form of trade unions.

Burke's *Reflections on the French Revolution,* as early as
1790, gave a good presentation of the latter's case.

It must be emphasized that there was nothing "national"
about the French Revolution in its early stages. On the contrary, and consistently, its makers, imbued with eighteenth-
century ideas, were thinking in terms of Man and of Society
in general; the changes brought about in Paris would be just
as valid and good in London or Berlin, or in Pekin for that
matter. As we have had occasion to see again in our own day,
such ideological struggles cut across state or national lines
which to them have no relevance or meaning. It is an easy
step from this to a situation where French intervention would
be the best hope of certain elements abroad, while conversely
the best hope in France of other forces would be that of
foreign intervention.[16]

b. FRENCH ELEMENTS FAVORABLE TO FOREIGN INTERVENTION.
This did not necessarily mean war. In England, Pitt was satisfied to let France work out her own disputes at home while he
pursued his own domestic program undisturbed. The most
important continental personage at this juncture was Leopold,
the Austrian Emperor, brother of the French Queen. He
showed at first little inclination to become involved in French
affairs for her sake, but his successor Francis was less reticent.[17]

On the French side, after the failure at Varennes of his attempted flight in June, 1791, Louis XVI was essentially a
prisoner of the revolution. From 1789, following the early
example of the king's brother, the Count of Artois, a steadily
increasing stream of noble emigration had left France and
scattered in various countries, particularly in the Rhineland.
The *émigrés* constituted centers of agitation, untiringly seeking to procure the king's "rescue" through foreign intervention.

c. THE DECLARATION OF PILLNITZ. In August, 1791, Emperor

---

[16] The situation is wholly comparable, in this respect, to that created in
our own day by the Russian Revolution. It is perhaps a good occasion to
recall the phrase: "if this is treason, make the most of it."

[17] The Polish situation is of importance in considering the policies of
Austria, Prussia, and Russia. There were marked signs of national revival
in Poland at this time, and the year saw the drafting of an interesting and
enlightened constitution.

Leopold, meeting the King of Prussia, issued the famous Declaration of Pillnitz: the Emperor would intervene in France if other powers did likewise. The "if" was large, but the *émigrés* pretended to ignore it, and so likewise did the revolutionaries in France, who, rather than cowed, took up the challenge and began to talk in terms of a crusade of peoples against tyrants.[18]

2. The Outbreak of War. The representatives of France were now the just elected Legislative Assembly.[19] The two most active tendencies in that body were the constitutionalists who favored the application of the constitution as it was and feared a further curbing of the royal power, and the more radical Girondins, highly suspicious of the latter and of its use.[20] Of extreme radicals, or Jacobins, only a handful were present: despite discontent with conditions, the Assembly had been elected by the highly restricted body of some 50,000 electors.

For a variety of reasons, it so turned out that all, save the extreme radicals, were in favor of war,[21] and in the mounting excitement, revolutionary enthusiasm, and national fervor, the initiative of a declaration of war against the King of Hungary and Bohemia came from the French Assembly in April, 1792.

The war thus begun was to furnish another illustration of the unpredictability of the course and outcome of armed adventures. Not until 1815 did it really end, having proved

---

[18] The French annexation of Avignon and the actions in Alsace may have been justified applications of the newfangled principle of popular sovereignty. They were also clear cases of unilateral violations of existing international obligations.

[19] The Constituent Assembly had decreed the noneligibility of its members. This was a self-denying but short-sighted ordinance, for it deprived the country of the services of some of its ablest representatives, who had moreover been gaining experience in the process of constitution making and of administration.

[20] The Girondins belonged in large part to the Jacobin Club. This, like other groups, or clubs, was very active at this time. These clubs were centers of political education and activity, with branches throughout the country, and they exercised a powerful influence.

[21] The royalist faction favored war as a way to force foreign intervention, which they expected would result in defeat, hence restoration; their opponents saw in it a way of consolidating and extending the revolution. Robespierre, for the radicals, spoke passionately against it, giving a remarkably accurate forecast of the course of events as it actually materialized.

false the calculations of its initiators on both sides, and by that
time Europe had undergone unforseen convulsions. The first
and most marked effects of war, however, were felt in France
herself.

III. THE SECOND PHASE: THE DEMOCRATIC
REVOLUTION

A.   The War and Its Effects on the Revolution

Militarily, France was unprepared for this war. Her armies
were in a state of disorganization, if only because of the emigration of a large section of the officer corps; of the remaining
ones, not all were loyal, and suspicion was often mutual between them and the new recruits. French diplomacy at this
juncture was no help to the military, and the belief that French
armies would be welcomed abroad could hardly be tested so
long as they were not able to cross their own frontiers.[22]

French setbacks were openly welcomed in France by
enemies of the Revolution, who saw in them hope of prompt
restoration for themselves and the King. Feeling ran correspondingly high among revolutionaries, who represented a
decreasingly large but growingly determined section of the
nation. The Paris sections,[23] and local administrations throughout the country, began to take matters into their own hands
in curbing counter-revolutionary activity. Cries of treason
were often heard; incompetent or unreliable generals, ex-
nobles, non-juring priests, were all suspect. Revolution was
young in those days and the naive enthusiasm of some of its
adherents was boundless. The success of the *Marseillaise*, com-
posed at the army of the Rhine and popularized by the volun-
teer contingent marching up from Marseilles, is apt expression
of one aspect of the existing temper.[24]

---

[22] The poor management on the French side was only second, if that, to
the quality of direction of the Austro-Prussian coalition, a combination badly
organized from the start.

[23] These were the districts into which Paris had been redivided in 1790
and which became the active centers of municipal activity under the leadership of the more radical leaders.

[24] The high excitement attending the chaotic dawn of the new age is
best conveyed by literary works. Anatole France's *The Gods are Athirst* may
be cited as a good illustration among an extensive literature.

1. Brunswick's Manifesto. The allies, too, were unprepared, but the conditions prevailing on the French side enabled them to advance into France. At the beginning of
August the news became known in Paris of Brunswick's Manifesto. The Duke of Brunswick, leader of the Austro-Prussian
armies, chose to threaten reprisals on Paris in the event that
the safety of the royal family should be impaired.

2. August 10 and the September Massacres. This psychological blunder, coming in the midst of the high state of
tension, served to precipitate the rioting of August 10. The
more radical elements of Paris seized control; the Tuileries
were invaded by the mob, the royal family was imprisoned,
and the terrorized Assembly acknowledged under pressure
that a new constitution, more democratic in character than the
existing one, should be enacted. The situation created as the
result of the march on Versailles of October, 1789 was now
bearing fruit, and we shall again have occasion to observe the
disproportionate influence of the great city and its proletariat
on the course of events.

This has been called the opening of the "second revolution";
certainly the call for new elections under universal suffrage
opened up a new phase of development. It was a more funda-
mentally important event than that more lurid manifestation
of collective hysteria, the September massacres. In the early
days of that month, the prisons were broken into and counter-
revolutionaries, nobles, priests, and sundry suspects were executed after summary trials.[25]

B.   The National Convention, First Phase

1. September, 1792. Hysteria and exhilaration, base fear
and noble hope, were abroad in the streets of Paris in these
September days. The Convention met on the twentieth, the
same day that the news of Valmy meant that the Revolution
was, for the moment, saved. If the heroic legend of Valmy—
raw, unshod recruits successfully matching their enthusiasm
against the guns of armies that were trained but not inspired
by an idea—has largely been exploded, its symbolic value re-

---

[25] In order to retain a sense of proportion, it should be realized that,
as such things go, this first Terror was a comparatively mild· affair. The
number of victims of the September massacres was slightly over 1000.

mains. The Revolution being saved, the first act of the Convention was to proclaim the decadence of the monarchy: France would henceforth be a republic, one and indivisible.

2. War and the Foreign Situation

a. FRENCH MILITARY SUCCESSES. The allies having decided to withdraw, the French pursued their advantage. Jemmapes in November, though less sensational than Valmy, represented a more substantial victory. It was a real battle which the revolutionary armies won. Belgium and the Rhineland were overrun and the revolution took conscious steps to exploit the value of its propaganda abroad.

b. THE POLISH QUESTION. There was another factor that contributed importantly to the success of the struggle of revolutionary France against her foreign foes. It was in January, 1793 that arrangements for the second partition of Poland were completed between Catherine of Russia and Prussian Frederick William; Austria was being excluded. The danger inherent in revolutionary ideology in France and the desire or desirability of restoring the French king to his rightful position were important enough matters; but Polish territory was more concrete. The diplomatically ill-contrived Austro-Prussian alliance virtually ceased to function, or at least its effectiveness was largely destroyed by the concern of its members for developments in eastern Europe.

c. EXECUTION OF LOUIS XVI. It is at this time that the fate of Louis XVI was decided. Already deposed, he was now placed on trial and found guilty of treasonable conspiracy against the nation. On January 16, the death sentence was voted in the Convention, and he was guillotined on the 21: the dignity of his death has caused it to be described as the one proper act of his life.

d. WAR WITH BRITAIN. This execution, too, was a symbolic act, a gesture of defiance to all kings. It created the proper degree of horror and indignation in England, and, though not the cause, it was a factor that helped bring about the breach between that country and France.[26]

The initiative came again from revolutionary France which, on February 1, 1793, declared war on both England and Holland. The step was a fateful one. England was not prepared for war on land; she proceeded therefore in her usual manner to raise, finance, and sustain a coalition against France.[27] Many were the coalitions that had to be raised before the drama was played out, but raised they were, and England was their heart until she had her way with the enemy.

3. The Course of the Revolution in France

a. DISAFFECTION AT HOME. The successes of the autumn of 1792 were followed by reverses in the following spring, and these in turn increased internal stresses, for this was a new type of conflict, ideological as we should call it now, that cut across frontiers. On the one hand, the revolution, or at least the revolutionary government, was far from commanding the undivided allegiance of the country. Aside from *émigrés*, active beyond its boarders, large-scale risings occurred, especially in the Vendée, while some of the larger towns, such as Lyon, were in open rebellion.

b. WEAKNESSES OF THE COALITION. But on the other hand, balancing the effects of disaffection in the rear and even at the front,[28] the coalition was hampered, not only by the usual bane of coalitions, divergent aims, and internecine jealousies,

---

[26] The French policy of annexation, as in Savoy for instance, on the plea of national sovereignty, especially when combined with a revised version of natural boundaries, looked to England like familiar ground. On the issue of the control of Belgium, and in particular of the mouth of the Scheldt, England was especially sensitive and adamant, as she has been before and since.

[27] The so-called First Coalition was a loose arrangement. After she entered the war, England during 1793 made separate treaties with Russia, Spain, Portugal, Sardinia, Naples, Austria, and Prussia. Other Italian and German states were also brought in. Not all members participated in active hostilities (e.g., Russia) but in one form or another France had against her virtually the whole of Europe.

[28] Dumouriez himself went over to the enemy.

but also by the fact that it had no effective answer to the challenge to the existing order implicit in the revolution.

Allowing that popular education and propaganda were still in their crude infancy, the revolutionaries enjoyed the large asset of being the ostensible advocates of progress, change, and of improving the lot of the downtrodden masses. As has been pointed out, the members of the coalition distrusted their own subjects almost as much as they feared the enemy, and this fact, though impossible of accurate statistical assessment in its effects, was an important element in the final outcome.[29]

c. The Parties in the Convention. It is well to bear in mind at this point the composition of the Convention. It may be said, broadly speaking, to have consisted of three groups. The old Girondins, formerly active movers of a greater installment of reform and of war, were still there; but they now constituted the conservative wing of the assembly. Their former place had been taken by the Mountain, so-called from the seating location of its members, the band of radical Jacobins destined to direct for a time the course of the revolution. Between Gironde and Mountain stood the Plain or Swamp, a large mass of members, moderates of not too deep conviction or too strong moral fiber, who in emergencies and crises would abdicate and follow whoever gave the more determined leadership.

C. Second Phase of the Convention: The Dictatorship of the Mountain

The revolution was a force unleashed which now went on seemingly according to laws of its own nature. In the chaotic circumstances of the spring of 1793, foreign successes, domestic disaffection, mounting economic and financial difficulties, either it must disintegrate or else resort to more ruthless action.

1. Elimination of the Girondins. Between the Gironde

---

[29] As usual also, in such circumstances, some of the very policies, economic, political, and military, introduced by the revolutionaries, had, in part at least and from sheer necessity, to be imitated by their enemies, thus by indirection spreading revolutionary change abroad. This is the usual dilemma, as we are witnessing again in our time, of *status quo* powers fighting forces of change.

and the Mountain, the struggle was now one to the death. The Mountain in this contest had the advantage, weapon of double edge, of being able to call on the Paris sections and to organize a *journée*, or popular demonstration. Such a demonstration took place at the turn from May to June (May 31-June 2) when once more "the people" overawed their representatives. In brief, this was the death of the Gironde. Its members, placed in accusation, either found their way to the guillotine or disappeared, to be hounded to the last. The terrified and surprised Plain acquiesced and gave the stamp of formal legality to the proceedings; many of its members, too, thought it wisest to go into hiding for a time while the storm was raging at its worst.

2. The Committee of Public Safety. Reminiscent in some respects of Commonwealth England of a century earlier, a rump now governed France. More narrowly still, the active agency of effective rule was the Committee of Public Safety. This body of twelve men, monthly renewable, exercised in effect a dictatorship. For about a year, the figure of Robespierre was its dominant leader whose policies generally had their way.

3. The Terror. The personality of Robespierre has been and will continue controversial. No doubt he did preside over the most extreme phase of the revolution, that associated with the Terror. Terror was, to be sure, the instrument of government for a time, and for that time effective in that it did contrive to master enemies both domestic and foreign.

By the standards of our own age, the French Terror was a mild affair. In a country of some 25,000,000 its victims were less than 50,000;[30] it was nevertheless an effective enough

---

[30] D. Greer in *The Incidence of the Terror* (Cambridge, Mass., 1935) arrives at a figure of between 35,000 and 40,000. Actual sentences of revolutionary courts totalled 17,000, but this represents only a part of the total, the estimation of which contains an element of definition and hence some arbitrariness. The revolutionary tribunal of Paris accounted for 2639 victims.

It is of interest that the Terror did not operate blindly and indiscriminately against beneficiaries of the old regime; most of its victims were of the Third Estate, and its general and broadly dominant motivation was the suppression of opposition, especially in regions of danger, the capital, the Vendée, etc.

instrument through the impressiveness of its performance, the ceremonial of the executions, especially in its last and most violent phase. Denounced and imprisoned "suspects" were vastly greater numbers and the Revolutionary Tribunal a proper object of dread.

a. ROBESPIERRE. As to Robespierre himself, a native of Arras and lawyer by profession, he had shown ability in his early career. Thoroughly steeped in the eighteenth-century background, he had from the beginning of the revolution been a defender of the more democratic or radical tendency, and also a humanitarian opposed to the death penalty. Such are not the rare vagaries of unbending, uncompromising, abstractly rational, lovers of mankind, often callous where the fate of individual men is at stake.

Of his high-minded devotion to the revolutionary ideal there is no cause to doubt—Incorruptible was his nickname—yet not devoid of the capacity for cool political appraisal, Robespierre understood the mechanism of organizing a popular demonstration. But if the mob could be used, it should be held in check. Robespierre who almost ostentatiously eschewed the cruder outward signs of catering to popular favor—witness his "fussy" personal appearance and clothes—endeavored to contain the more radical elements, the *enragés*, and for that reason has been called by some betrayer of the revolution.[31] For all the violence and bloodshed, it must be recognized that the economic policies that the revolutionary government found itself driven to adopt, controls of various sorts, were half-hearted and seemed to run against the grain.[32]

b. THE CLIMAX OF THE REVOLUTION. Some of the more picturesque manifestations associated with the Convention were little more than that. Even the calendar was made over, from the Year One when the Republic was born, and the months were given names, attractive in themselves but of synthetic

---

[31] This is the Marxian view, according to which the mass of the people, represented by the *enragés* (extreme, uncompromising radicals), was frustrated of its victory by the bourgeoisie and its agents, of whom Robespierre was one.

[32] One may see in this the influence of physiocratic, *laissez faire* ideas in combination with the fact that there was no adequate mechanism in existence for the effective operation of controls.

derivation. The *décadi*, a ten day period, displaced the week, and was a less than popular reform.

With the Church, and even more broadly with Christianity, the break was complete. The new society was based on Reason, and would bow to no other deity. By the time the Cult of Reason had taken over Notre Dame, with an actress impersonating the divinity, one can only wonder at the humorless vagaries to which the use of the rational faculty may lead.

But all this, if symbolic, was secondary. Of greater moment was the fateful course of revolutionary events. Again, an oft-repeated phenomenon occurred: suspicion was abroad, and with untiring ruthlessness the Revolution began to devour its own children. The more radical faction, led by Hébert, was defeated and paid the then customary price of political failure. Even great Danton himself, fiery orator and leader, moving force of the early Terror, demanding ever more blood, after a time fell under suspicion. He, too, paid with his head for the crime of relative moderation. Robespierre was uncontested master in the spring of 1794.

IV.   THE REVOLUTION TAMED

A.   Third Phase of the Convention: The Thermidorean Reaction

1. The End of Robespierre. Yet he, too, was about to meet his fate. For there was much weariness of the everlasting turmoil and uncertainty; the Terror may, to a point, have had justification, but not after it had served its purpose. The Revolution seemed no longer threatened, either from within or without.[33] The government was a dictatorship, but without clear justification and with diminishing support. Increasingly alone, Robespierre became the central butt of discontent. The sessions of the 8th and 9th Thermidor (July 26 and 27) were dramatic. At the last moment, having apparently once more silenced his critics, Robespierre, ailing and weary, failed to press his advantage to the end. Quite suddenly, the tide turned. Placed under accusation himself, after a day of confusion and some involved maneuverings, he was found guilty and executed

---

[33] On the war situation, see below, p. 226.

the next day. For two days, the guillotine worked overtime disposing of the leaders of the Terror.

Events had moved with bewildering rapidity. Robespierre himself a betrayer, the Incorruptible false to the Revolution, were things hard to believe, yet out of the universal weariness no one rose to defend him. Instead, the more moderate—and timid—leadership, the frightened Plain, possessed of numbers, came back into its own. It was as if the revolutionary fever had burst its abcess, and a widespread, if tacit, demand for repose were the universal wish.

2. The Work of the Convention

a. THE CONSTITUTION OF THE YEAR I. The Convention had met initially, in September, 1792, in order to draw up a new constitution. And this it did. Despite the turmoil and excitement, by June, 1793, the Constitution of the Year I was ready. It is an interesting document, far more democratic and radical than the constitution of 1791, as it was meant to be. But its interest is little more than historical, for, owing to the circumstances of the moment, it was immediately suspended, and the country drifted into dictatorship and Terror as has been described.

b. THE CONSTITUTION OF THE YEAR III. The events of Thermidor had the immediate consequence of a return to more moderate direction, the so-called Thermidorean reaction. Reaction it was indeed, by contrast with what went just before, but the whole quarrel was an internecine one within the Revolution: the leaders of the now controlling faction, if more moderate, did not wish to restore the King. They represented to a large extent the initial movers of the Revolution, the bourgeoisie, to which may be added those, new bourgeois and *nouveaux riches*, whom the confused conditions of the day had given opportunities for enrichment. Freedom of enterprise, elimination of controls with the consequences of inflation and rising prices, were the order of the moment. To a degree, frightened bourgeois, just because they had been so frightened, would retaliate in kind against a democracy that was equated with mob rule and bloodshed. The Terror only gradually subsided, being turned for a time against the original terrorists.

The mob still played a role, only it was a different mob, bourgeois rather than proletarian; the *jeunesse dorée* hunting down and persecuting erstwhile Jacobins. A White Terror took the place of the Red.

This did not go without grumbling on the part of a frustrated proletariat. But it had lost its leaders, and the attempted insurrection of Prairial in the Year III (May 1795) was handled with determination—a whiff of grapeshot that the army was called on to administer. But, to repeat again, the Convention, if it would condone reaction, would do so within definite limits only. Agitation from the Right was equally put down, again with the help of the army, where a young officer, Bonaparte by name, was present.

The Convention proceeded to draft yet a new constitution, so-called of the Year III, which began to operate at the end of the year 1795, bestowing upon France yet a new system, the Directory. The Directory, so named from its executive, was still Republic. The role of the army, adumbrated in the last year of the Convention, was to become ever larger in it. But before going over the story of the Directory, we must bring up to date that of the war situation.

B. The War to 1795

1. The New Army. The Republic could not have survived in 1793 had foreign armies come to Paris. It was saved at the time by the combined ineptitude and the dissensions of its enemies, among whom such issues as the Polish loomed large. The summer was used in gathering and training new recruits. A novel kind of army was being forged as a tool of the revolution, and to this end the Committee of Public Safety spared no pains.

Man power was no problem in the most populous country of Europe, once the principle of conscription and the *levée en masse* had been adopted. The problem was on the one hand that of training and cadres, of supplies on the other. Carnot, though not alone, but outstanding for his organizing and directing genius, earned the epithet "organizer of victory." The new recruits, at times as enthusiastic as they were unskilled, were fused in the ranks of the old army. Officers were a great problem, for many had emigrated and others

were not trusted. The government resorted to drastic measures. Failure in the field might be punishable by death; representatives were detached from the Convention and sent "on
mission" to watch and supervise the conduct of operations.
The new army was successfully forged on the field of battle.

Most important perhaps, it was an army of a wholly different character from the classical armies of the time. It was
the first truly "national" army, politically conscious of fighting
for the nation from which it was drawn. The depletion of the
old officer ranks and the new possibility for talent to assert
itself and rise were to produce a bevy of military names of a
high order of competence that was to give France the military
leadership of Europe for a generation.

The successes of 1793[34] had carried France to her "natural"
frontiers, confirmed by annexations up to the Rhine and along
the Alps.[35] These were, however, unilateral actions and did not
end the war. But in 1794 negotiations were going on with
some of the enemy countries.

2. The Third Partition of Poland. The Polish question
again played an important role, for the second partition was
but a transitory solution. Catherine was not loath to see both
Prussia and Austria embroiled in the west; her wish to see
them destroy revolutionary France was all the more sincere
that it gave her a free hand in Poland. She now proceeded to
deal with Austria to the exclusion of Prussia, reversing the
situation of 1792. In January, 1795 the third partition of
Poland was arranged between the two who, though not con-
sulting him, allowed Frederick William some compensation.

3. Peace with Prussia, Holland, and Spain. These negotiations, secret but not unknown, made Prussia all the more eager
to negotiate with France in order to be free in the east. The
French revolutionary government put forward large claims,
but Barthélemy, its representative in Switzerland, where negotiations were conducted, was more moderate. By the treaty

---

[34] The favorable war situation made it possible to use armies for the
purpose of dealing with domestic rebellion. It was late in 1793 that a
successful campaign broke resistance in the Vendée.

[35] Whether these annexations should be made conditions of peace or
used as bargaining counters was one of the issues debated on the French
side, especially after Thermidor.

of Basle of April, 1795 peace was re-established. If France failed to obtain the concrete advantages that she had sought, Prussia's secret abandonment of Holland, and even more the moral victory entailed in the recognition of the Revolution by a major European power, constituted a substantial achievement.[36]

Left to herself, since England could offer no tangible land assistance, Holland yielded at the Hague in May to harsher terms.[37] Spain was next to make peace, in July, essentially on a *status quo ante* basis. The coalition had largely disintegrated, being reduced, apart from minor states, to England and the Emperor. By the second half of 1795 revolutionary France had recovered a place, though still an uncertain one, among the European powers.

V. THE DIRECTORY

A. Nature of the Regime

1. The Government. Internally, the task of stabilization went on, of which the drafting of the new constitution was one of the manifestations. After four years of storm and stress, France was back near the place she had reached in 1791. The most significant feature of the Constitution of the Year III was the qualification hemming its franchise: seemingly very wide, the device of indirect election vested control in a body of some 30,000 qualified by the large property they held.

There was to be a bicameral legislature: the Five Hundred, and half as many Ancients. A group of five Directors—hence the name of the regime—chosen by the Ancients from a list submitted by the Five Hundred, constituted the executive, to whom the ministers, appointed by it, were responsible. The powers of the executive were broad.

---

[36] The question of the Rhine was left unsettled, Prussia merely withdrawing from the war. England was naturally disappointed at the Prussian defection, though her own niggardly policy in the matter of subsidies helped produce this result.

[37] Besides territorial losses Holland was liable to an indemnity. The financial difficulties of France were naturally reflected in difficulties in maintaining her armies. This in turn had the consequence of causing a mulcting of the vanquished, a fact which made the revolution less than popular abroad, especially when coupled with the rash emulation of certain reforms (e.g., religious) introduced in France.

One curious feature of this constitution was the lack of contact or coordination between, rather than separation of, the executive and the legislature, as well as the difficulty of amendment. The rigidity of this constitution would contribute to its violent demise. The makers of this instrument, if they were moderate bourgeois reformers, highly respectful of property, had cause to fear reaction of too extreme a sort. Reversing the self-denying ordinance of the Constituent Assembly of 1791, they provided instead that 500 out of 750 legislators to be elected must come from their number, thus insuring continuity of control and direction.[38]

2. Transitional Character of the Directory. The regime of the Directory lasted four years. It was the anticlimax of the revolution in a sense, a period of transition to something else. If France was still a Republic, the revolution had spent itself, and the regime had little enough active support from any quarter. The Thermidoreans were not royalist, but they had initiated a backward movement by comparison with the initial revolutionary impulse that reached its peak in 1794.

Reaction might go further yet, for the monarchist idea had too deep and ancient roots so easily to vanish. But it could not, in any event, be the monarchy of pre-1789; had the Count of Provence, Louis XVI's brother and heir, understood this in 1795, there might conceivably have been some chance of restoration already then, but his intransigeant position nullified it. For all the discontent and disillusion, too many had acquired a vested interest in some at least of the changes that had come to pass.

3. The Directory to 1797. The discontent existed and manifested itself in such outbursts as the conspiracy associated with the name of Babeuf, heir to the *enragés* and advocate of advanced ideas of socialistic nature. To question property rights was certain to touch upon a sensitive chord among those in control of the state. In 1796 the Babouvists were dealt with with expedition and determination.

---

[38] For this provision, the reelected *Conventionnels* were derisively known as "perpetuals." Their re-election was left to chance, with the provision that those elected would "co-opt" as many as necessary in the event of failure to secure the re-election of 500 members.

So the Directory went on, in a sense by default. It was a time of marked relaxation from the tension of the preceding years. Economic difficulties, unsound finance, inflation, profiteering, widespread corruption that reached its brazen height among the Directors themselves accepting bribes from foreign powers, exaggerated fantasy in the very clothes of the *incroyables*, set the tone of the period.[39]

When elections took place in March 1797—the first free elections under the new constitution—for the renewal of one-third of the membership of the legislative councils, virtually all the "perpetuals," as they were called, were eliminated, and there was a marked royalist swing. But the foreign situation must first be considered in the preceding interval, for it was of crucial importance in 1797 when domestic and foreign affairs became thoroughly entangled.

B. Continued War

After the treaties of 1795, when England and the Emperor were left virtually alone at war with revolutionary France, a temporary stalemate ensued into which, however, a novel force was about to intrude, a force by the name of Napoleon Bonaparte.

1. Emergence of Napoleon. Bonaparte was a young officer, aged twenty seven in 1796, to whom the revolution had given an unexpected opportunity for advancement.[40] He had participated in the recapture of Toulon from the British, and in Paris in 1795 had defended the Convention against a royalist attempt. With this background, ability that had attracted

---

[39] As usual in such circumstances it should be borne in mind that the more extreme manifestations were in the cities, especially in Paris. Overwhelmingly agricultural France went about its wonted occupations though it, too, was affected by economic conditions and the price situation in particular.

[40] He was born in Corsica in 1769, just after the purchase of that island by France from Genoa. His family rallied to French rule and he received his education and military training in France. The outbreak of the revolution found him hesitant for a while, but when the rival Paoli took the leadership of the movement for Corsican independence, Bonaparte was confirmed in his French, and revolutionary, allegiance.

Carnot's attention, and his recent marriage to Josephine,[41] Bonaparte received the command of the southern armies operating along the Italian border.

a. BONAPARTE'S FIRST ITALIAN CAMPAIGN. This army, which he found demoralized and unpaid, he turned into an instrument of victory. With lightning speed, in the spring of 1796 he overran Piedmont, forcing the King of Sardinia out of the war (May, 1796), and proceeded to pursue the Austrian forces across the rest of northern Italy.

The results of these victories were considerable. Not only were the French armies clothed and fed out of the large indemnities levied on the conquered lands,[42] but, even apart from much private speculation, there was money to spare for sending home to the harassed Directors. Bonaparte could and did, in the circumstances, adopt and follow an independent policy of his own. The fact that comparable successes did not attend French arms in other quarters made him stand out all the more as a young general of promise, and increasingly as time passed, as *the* hope of the country, or the government, or the Revolution.

2. The War and the Domestic Situation. While England, by reason of lack of success in the war and of her domestic conditions, was induced to enter negotiations at Lille in 1796-1797, Bonaparte on his own authority made an armistice with Austria, the preliminaries of Leoben, in April, 1797.[43] The above mentioned elections of March, 1797 had just taken place, which seemed to strengthen the party of restoration and of peace.[44] The desire for peace was widespread in France, but

---

[41] Josephine, born in Martinique, was the widow of Beauharnais, guillotined in 1794. Her liaison with Barras, one of the Directors, is generally considered to have been influential in procuring Bonaparte's appointment.

[42] The Revolution had many sympathizers in Italy, but the French exactions produced a considerable cooling off of enthusiasm and a willingness to be "liberated" from the "liberators."

[43] This arrangement, largely political, dealing with Italian and Rhenish territories, far exceeded the competence of a general, but was no less embarrassing to the Directors.

[44] A restored monarchy could easily have ignored the commitments of a republic bound by its constitution not to yield territory, such as for instance Belgium, unilaterally annexed.

the Republicans could brook no restoration, and thus they appeared as the party of war and annexations.

a. THE COUP OF FRUCTIDOR (SEPTEMBER, 1797). Despite Bonaparte's arbitrary behavior in Italy, here was the basis of an alliance between himself and the Republicans. While negotiations were dragging on inconclusively, with the English at Lille, at Udine with the Austrians, the situation was resolved by the coup of Fructidor (September 4, 1797). With the connivance of Bonaparte supplying the armed force,[45] the republican elements caused the Councils to annul the elections. If thereby they had saved the Revolution, as their justification went, they certainly had broken the constitution. Of their dependence on the army there could be no question.

b. THE TREATY OF CAMPO FORMIO. The intransigeance of the reorganized Directory caused the failure of negotiations with England, but with Austria peace was made by the treaty of Campo Formio in October, 1797, largely in accordance with Bonaparte's ideas. The French annexations in the north—Belgium and the left bank of the Rhine—were recognized, and there were in addition substantial changes in central Europe.

In Italy, the newly formed Cisalpine Republic was modeled after the French of which it was a satellite. As to the Empire, the dispossessed princes of the left bank of the Rhine would be compensated from ecclesiastical territory elsewhere, and in this domestic imperial rearrangement France was to have a say.[46] In a few years, the young republic had achieved the long term goal of the monarchy of giving France her "natural" frontiers, while having planted a controlling influence in northern Italy.

Bonaparte had dealt with Austria as if he were an independent power. His "court" in Italy carried similar implications. The victorious general was welcomed with due honors and respect in Paris by a grateful, if perhaps suspicious, government, at once increasingly ineffective and dictatorial, and also increasingly at the mercy of the military arm.

---

[45] He himself did not come to Paris, whither he sent his lieutenant Augereau.

[46] Austria was compensated at the expense of Venice, now destroyed. But at the exit of the Adriatic, Bonaparte insisted on retaining control of the Ionian islands.

3. The Egyptian Expedition. But the time was not ripe. If peace reigned on the continent, it was precarious peace, for the foreign policy which the Republic was pursuing contained the seeds of further growth. Moreover, war with England was still going on. As the prospect of an invasion of England offered little promise of success, Bonaparte instead devised the scheme of an eastern expedition, to Egypt, which would have the incidental advantage of removing him from France during a period of inactivity.

The expedition in some ways was rash, but Bonaparte for a long time, in addition to his ability, had luck. Evading the British fleet, Malta was seized on the way, and an army successfully landed in Egypt.[47] On land and locally the expedition was successful; Egypt was conquered. But the conquest was barren of results. At Aboukir, on August 1, 1798, Nelson virtually destroyed the French fleet, bottling up the French forces in Egypt while in Europe the whole issue was being reopened.

4. The Second Coalition

a. FRENCH ENCROACHMENTS IN EUROPE. At the beginning of 1798, a Dutch assembly set up a Batavian Republic, new satellite of the French. The Cisalpine Republic was a natural focus of agitation for the entire Italian peninsula. In the confused situation, rife with incidents, French forces appeared in Rome, where another republic was installed.[48] These French encroachments were naturally resented abroad; more narrowly, the French interference at the Congress of Rastatt where the Empire was being territorially reorganized, irritated the Emperor.

b. FORMATION OF THE SECOND COALITION; ITS INITIAL SUCCESSES. The Russian Tsar, with more enthusiasm than balance,

---

[47] Egypt was at this time Ottoman territory, but this French intrusion in the eastern Mediterranean was of equal interest to Britain and to Russia. The French expedition was the beginning of the long story of French interest and influence in that quarter during the nineteenth century. The expedition had incidentally considerable scientific and archeological importance.

[48] Pope Pius VI, on very bad terms with the Republic, was sent off to Siena. Switzerland also, in 1798, became the dependent Helvetic Republic.

entered the antirevolutionary list,[49] and English subsidies were available for his armies. The Neapolitan King acted prematurely, with the result that a Parthenopean Republic appeared at the end of 1798, but with the entrance of Austria in March, 1799, the second coalition had come into existence.[50]

Briefly, the spring of 1799 saw the undoing of most of the earlier French successes. Italy was overrun, or liberated, Suvarov's Russians appearing as far as Piedmont and Switzerland. Although the allies failed to press their advantage as much as they might have during the summer, the situation was potentially serious for the Directory. To a degree matters were retrieved in the autumn, but best of all, the news, as unexpected as welcome, spread in France that general Bonaparte, the lucky and invincible, had landed at Fréjus and was going to Paris.

5. Brumaire. The news was correct. Stranded in Egypt, the French army was left to fend for itself, but Bonaparte's lucky star had enabled him to evade the British once more and return home. Ostensibly, he was a general momentarily without employ who might be expected to receive an important command on the continent. The military situation, however, was not immediately alarming and could therefore wait, while that in Paris was now ripe for change.

Among the forces in control of the state, there were elements who wished to effect such change. Siéyès was the most active connection and go-between, and, once more, the army would have to be relied upon. The coup was clumsily contrived and arrangements almost went awry, for opposition was strong among the legislators to military dictatorship, and Bonaparte, appearing before them in person, made a poor and awkward impression. The day was saved in part by Bonaparte's brother, Lucien, who rallied sufficient troops to drive the legislators out of their meeting hall. A rump sanctioned the coup and entrusted the drafting of a new constitution to

---

[49] This served well enough the purposes of Russian policy. Turkey being at war with France as a result of the Egyptian affair, Russia obtained the opening of the Straits. A Russian fleet appeared in the Mediterranean and captured Corfu.

[50] The fact that Austria entered the struggle independently and without prior arrangements made in some ways the second coalition even more flimsy than the first.

three Consuls that were to supersede the Directors. The day was the 18 Brumaire of the Year VIII (November 9, 1799).

a. SIGNIFICANCE OF THE COUP. As it turned out, the consequences of this particular coup d' état were far reaching and lasting. The argument could no longer be used as two years earlier that force had been resorted to as the sole means to save the constitution.[51] That instrument itself was now being destroyed. Also, the role and preponderance of the military were clearly sanctioned in the elevation of Bonaparte, despite his illegal age, not only to the Consulship, but to primacy among the Consuls.

The coup is usually considered the ending of the French Revolution. Allowing that the Revolution may be said to have been fought out far into the nineteenth century, if not beyond, it is fair to consider now closed the chapter of French history that opened ten years earlier. The significance of the coup lay in stabilizing an equilibrium reached between the contending forces of that decade. The moderate group in the Convention, neither extreme radicals nor reactionary monarchists, the upper layer of the Third Estate, had won, not only recognition, but dominant control, having survived and then suppressed the twin dangers of radicalism and of reaction.

But if this broad interpretation of the operation of historic forces is warranted, what makes the coup of Brumaire a stopping point of greater significance than others lies in considerable measure in the accident of personality. When fate, or the political forces of the day, or Siéyès, brought Bonaparte to a position of important power, they raised in him one of those men of such marked genius that a whole era has received his name. For the better part of a generation, not France alone, but Europe, was to be dominated by the little Corsican. This era is named after Napoleon who may now be said, symbolically, to have superseded Bonaparte.

---

[51] The plea of terrorist plotting and some even more fantastic arguments were used by Lucien Bonaparte.

ADDITIONAL READINGS

Brinton, Crane, *A Decade of Revolution, 1789-1799* (1934); Brinton, Crane, *The Jacobins* (1930); Cobban, Alfred, *Edmund Burke and the Revolution against the Eighteenth Century* (1929); Farmer, Paul, *France Reviews Its Revolutionary Origins* (1944); Gaxotte, Pierre, *The French Revolution* (1932); Gershoy, Leo, *The French Revolution and Napoleon* (1933); Gooch, G. P., *Germany and the French Revolution* (1920); Gottschalk, Louis, *The Era of the French Revolution* (1929); Greer, Donald M., *The Incidence of the Terror during the French Revolution: a Statistical Interpretation* (1935); Hyslop, Beatrice, *A Guide to the General Cahiers of 1789, with Texts of Unedited Cahiers* (1936); Lefebvre, Georges, *The Coming of the French Revolution* (1947); Mahan, Alfred Thayer, *The Influence of Sea Power upon the French Revolution and Empire, 1793-1812* (2 vols., 1893); Mathiez, Albert, *The French Revolution* (1928); Mathiez, Albert, *The Fall of Robespierre, and Other Essays* (1927); Taine, Hyppolite, *The French Revolution* (3 vols., 1878-1885); Thompson, James M., *The French Revolution* (1943); Thompson, James M., *Robespierre* (2 vols., 1935).

CHAPTER 14

Napoleonic Europe

I. THE CONSULATE

A. Europe in 1799

When Napoleon became First Consul, his ability to guide and mold the domestic course of events was unknown and untested. As it turned out, the five year Consulate was a period of most intense and fruitful activity in the domestic field; many would say the more solid basis of Napoleon's title to fame.

1. The Second Coalition. But the foreign, more narrowly the military, situation was unresolved, and in this field his proved ability could well be expected to operate with success.

a. DIVERGENCES AMONG THE ALLIES. The second coalition had undone much of the accomplishments of two years earlier, especially in Italy from which French influence had been expelled. Its place had been taken by Austrian, and—forecast of 1815—this state of affairs might, from the Austrian point of view, prove the basis of an acceptable settlement, for in some ways it constituted advantageous compensation for the loss of the remote Netherlands. It rather depended upon France whether she would acquiesce in such a view of compensations. She still controlled Holland and, in the south, could use the Spanish alliance.

Prussia was neutral and enjoyed the advantages of this status, especially while Austria was at war. This fact was source of Austrian irritation, all the more that Austrian influence was

finding difficulty in maintaining itself in the Germanic world.[1]
Tsar Paul, unstable and erratic, had recalled Suvarov from
his western successes, and Russia seemed to show more interest
in affairs nearer home and in the Mediterranean.[2] The seeds
were sprouting of the future nineteenth-century Anglo-Russian
rivalry in that sea, the strategic significance of which was beginning to assume major proportions in British eyes.[3]

Like all coalitions, this one suffered from the usual divergence among the interests of its constituent members. In
actual fact, the role of England was a relatively passive one
in the war, while the burden of active operations was Austria's.
England's activity was chiefly maritime, a blockade of limited
effectiveness and the extension of her empire overseas; her
contribution to warfare on land was essentially financial.

b. UNITY OF THE PERIOD 1792-1814. Such the picture of the
general situation in Europe as France was opening a new
chapter in her history. Having disposed with expedition of the
situation in Paris—to which we shall return—Napoleon turned
to the foreign scene. From the point of view of Europe as
a whole, the French Revolution and the Napoleonic period
constitute a single unit in which the latest French development introduced a new factor and gave an unexpected turn
to issues, rivalries, and quarrels of long standing. From 1792
to 1814 there raged a conflict of European, indeed of world,
dimensions. The story of it is complicated by the fact that
the conflict was broken up into a series of wars, interrupted
by many peaces, really truces, with some or all of the bellig-
erents. The war of the second coalition of 1799 is but one
of these.

2. The Treaties of Lunéville and of Amiens. Russia having virtually withdrawn from the coalition into an armed

---

[1] The Empire, long impotent as such, was further discredited as the result
of the Congress of Rastatt, preview of its impending formal dissolution.

[2] The accident of the French expedition to Egypt, placing Russia and
Turkey in the same camp, had brought the Russian fleet into the Mediter-
ranean where Russian influence reached a point never since duplicated.
The Tsar had taken the Order of Malta under his protection and asserted
claims on the island, while he encouraged Naples in her revolt against
French rule.

[3] Britain had secured control of Sicily where the King of Naples continued
to rule under her protection.

neutrality, the real enemy was Austria. Crossing the Alps, Napoleon fell upon and defeated the Austrians at Marengo in June, 1800 and, in brief, produced a second edition of his Italian campaign of five years earlier. The result was now the same as then. The treaty of Lunéville in February, 1801 duplicated the terms of Campo Formio. This left England alone in the struggle to which, largely for domestic reasons, she was willing to put a stop. At Amiens in March, 1802, a decade of Anglo-French hostilities was closed on terms highly advantageous to France.

Not only was the Republic now universally recognized, and that within the "natural" boundary of the Rhine, an ambition that French kings had never been able to realize, but through the satellite republics on her borders, Batavian, Helvetic, Cisalpine, and Ligurian, her influence was paramount far beyond these borders.[4] For a year Europe was to know a universal, if uneasy, peace.

B. The Organization of France

Napoleon was now free to devote more attention to the task of consolidation of the structure and organization of the system adumbrated after Brumaire.

1. *The Sources of Napoleon's Success.* One of the sources of Napoleon's strength was that he was, in the context of his own time, a modern man. Personally ambitious and in love with power, egotistical and vain, all this he was; but above all, in addition to a colossal energy and a capacity for work unrivaled, he had a clear and orderly intelligence that made him appraise and understand the moving forces of his time. His success and the lasting mark he made are basically due to the fact that he worked with instead of against these forces to which he himself gave an added impulse. In the obverse of these qualities may also be said to have lain his limitations and the ultimate cause of his failure. If intelligent efficiency were the sole and ultimate purpose of the ordering of society

---

[4] England was to retain Dutch Ceylon alone, withdrawing from the Mediterranean islands and from Trinidad. The retrocession of Louisiana by Spain to France in 1800 gave point to the revival of French colonial ambitions.

and of the governance of men, the world might well be handed over to Napoleons.

2. The Constitution of the Year VIII. The coup of Brumaire was quickly followed by a new constitution, of the Year VIII, for which Napoleon, understanding the psychological value of the endorsement of numbers, obtained overwhelming popular ratification. The plebiscite has ever since been a seemingly democratic, but often in practice dangerous, tool of government.

This constitution was purposely involved in its provisions. If the franchise was wide, it would serve only to elect a restricted body of "notables," out of which the ostensibly governing bodies would be chosen: a Legislative Body which enacted laws, but did not debate them; this function devolved on a Tribunate, which in turn had no powers of enactment. A conservative Senate was charged with appointive functions; but in any event the reality of power was situated in a Council of State where legislation was initiated, and, more narrowly still, in the hands of the First Consul, on account of his powers and of the active nature of his leadership.

This was not a division as much as a fragmentation of power. The extension for life of Napoleon's tenure of the Consulship in 1802, his assumption of the imperial title two years later, introduced little real change in what was from the beginning a dictatorial situation.

3. Real Nature of the Regime

a. TECHNICAL EFFICIENCY. Yet there was a surprising degree of acquiescence in the Consulate. Doubtless, this was due in part to the weariness induced by the years of turmoil and uncertainty, especially as it soon appeared that the newly established regime meant stability, order, and domestic peace.[5]

Napoleon has been described as an enlightened despot in the tradition of eighteenth-century predecessors such as Frederick the Great. This is not an unfair characterization, for his conception of government was not colored by abstract ide-

---

[5] Even foreign peace was vouchsafed for a brief time after the treaties of Lunéville and Amiens, a result all the more welcome that it was an advantageous peace of victory.

ology, but rather steeped in the concept of technical efficiency. Given his organizing abilities, he carried this conception to a high point of perfection. He had little concern with philosophical preconceptions and would take in his camp former monarchists, ex-regicides, or the ubiquitous Talleyrand, if only they had ability that they would put in his service. This made for a considerable degree of acceptance and reconciliation and enabled him to enlist the wide basis of support that was soon his.

b. THE RELIGIOUS ISSUE; THE CONCORDAT OF 1801. No issue had had more disastrously divisive effects than the religious quarrel. Napoleon was an emancipated eighteenth-century realist, indifferent toward religion, but he understood the usefulness of the church in society. In 1801, formal relations with the papacy were resumed through a Concordat more advantageous to the state than its predecessor. The chief thing was the fact of peace itself, the Revolution being sanctioned by the Pope, as well as most of the material changes it had brought to the Church.[6] In compensation, the state would henceforth pay the clergy's salaries, though this measure would equally apply to Protestants and Jews.[7] Complete freedom of religion obtained, and the Pope had to be content with the incontrovertible statement that Catholicism was the religion of the majority of Frenchmen, which indeed it was.[8]

c. ADMINISTRATIVE REORGANIZATION. The old administration of the *ancien régime* had been destroyed. Napoleon retained the framework designed by the Revolution, but gave it really solid content. The prefects at the head of each *département* became the trusted agents of the central government. France thus became uniform, centralized, and bureaucratic to a far greater degree than other states, though it should be pointed out that in this respect (allowing for the momentary federalizing tendency in the early days of the Revolution) the Mon-

---

[6] This had the great advantage of giving wholly clear title to those who had acquired Church property.

[7] The emancipation of Jews in Europe, fruit of the eighteenth-century Enlightenment, was initiated by the French Revolution and gradually spread over Europe until the retrogression of our own time.

[8] Relations with the papacy did not long remain cordial, but the Concordat survived the quarrel and remained in force until 1905.

archy, the Revolution, and Napoleon operated along the same stream of development.

d. Financial Stabilization. Financially, the Revolution had meant a culmination of the chaos out of which it was born. Inflation, depreciation, repudiation had become familiar, together with all the disorder that they inevitably induce. Yet, even before the Revolution, the trouble with French finances was merely one of management. With her resources, France could easily carry the financial burden that was hers. As when Henry IV had in a short time restored French finances to health, following the disorders of religious wars, so now Napoleon, instituting a rational system of impositions and their collection, soon restored both finances and currency to soundness.

Part of his reorganization entailed the creation of the Bank of France. During the whole period of his tenure, allowing that he called upon his conquered enemies and satellites for substantial contributions to his large schemes, the finances of France easily bore the burden that he imposed on them and remained sound. One important feature of his system, of revolutionary origin also, was the absence of all the discriminations and inequalities that had burdened and finally wrecked the old regime.

e. Judicial Reform; the Napoleonic Codes. Napoleon is credited with the observation that the French people were deeply concerned with equality, but little with liberty. Equality before the law, though somewhat qualified,[9] was, broadly speaking, and certainly by comparison with earlier practice, essentially enacted. Along with this fundamental principle, and the better to realize it, order was brought into the ancient jumble and diversity of laws that had prevailed over the lands of France, and to which had been added the considerable accretion of ten years of revolutionary legislation. The old was not rejected, but coordinated, made uniform, molded into consistent shape, in short codified.

Had he done nothing else than cause this to be done, Napoleon's name would loom large in the annals of history, for the Napoleonic codes rank in importance with the Justinian

---

[9] The testimony of a workingman did not carry the same weight in court as that of his employer in a dispute between them.

compilations, and their clear advantage has caused them to be spread far beyond French borders. The expedition with which the task was done was a reflection of the temper of its mover.

4. Acceptance of the Regime

a. ITS DICTATORIAL NATURE. Such achievements as have just been related—and they were achievements in effect, not paper programs—explain the hold of the First Consul on the nation. There were irreconcilables, those who would be content with nothing less than the *ancien régime* restored, and those who thought that the Revolution had been betrayed. Both represented diminishing extremes, but the system was none the less a dictatorial one of personal power and Napoleon felt that he could not dispense with the apparatus of coercion that usually accompanies such systems.

Mild by the more efficiently refined standards of our age, there was nevertheless control and supervision of opinion. The press was closely censored, while education was intended to inculcate loyalty to the regime. The able but repellent Fouché found scope for his talents of secret supervision, and an occasional act of terrorism, even if unnecessary, such as the abduction and execution of the Duke of Enghien, was designed to strike preventive fear among potential conspirators.

b. THE PERSONAL RULE OF NAPOLEON. Important as these things are in principle, they fill but a small part of the Napoleonic canvas. As stated earlier, in 1802, Napoleon's popularity was such that he became Consul for life. In 1804, logical sequel, a new constitution proclaimed that an Emperor would henceforth head the government of the Republic. General, then Consul, Bonaparte now in the eyes of all would be Napoleon I, Emperor of the French. Both acts, in 1802 as well as in 1804, were acts of arbitrary power, yet it cannot be said that at the time they took place against the will of the French nation.

C.   The Return to War

As a ruler among rulers Napoleon was a *parvenu*. Yet his power was such that he could cause Pope Pius VI to journey all the way to Paris to consecrate with his participation the ceremony of the imperial coronation. The sanction of the West's oldest existing institution was thus placed on the Revolution and its extraordinary offspring.

1. Reorganization of the Germanic World. The peace established in 1801-1802 was a flimsy structure. It might conceivably have lasted had France been willing or able not to exert her influence beyond her new frontiers on the continent. But the dynamism of change was not exhausted, and power tends to feed upon itself. The treaties of Campo Formio, confirmed at Lunéville, forecast internal change in the old Holy Roman Empire. It was now time to implement these, in the making of which French influence and power had an important voice.

The territorial rearrangements produced an undignified scramble, the "shame of princes," competing against each other for French favor. The outcome, registered in the *Reichsdeputationshauptschluss,* was considerable simplification of the political map. The vast majority of ecclesiastical principalities and free cities simply disappeared through incorporation into larger neighbors. The process of consolidation, important step toward further future change, redounded mainly to the benefit of these larger states, most of which had as a consequence a stake in the fortunes of the French Empire.

2. The Renewal of Hostilities. This extension of French influence beyond the Rhine, when Italy was also largely satellite, did not fit the British and the Austrian books. Britain, contending that Napoleon was not living up to the terms of peace, refused to evacuate Malta. When he in turn protested, she declared war in May, 1803,[10] and endeavored to organize a new coalition. It was in May, 1804 that the Empire was proclaimed in France and three months later that the Austrian Empire came into existence, in effect superseding the Holy Roman Empire defunct beyond retrieval. The French Empire opened its course under the sign of Mars.

---

[10] The difficulty of maintaining overseas communications caused Napoleon to abandon imperial ambitions at this time. Cutting his losses, he decided to sell to the United States the possession of Louisiana, retroceded to France by Spain in 1800.

II. THE EMPIRE

A. The Third Coalition

Not until 1805 did Britain succeed in fully welding the Third Coalition, with the accession to it of Austria and of Russia. The community of interest between Britain and Austria was more real than that between either of them and Russia.

1. *Tsar Alexander and Russia*. The autocratic constitution and backward condition of that country made her policy particularly responsive to the whims of her rulers. Tsar Paul had joined, then abandoned, the Second Coalition. His son Alexander succeeded him in 1801 in circumstances surrounded with suspicion. Tsar Alexander, during the quarter century of his rule, was to display the psychological consistency deriving from the impressionable disposition which allowed shifting influences and moods as guides to action in place of cooler judgment and steadier purpose.

In his own eyes, Alexander was a more genuine liberal than Napoleon, whose abduction of Enghien, for instance, had horrified him. Horrified also at the callousness that had destroyed the Polish state, he would have reconstituted it—with himself as ruler. Such solutions as this, neatly reconciling Russian aggrandizement with purer purpose, puzzled his brother rulers: Alexander must be charged with the variation of well-meaning inconsistency rather than the clear purpose of crafty calculation.

The basis of the Third Coalition lay in the common wish to oppose the extension of French influence into the heart of Europe. Issues dealing with the Ottoman Empire and the Eastern Mediterranean were left out of the Anglo-Russian treaty of 1805, which spoke instead of Russian troops and British subsidies.

2. *The War of the Third Coalition*

a. The Projected Invasion of England. Already in 1803, when hostilities with Britain had resumed, Napoleon had thought of the possibility of disposing once and for all of his most stubborn and least accessible foe. Near Boulogne, on the Channel coast, he gathered an army and began extensive preparations for a sea-borne descent on England. French naval power, though inferior to British, was substantial; all that was needed was control of the narrow seas for a time long enough to effect a crossing of troops. If any appreciable numbers could secure a lodgment, it might go hard for England, militarily unprepared in 1803—as in 1940. Excitement and alarm with cause ran high in Britain where, as in the days of the Armada, hasty preparations for interception and resistance were made. Needless to say, this was inducement to portray "Boney" in the dark hues of a child-eating ogre, the very quintescence of all that was evil.

b. AUSTERLITZ. It was also added inducement to England to bring land powers into the struggle. The coalition once organized, Russian and Austrian armies began to move during the summer of 1805. Napoleon had missed his chance, but he was not one to shed tears over this turn of fate. With the promptness of decision and the capacity for execution that were one of his chief assets in war, abandoning Boulogne, he brought his forces into Germany. An Austrian army had to surrender at Ulm in October, and six weeks later, on December 2, 1805, the "sun of Austerlitz" witnessed one of the great victories of his career when he crushed the combined Austro-Russian forces.

c. THE TREATY OF PRESSBURG AND THE CONFEDERATION OF THE RHINE. If the Tsar could withdraw into Poland and even beyond, Austria had met defeat at home.[11] The treaty of Pressburg registered this defeat, the price of which was the loss of Venetia, added to the Italian Kingdom. This was occasion also for further rearrangements in the purely Germanic world. The formal demise of the Holy Roman Empire was less significant than the creation of the Confederation of the Rhine, of which Napoleon would be "protector." The Confederation consisted of territory on the right bank of the Rhine whose dependence on French power was emphasized by the fact that Bavaria and Württemberg received from it their royal titles.

d. THE COLLAPSE OF PRUSSIA. Prussia had held aloof from the Third Coalition, but now taking foolishly belated alarm at the

[11] Austerlitz is in Moravia.

progress of French power, chose this inauspicious moment to
enter the fray. She demonstrated more conclusively than ever
that Frederick's soldiers "grown twenty years older" were no
match for the young armies of the Revolution.[12]

e. NAPOLEON AND ALEXANDER; THE TILSIT MEETING. The
following year the Russians, though with less ease, were also
defeated at Eylau and Friedland. Nothing on land it seemed
could stand up to the little Corsican's military genius.

With Russia willing to make peace, the Third Coalition was
destroyed. This peace was the result of the meeting between
Napoleon and Alexander that took place on a raft on the
Niemen River. Napoleon, who knew how to use charm and
could be diplomatic when necessary, had little difficulty in
capturing the imagination of the impressionable Tsar. Casting
England in the role of chief villain—a case that could be made
with ease and plausibility—the two emperors toyed with
schemes of world dominion. West of Russia, in Europe
proper, Napoleon would be supreme. In the vastness of Asia,
toward India, Alexander could extend his power indefinitely.
The awkward issue of the Ottoman Empire at the eastern end
of the Mediterranean was tactfully left unresolved. On this
basis the two rulers entered into alliance.

Unwise and timid Frederick William of Prussia was saved
by the Tsar's friendship from the complete destruction of his
state which was, however, much reduced and badly humiliated
in addition: it would not extend beyond the Elbe on one side,
and on the other lost its Polish booty that went into the
making of a Grand Duchy of Warsaw. In northern Germany,
a new synthetic Kingdom of Westphalia was created, at the
head of which Napoleon placed his brother Jerome, and which
was added to the Confederation of the Rhine.

B. Consolidation of Napoleon's Power

The next few years saw Napoleon's power at its height.
To be sure, he had difficulties, and the seeds of his undoing
were starting their slow work of germination, but outwardly
at least he was master of circumstances.

---

[12] A parallel might be drawn between the Prussian collapse of 1806
and the contemporary French performance of 1940.

1. The Continuing War with Britain. His brilliant military campaigns had destroyed the Third Coalition; Prussia and Russia, by coercion or choice, were his allies. The main significance of their alliances—especially the Russian, for Prussia could easily be controlled—from Napoleon's point of view lay in the continuing war with Britain.

a. TRAFALGAR. For at the very time that Napoleon had been launching his campaign, at Trafalgar, on October 21, 1805, the British fleet under Nelson had conclusively disposed of the combined French and Spanish naval forces. If censorship kept the news out of the French press for years, the results were no less significant, for this marked the end of serious French attempts at competing with the British at sea.

b. ECONOMIC WARFARE. The consequence of Austerlitz, Trafalgar, and Tilsit was a state of affairs which other occasions in history have seen,[13] when two powers, each supreme in his own sphere of land or sea, respectively, stand perplexedly face to face. Existing armed force being impotent, either power must in the end produce the sort of weapons in which the other has supremacy.[14] But meantime other less direct weapons may be resorted to, of which economic warfare is the outstanding.

2. The Continental System. If Britain could not be defeated at sea, or invaded at home, perhaps she could be commercially hurt into surrender.[15] Though agriculture was still an important pursuit in Britain, manufacture and trade (her own and re-exports) were of sufficient consequence that if the entire continent were closed to her trade the effects on British economy and finance might prove disastrous. To most of the continent Napoleon could dictate orders, and already after the battle of Jena, at Berlin in 1806, he had issued the decree named from that city which inaugurated the so-called Continental System. This was a counterblockade closing Europe

---

[13] After the fall of France in 1940, to take the most recent instance.

[14] Historic precedent, for what it may be worth, tends to show that in such cases the ultimate victory goes to the sea power.

[15] The state of the British economy at this time, when industry was still in its early stages, precluded the twentieth-century possibility of starving her into surrender through a blockade of food imports.

to British imports, which the Tilsit meeting caused Tsar Alexander voluntarily to join.[16]

This sort of economic warfare requires a large personnel to operate its elaborate system of control, and this was more than the time could furnish. Prohibitions were honored in the breach and smuggling flourished, even in France herself. Even so, the controls, especially if prolonged, were irksome, and particularly so to those who had no direct stake in the Napoleonic structure.

a. PORTUGAL AND SPAIN. Portugal, a British satellite, had to be invaded in order to bring her into line, and this meant bringing Spain into the picture.[17] The Spanish royal house, King Charles IV, his son and heir Ferdinand, his wife, and Godoy, constituted a sorry assemblage. A curious mixture of diplomacy, duplicity, and force procured the abdication of Charles and of Ferdinand, and another of Napoleon's brothers, Joseph, was installed on the Spanish throne.

French ideas and methods of administration represented for Spain a vast improvement, but, apart from the vested interests that they disturbed, they suffered from the stigma of being French, that is, foreign. Spanish national pride and bigotry were easily aroused and the French forces in Spain found themselves involved in a new type of warfare, guerrilla, for which their methods were not suited. England sent some forces to Spain, harbinger of later larger efforts, and the French suffered some reverses. The Peninsular War inconclusively dragged on, a festering sore in the Napoleonic structure. By itself, it was a minor matter, and the hopes that it raised of successful rebellion elsewhere were premature.

b. THE ERFURT CONGRESS. If the crisis of 1808-1809 was successfully surmounted, it was a crisis none the less. At Erfurt, in September, 1808, Napoleon had caused to be gathered much of the royalty of Europe, from whom he received evidence of adequate subservience. But if frightened German princes would fawn, Tsar Alexander was not overawed. What is more, Talleyrand, now Napoleon's foreign

---

[16] It was as a consequence of these measures that Britain took the initiative of bombarding Copenhagen and seizing the Danish fleet. This in turn caused Denmark to join the French camp.

[17] The same necessity led to the invasion of the papal domain.

minister, highly intelligent, clear sighted and unprincipled, felt that his master's plans exceeded bounds of reasonableness and did not hesitate so to inform the Tsar.

3. War with Austria, 1809. But if the Tsar would not actively support Napoleon against Austria, neither would he forcibly oppose him; he was content to watch events and wait. Luckless Austria was ill-advised to try the test of force alone in 1809. The war was brief, won after Wagram in July. Once more, at Schönbrunn in October, she had to pay the price of failure. From her territory, the Grand Duchy of Warsaw was enlarged; though this might be called restitution, the fact did not please the Tsar. Napoleon was ever interested in eastern matters: the eastern shore of the Adriatic, under the name Illyrian provinces, was also severed from Austria, soon to be formally incorporated into the French Empire itself.

C. The Apogee of the Empire

1. Napoleon and Austria. In 1809, at forty, the little Corsican corporal had reached incredible heights of power, on which moreover he sat seemingly secure. Austria's last effort had merely served to demonstrate its futility. Metternich, who now came to the helm of the Austrian state, old Kaunitz's grandson-in-law, a diplomat of the old school, ex-ambassador to Paris, like Talleyrand thought in terms of the balance of power. Under his guidance, despite humiliation, Austria gave Napoleon the sanction of recognition and reconciliation to the extent of acquiescing in the marriage of the Emperor's young daughter, Marie Louise, to the upstart adventurer.[18] The irony of fate was deep when the son of the regicide Revolution, through marriage in the Austrian house, found himself related to the Bourbons. The marriage in 1810, followed in 1811 by the birth of a son, immediately titled King of Rome, seemed to promise permanency to the results of meteoric rise.

2. Europe about 1810. These events marked the apogee of the Napoleonic adventure. The structure which he had given Europe must for a moment be examined; for all that it

---

[18] Napoleon was concerned with his failure to have an heir from Josephine, who, however, had had two children by Beauharnais. He had his marriage with her dissolved, and when his discreet inquiries at the Russian court were discreetly rebuffed he turned to Vienna.

EUROPE AT THE HEIGHT OF NAPOLEON'S POWER

Confederation of the Rhine
Westphalia
Saxony
Saxon Duchies
Bavaria
Wurtemberg
Baden

French Empire

Grand Empire

Allied with Napoleon

St. Petersburg

Finland to Russia, 1808

RUSSIAN EMPIRE

Moscow
Borodino

SWEDEN

DENMARK

Heligoland

Swedish Pomerania

Hamburg
Bremen
Berlin
PRUSSIA
Tilsit
Königsberg
Friedland
Eylau

GRAND DUCHY OF WARSAW

Bessarabia
to Russia, 1812

BLACK SEA

Jena
Erfurt
Ulm
Austerlitz
Wagram
Vienna
AUSTRIAN EMPIRE

Slavonia
Croatia
Venice
ILLYRIA
Trieste

OTTOMAN EMPIRE

UNITED KINGDOM OF GREAT BRITAIN AND IRELAND

London

CHANNEL IS.

Paris

FRENCH EMPIRE

Genoa
Leghorn
KINGDOM OF ITALY

Rome
KINGDOM OF NAPLES

Sicily
Straits of Messina

Malta

IONIAN IS.
Corfu

Sardinia

Corsica

BALEARIC IS.
Minorca
Majorca

SPAIN
Madrid
Baylen
Gibraltar

PORTUGAL
Lisbon

CAPE TRAFALGAR

Cyprus

was transitory, some of the consequences went deep. This was especially the case when it comes to the impact of internal change that followed in the train of French influence. The sheer fact of military conquest and annexations left less permanent traces, though some of its indirect repercussions were also long lasting.

a. THE FRENCH EMPIRE PROPER. At the center of the whole system was naturally the French Empire, the core of which was France, but which extended far beyond even her "natural" frontiers, Beyond the Rhine, in the. north, the Batavian Republic had once more become kingdom after 1804, with Napoleon's brother Louis as king. Louis' independence had led to his deposition and the direct incorporation of Holland into the French Empire.

Beyond Holland, and for much the same reasons of economic warfare, the entire North Sea coast of Germany, even to Lübeck on the Baltic, was also incorporated into France. Likewise in the south, across the Alps, Piedmont, Genoa, and the whole western half of central Italy, including Rome, were annexed outright to the Empire. A France including Hamburg, Bremen, Genoa, and Rome was somewhat less than purely French; her original eighty-three departements had grown to one hundred and thirty, and the same centralized administration directed from Paris through the prefects applied equally to them all.

b. THE IMMEDIATE SATELLITES. Beyond and immediately surrounding this greatly expanded France, there was a ring of closely dependent satellites. Napoleon's brother Joseph was king in Spain, having yielded his temporarily occupied Neapolitan throne to Napoleon's brother-in-law, the dashing and somewhat erratic Murat. The rest of the Italian peninsula was formed into a Kingdom of Italy where Joseph Beauharnais, Napoleon's stepson, was Viceroy.

Switzerland was a dependent Helvetic Republic, to the north of which the Confederation of the Rhine comprised the rest of Germany outside of Prussia.

c. PRUSSIA, AUSTRIA, RUSSIA, AND BRITAIN. Prussia existed as an independent state, but she had been thoroughly humiliated and frightened and reduced in power to second or third rank.

The Austrian Empire also subsisted in independence, and, despite its defeats and losses, commanded more power and respect than Prussia. To the east, Russia was fully free, an equal, and still ostensibly Napoleon's ally. Britain alone, of all Europe, persisted at war with him. So far uninjured and implacable, to his undoing she was dedicated, mainly for the reason that she felt, then as always, that the bulk of the European continent under one single rule or dominant influence constitutes too great a threat to her security, hence is not to be tolerated.

d. THE REST OF EUROPE. To complete the map, Denmark, and with it Norway, was also Napoleon's ally. In Sweden, Napoleon's ex-marshal, Bernadotte, had in 1810 been formally adopted as his successor by King Charles XIII.[19] The Grand Duchy of Warsaw was an outpost of French power in the east. Though greatly diminished by comparison with former Poland, this state held the seeds of restored independence for the whole, and, for that reason, was a genuine ally of French power. The Ottoman Empire was essentially outside the sphere of Napoleonic Europe.[20]

3. Napoleon's Impact on Europe

a. THE LIBERATION OF NEW FORCES. As might be expected, the effects of French influence, whether through conquest or imitation, were greater the nearer one went to its center. The annexed areas, as pointed out, were thoroughly assimilated to French administration and law, but in the rest of Italy and in the Confederation of the Rhine new constitutions of French model also displaced the old regimes. Napoleon was here the carrier of the Revolution, in the aspect at least which derived from the eighteenth-century Enlightenment. Liberalism and democracy in our sense of the words there was none, but the fundamental aspect of equality—equality of opportunity, careers open to talent—was in large measure realized.

Government was a technical matter to be left in the hands of the qualified and the competent; but government should be orderly and efficient. Napoleon believed in constitutions,

---

[19] Russia had secured Finland from Sweden in 1809.

[20] With the liquidation of the Egyptian expedition peace was restored in that quarter.

not in the sense of charters guaranteeing popular rights,[21] but in the sense of rational devices of procedure for the management of the state. By contrast with the *ancien régime* this undoubtedly represented progress, or at least modernization. If the disturbed vested interests of this *ancien régime* everywhere objected to these changes, there was also widespread support for them in many quarters; the bourgeoisie and many intellectuals reacted to them in the same manner outside as well as in France, and, partly for that reason, the rule of Napoleon was not oppressive—it had no need to be. Fouché's police was indeed active, but the actual instances of coercion and suppression are few.

b. NAPOLEON, CARRIER OF THE FRENCH REVOLUTION TO EUROPE. One aspect of the changes introduced or originating in France was the greatly increased effectiveness of the new state. Granting that France in Napoleon's time was much the most populous country of Europe,[22] the fact remains that she apparently possessed sufficient power to master the totality of the continent. Napoleon's military genius doubtless played an important role in this accomplishment, though he acknowledged his debt to such predecessors as Frederick of Prussia; but of equal importance at least was the fact that Napoleon had known how to remold the broken fragments of the old into a more effective structure. French resources, and others after a time, were husbanded with greater efficiency than those of other states. Even among those who would overthrow French dominance, in humiliated and disgruntled Prussia for instance, many came to realize that much of the French innovation must be accepted and adopted. In this wise, and through Napoleon, the French Revolution spread in widening circles over Europe. The old order was aware of this, and in its eyes Napoleon was truly the son of the Revolution that he proclaimed himself to be.

c. THE CASE OF BRITAIN. Here also, the English case is an exception. The early impact of that other revolution, contemporary with the French, but less spectacular and less

---

[21] Napoleon was fully aware of the value of popular support and of propaganda, as we now call it. He knew how to expatiate on the themes of liberty and tyranny.

[22] Even Russia's population did not pass France's until around the turn of the century.

sharply defined in time, that is associated with the coming of industry, was at the turn of the century most markedly felt in England. The prolonged struggle in which Britain was almost uninterruptedly engaged for more than twenty years had the effect of diverting her energies away from domestic political and social change toward the overriding necessities of the foreign situation. The consequence was hardening, even retrogression, where her political evolution was concerned, very possibly the postponing for some decades of the crisis that came to her in the eighteen thirties.

III. THE FAILURE OF THE NAPOLEONIC SYSTEM

A. Economic and Political Developments

1. The Continental System. The economic consequences of this protracted warfare were also considerable, though perhaps not quite the expected. In theory, Britain maintained a blockade, while the Continental System excluded her goods from the continent. French claims to rights of seizure in answer to requirements imposed by Britain produced in turn the retort of Orders in Council. The controversy raged over the rights of neutrals at sea, each side espousing the view most advantageous to itself.[23]

On balance, Britain did not suffer from this state of affairs, and her national income grew during the period of hostilities. In control of the seas, she developed substantially her extra-European trade, while that with Europe proper altered in its composition. She controlled all the islands adjacent to the continent of Europe, and many of these became flourishing entrepots for trade and smuggling.

a. CAUSES OF FAILURE OF THE CONTINENTAL SYSTEM. Napoleon's were the two related aims of destroying English trade, hoping thereby to force Britain to terms through economic pressure, and at the same time usurping Britain's place in continental markets.[24] France's trade with the rest of

---

[23] One aspect of this dispute was the Anglo-American War of 1812, an incident of little consequence or purpose in the story here being told.

[24] There were substantial food exports to Britain from the continent. This did not matter, from Napoleon's point of view, his aim being to injure British commerce, not to blockade England or to curtail continental exports.

the continent, before the Revolution, had been very substantial and larger than that of Britain. To a degree, efforts were made to enlarge French production and give it the benefit of the whole continental market.[25]

From the point of view of the non-French part of the continent, it might not matter much whether its needs for manufactures were supplied from British or French sources. There certainly was no a priori reason why other nations should favor an England the primacy of whose concern for her own selfish interest was well-known; but neither was there cause for privation for the sake of a system that might be European, but at the moment seemed French and ever more devised to French advantage. Apart from difficulties of enforcement, the main reason for the failure of the Continental System was France's inability to supply the needs of the European market, thus leaving in existence a demand for British goods.

2. *Political Difficulties*

a. THE UNIVERSALISTIC CHARACTER OF THE REVOLUTION. But the economic is only one aspect of the story. What may broadly be called the political is even more important. Just as in matters colonial the view had gained currency that the very effort to develop overseas possessions would lead to their loss through their eventual demand for independent government (*vide* the North American example), so likewise the very spread of French influence carried the seeds of its undoing.

Napoleon himself was not particularly French; he was quite as much an Italian to whom France and her power were tools. Again, apart from the element of personal ambition and power, his outlook was the rationalistic, universalistic one of the Enlightenment. Good, that is rational, methods of government, if they were such in Paris, would have the same quality in Berlin, or Vienna, or wherever men lived in society. The Revolution in its early days had adhered to this humanistic, cosmopolitan, outlook. Although the Revolution had been

---

[25] This policy, carried to its logical conclusion, would have implied an economic integration of the continent which was at least premature. The internal economic structure within old France was vastly improved and rationalized, but these changes did not go the length of abolishing customs even within the new French Empire, as between say Holland and France.

French initially and war had been declared against all tyrants, the spread of conquest reintroduced the cosmopolitan element: Napoleon's armies consisted of increasing quantities of Italians, Germans, and Poles.

b. THE DEVELOPMENT OF "NATIONAL" OPPOSITIONS. Nevertheless, the core of armies, administration, and political direction remained French. This tended to emphasize the factor of "foreignness," the simplest and most effective way to evince a reaction of opposition and to develop a consciousness of difference in customs and outlook. By simple standards of rational efficiency, French control generally meant improvement in the quality of administration. But the Spanish people, for example, would not see it as such; in their own eyes, Napoleon's brother Joseph brought not so much the benefits of latest modernity in government as the horrors of the godless republic beyond the Pyrenees.

Even in Italy, where Napoleon's rule was less markedly "foreign," there was opposition and restlessness, though not armed rebellion as in Spain. The case of Italy brings out another significant facet of the Napoleonic episode. The combination of the French example with the fact of having violently destroyed existing administrations and boundaries was the first preliminary step that was needed before the hope of a united Italy could take on connotations of achievable reality. But the most important case of all was that of Germany.[26]

B. The German Rebellion

1. Nationalism and Romanticism. Eighteenth-century Germany, or rather the Germanic people, knew little nationalism; as to German national consciousness, it was little developed by comparison with that of the French or English, whose national unity had found political expression long ago. The logical, rationalistic climate of the Enlightenment was unfavorable to the growth of distinctive national consciousness. Man was man, whether in Pekin or Rome, to be guided by the dictates of reason, a faculty of universal application, independent of race or language.

---

[26] If the achievements of Italian and German national unity were glorious deeds, then the first Napoleon well deserves having statues in the public squares of both countries.

To speak of "German" reason, in contrast with English or French, would be as absurd as to make the validity of geometric theorems a function of climate and season. But there is more to man than reason, and if one began to think of a German or other "soul," one entered a murky realm full of unverifiable possibilities, yet none the less real for all its lack of the sharp clarity of rational endeavor.

a. HERDER AND THE VOLKSGEIST. This is precisely what may be associated with such a name as Herder,[27] to cite a typical example. The rebellion against French ways and influence for which he stood antedated the Revolution and was essentially on the cultural level. German ways were different from, rather than worse or better than, French or others, and their distinctiveness should be recognized and cultivated in order to give expression to the true potentialities of the Germanic genius, which foreign imitation would only stifle and distort.

This innocuous, indeed valuable,[28] approach found expression in the concept of *Volksgeist*, the distinctive national character and spirit, sole sound basis of the flowering of civilizations. By contrast with and in reaction to the prevalent mood, the notion easily led to the search into, then exaltation of, the romantic German medieval past. This is one aspect of the Romantic movement, of which Germany is the native home par excellence. Its subjective aspect must be stressed and its marked antithesis with the universalistic outlook of the rationalistic Enlightenment.[29]

---

[27] Herder (1744-1803) was a Protestant pastor, somewhat irked by what seemed to him the "frivolity" of French ways. His reasonable enough stress on cultural diversity could be, and later on was, distorted and annexed by advocates of the more bigoted nationalism that insists on equating distinctiveness with superiority. Herder's important book, *Ideas on the Philosophy of the History of Mankind,* dates from 1784.

[28] The great and rich cultural diversity of Europe over its relatively small area is one of the chief titles of that continent to significance and the fruitful source of many of its contributions. The cultural aspect of nationalism may indeed be regarded as a valuable, creative, element.

[29] The observation, *"vérité en deça des Pyrénées, erreur au-delà,"* (truth on one side of the Pyrenees is error on the other), belongs to the seventeenth century, when it was meant as a comment on human frailty. Under the new dispensation of the Romantic *Volksgeist,* the same observation would be taken to justify a subjective (national, *volkisch*) approach to absolute abstractions, like justice and truth.

2. The Leadership of Prussia

a. THE PRUSSIAN COLLAPSE. To this development, the events whose motive force lay in France gave a new turn, the net result of which was that Prussia, the least German among the German states, emerged to the leadership of German national-ism.[30] Within this Germanic world, Prussia, despite her power, had not been looked upon as an exponent of higher culture worthy of imitation—if anything the opposite.

Even in terms of power, the myth of Prussian effectiveness for a time seemed exploded. When Prussian armies had faced those of the Revolution their performance had seemed one of thorough impotence. Worse still, Napoleon's victory at Jena in 1806 was the signal for rather ignominious collapse.

b. PRUSSIA'S RECOVERY. Prussia was severely punished, drastically reduced, and deeply humiliated. Occupied by French forces, she was coerced into reluctant support of the Napoleonic system, though she was allowed to retain her own institutions and government.

This put Prussia in a category apart. The rest of Germany had been completely remolded and reorganized into the satellite Confederation of the Rhine, and, after 1809, even Austria seemed to give the sanction of willing acquiescence to Napoleon's rule. Thus Prussia, despite her poor military per-formance, came to be the rallying point of what there was of German opposition to this rule, and Berlin the focus of German hopes of liberation. It was at the university of that city that Fichte, in 1808, delivered his *Addresses to the German Nation*,[31] a landmark in the story of German nationalism.

c. THE REORGANIZATION OF PRUSSIA. But Prussia earned the right to leadership in other ways. However much Napoleon and all his works might be detested, the effectiveness of French power could not be gainsaid. And this effectiveness was due not to Napoleon's organizing genius alone, but quite as much to the deep changes that the Revolution had brought

---

[30] The consequences of this Prussian leadership for Germany, Europe, and the whole world, may well be called incalculable.

[31] Fichte, a professor of philosophy at Jena, then at Berlin, a disciple of Kant, initially approved of and admired the French Revolution, even in its more violent aspects. Adopting the idea of *Volksgeist*, he went a considerable step beyond Herder by insisting, not only on the distinctiveness, but assert-ing the superiority, of the German form of it.

about in French society, releasing untapped sources of energy in the subject become citizen. If power were to be met with power, some of these changes must be emulated; the Prussian army, and beyond the army, the state, must be reorganized.

This is the task that was undertaken in Prussia, though not particularly by Prussians.[32] Scharnhorst and Gneisenau attended to the army, but perhaps the outstanding achievement was that of vom Stein.[33] In 1807, Stein was able to abolish serfdom in Prussia, an abolition hedged with qualifications to be sure, for the result of further legislation was the ultimate enhancement of the *Junkers*,[34] but the rigid class structure of the Prussian state was loosened none the less. However, reorganized though she might be, Prussia alone was impotent; she must for the time being remain content with the role of keeper of the smoldering hope of eventual liberation.

IV. THE END OF THE NAPOLEONIC EPISODE

A.   1811, the Calm Before the Storm

It is a curious fact that, just as it fell to Prussia, looked upon as relatively barbarous by Germans of the west, to become the repository of German hopes, so likewise, on the larger European scale, it was Russia, most backward of European states, that came to be regarded as the hope of those who would not accept the Napoleonic dominance.

For in 1811 Napoleon seemed well entrenched in power. To be sure, unreconciled Spain was in the nature of a festering sore, one that, however, could remain under control, if alone. With Austria seemingly reconciled to the inevitable, Prussia's disgruntlement could also be ignored. Britain was safe

---

[32] King Frederick William was a timid and indecisive character, incapable of providing leadership. It is an interesting fact that the main leaders of the national and moral reorganization of Prussia, such men as Gneisenau, Stein, Hardenberg, and Fichte, were not Prussians, though Prussia made it possible for them to carry out their task.

[33] The French had not interfered with Fichte's lectures, but Stein was judged sufficiently dangerous to be forced into exile in 1808, when he found asylum in Russia.

[34] The *Junkers,* or landed aristocracy, imbued with a strong military tradition, constituted the backbone of the Prussian officer corps. Their influence, lasting to our day, has been considerable on the course of German affairs.

and powerful, but only on the sea. Russia alone of continental
European states was genuinely free and endowed with substantial power. For a time after Tilsit, Tsar Alexander had
been Napoleon's ally. Already in 1808, at Erfurt, the Tsar
was having doubts; by the end of 1810 he decided to resume
normal commercial relations with Britain.[35] The year 1811
was the turning point. Unable to deal with the last-named
country, Napoleon decided that he must settle the Russian
problem.

B.   The Last Coalition

1. *The War with Russia*

   a. THE GRAND ARMY. Preparations were made on a scale
hitherto unprecedented. By the time it crossed the Russo-
Polish frontier in June, 1812, the Grand Army was an
enormous force of more than 600,000 men, which represented
all of Europe. The largest single contingent was French, about
one third, but the German component, if one include in it
reluctant Austrian and doubtful Prussian forces, was nearly
as large. Italians and Poles were also present in substantial
numbers.

   b. THE RUSSIAN CAMPAIGN. From the start, Russian tactics
—elusion of the enemy, making allies of space and time—
thwarted the Napoleonic plan of quick decisive action. Into
the infinite vastness of the Russian plain the Grand Army
marched. Borodino was a major encounter, a hard-won, but
not decisive, victory for Napoleon. On to Moscow he went;
the city was set on fire; still the Tsar would not negotiate.
After too long a period of waitful hesitation Napoleon decided
to withdraw.

   It was an early winter and unusually severe. The tale of
the retreat from Moscow, amidst the combined enmity of
nature and of an elusive but forever harassing foe, is still
one of the great epics of misery and hardship. General Winter
had vanquished the Grand Army, most of which gradually
dissolved into a hungry and undisciplined horde. Some 100,000
men recrossed the border into Poland.

----

[35] During the interval of peace Russia acquired Finland in 1809 and
also undertook a war against Turkey. These were but secondary actions.

2. The Spread of War

a. THE LIBERATION OF GERMANY. Napoleon was no senti-
mentalist, one to shed futile tears over his wasted army.
Incognito, and at amazing speed (less than two weeks) he
dashed from Poland back to Paris, there to raise new contingents. For these the need was urgent, for the turn of events
naturally raised new hopes among his oft-defeated, but not
reconciled, enemies.

Prussia, as might well be expected, was first to turn, having
made with Russia an arrangement, the treaty of Kalisch, for
the future disposition of eastern territories. After some hesitation, Austria too joined in the war. The great encounter near
Leipzig, the Battle of the Nations in October, 1813, was
Napoleon's first real defeat in the field. As a result of it, all
Germany was liberated as French forces withdrew to and
beyond the Rhine.[36]

b. DIPLOMACY OF THE COALITION. Diplomacy took a hand
at this point, for the very successes of the allies had the wonted
effect of reviving their divergent interests. Tsar Alexander
wanted to redress in Paris the occupation of Moscow, but
Metternich saw clearly the danger of too great a Russian
influence in Europe which would invalidate the virtue of
eliminating Napoleon's too great power. A France reduced to
proper dimensions, but still strong, was necessary to the
balance of Europe. On the basis of the continuation of
Napoleonic rule within the natural frontiers of France he
would have negotiated peace after the success of Leipzig in
November, 1813.

But Napoleon would not come to terms. He felt too much
a *parvenu* in the society of rulers, lacking the sanction of
ancient and established dynasties, to be able to compromise.
Britain might have been expected to take a similar view to
Metternich's in the face of Russia's potential influence. But
it was still too soon for that. This was one of the few
occasions when she was resolved that nothing short of total

---

[36] Earlier in the year, the French had also been ousted from Spain, where
a British force was operating under Wellington, and France was being
invaded across the Pyrenees.

destruction of her enemy would suffice.[37] Her energies were bent on the prosecution of war, to which end she lavishly poured money in an effort to maintain the alliance in being.

Castlereagh's journey to the continent in January, 1814, with the same end in view, had its success facilitated by Napoleon's refusal of Metternich's approaches. In March, 1814 the treaty of Chaumont among the four chief members of the coalition sanctioned their alliance for a twenty year period and provided for contingents of specific size that they were to furnish for the purpose of implementing their common policies.

c. THE CAMPAIGN OF FRANCE. Meanwhile, since Napoleon would not come to terms, hence must be made to yield, the war was going on in France itself. It was conducted with skill by Napoleon, but he was now reduced to France's own resources of man power, which heavy demands over the years had depleted. The outcome of the unequal struggle was well-nigh inevitable, and by the treaty of Fontainebleau, in April, 1814, he finally consented to withdraw.[38]

3. The First Treaty of Paris. Napoleon might abdicate, but France remained. The settlement with her was relatively prompt and simple. The allied leaders met in Paris, where the ubiquitous Talleyrand was ready to receive and deal with them. Louis XVIII, Louis XVI's brother and heir, older and wiser now, came at last back into his "legitimate" inheritance. He would henceforth be King of France, a France brought back to the frontiers of 1792 before the long career of war had started. For the rest, and there was much else to be done in a Europe emerging from a quarter of century of wars and far-reaching readjustments, both domestic and international, a congress would meet in Vienna later on in the year. [39]

---

[37] The end of the great Anglo-French imperial struggle in 1763 was hardly out of living memory.

[38] Having abdicated the French crown, Napoleon received in full sovereignty the island of Elba, whither he went into exile, while financial settlements provided for himself and members of his family.

The short-lived episode of the Hundred Days in 1815, ending in Waterloo, is a picturesque, but not very significant, footnote to the Napoleonic epic. Napoleon surrendered to the British, who sent him to safer exile in St. Helena, thereby definitely closing his own story. He died in St. Helena in 1821.

[39] For the Congress of Vienna, see Chapter 15.

C. The Balance Sheet

In the spring of 1789 the Estates General of the Kingdom of France had met at Versailles, primarily to find some answer to the financial crisis that the existing government was unable to solve. The meeting turned out to be the catalytic agent whereby the pent up forces of nearly a century found release. Far beyond the expectations of the wildest dreamers had the explosion made its ripples felt: even distant Moscow had known the tramp of French armies. These armies that went to Moscow, after marching back and forth across Europe, apart from the fact that they were only partly French, were very different either from the eighteenth-century armies of the French king or from the early revolutionary rabble. They were the highly perfected tool of one of the greatest military leaders of all time.

But they were even more than that. Napoleon ever called himself a son of the Revolution. In a sense, in that it was the Revolution that made possible his rise, he certainly was that; nor did he cease to advocate the recognition of competence and talent and the reward of merit. But, great as he may individually be, Napoleon was in the last resort a passing meteor in the firmament of power, the instrument and agent of forces greater than himself. The things that he built up, codes, administrations, and highways, as much as those that he destroyed, ancient frontiers, moth-eaten imperial princelings, feudal survivals, equally served the entering course of progress, or if not progress, at least historic change.

If the political progress of Britain was perhaps somewhat retarded by reaction to the French Revolution and the Napoleonic episode, that of France and the continent was on the whole enhanced. Nor was other change, whether economic or cultural, impeded. Napoleon himself belongs in the classical tradition of France; rational order in the state (apart from power) was his ideal. The culture of his time, as of the Revolution, in France is strongly steeped in Roman emulation. Yet the whole episode may well be called romantic in its whole unfolding. The early romantic flowering in the neighboring Germanic world has been mentioned.

One aspect of this Romantic movement—less than fortunate in its ultimate consequences—was the exaltation of the national myth. Napoleon himself, for all the love he knew how to profess of the French nation, as indicated earlier, was no nationalist, but rather heir in many ways of the Enlightenment. However, to French arms he supplied an ample store of glory, and the military component too was to enter the Romantic-nationalist revival. As in most human developments of large magnitude, the whole quarter century episode was of mixed consequence and quality, yet, beyond question, one of the great epic tales of the checkered history of mankind.

ADDITIONAL READINGS

Aris, Reinhold, *History of Political Thought in Germany from 1789 to 1815* (1936); Brinton, Crane, *The Lives of Talleyrand* (1936); Bruun, Goeffrey, *Europe and the French Imperium 1799-1814* (1935); Buckland, C. S. B., *Metternich and the British Government from 1809 to 1814* (1932); Dard, Émile, *Napoleon and Talleyrand* (1937); Fisher, H. A. L., *Napoleon* (1913); Geyl, Peter, *Napoleon, For and Against* (1949); Gottschalk, Louis, cited in Ch. 13; Heckscher, Eli, *The Continental System: an Economic Interpretation* (1922); Lobanov-Rostovsky, Andrei A., *Russia and Europe, 1789-1825* (1947); Madelin, Louis, *The Consulate and the Empire* (2 vols., 1934-1936); Mahan, Alfred Thayer, cited in Ch. 13; Rose, John Holland, *Life of Napoleon I* (2 vols., 1902); Rose, John Holland, *William Pitt and the Great War* (1911); Seeley, Sir John, *Life and Times of Stein* (3 vols., 1878); Sweet, Paul R., *Friedrich von Gentz, Defender of the Old Order* (1941); Tarlé, Evgenii V., *Bonaparte* (1937).

PART IV

Epilogue

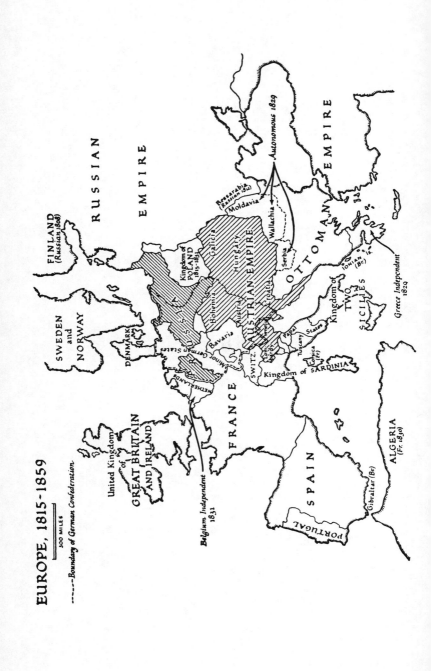

EUROPE, 1815-1859

300 MILES

------ Boundary of German Confederation

United Kingdom
of
GREAT BRITAIN
AND IRELAND

FRANCE

SPAIN

PORTUGAL

Gibraltar (Br.)

ALGERIA
(Fr. 1830)

SWEDEN
and
NORWAY

DENMARK

NETHERLANDS

Belgium Independent
1831

Minor German States

Bavaria

SWITZ.

Kingdom of SARDINIA

Corsica
(Fr.)

Lombardy
Venetia

Parma
Modena

Tuscany

Papal
States

FINLAND
(Russian 1808)

RUSSIAN

EMPIRE

Kingdom of
POLAND
1815-1831

AUSTRIAN EMPIRE

Galicia

Bohemia

Austria

Hungary

Tyrol

Croatia

Kingdom of
TWO
SICILIES

IONIAN IS.
(Br.)

Greece Independent
1829

Bessarabia
(Russian 1812)

Moldavia

Wallachia

Serbia

Autonomous 1829

OTTOMAN

EMPIRE

CHAPTER 15

The Struggle between Liberalism and Reaction: 1815-1848

I. EUROPE IN 1815

Napoleon had been an autocrat, in actual fact rather more arbitrary and powerful than his divine-right predecessors on the French throne. Yet Napoleon had called himself a son of the Revolution, and there is no denying that his armies had carried abroad with them some of the fundamental aspects of that upheaval. The example in practice of "the career open to talent," the recognition of individual merit irrespective of birth, and the institution of up-to-date constitutions on much of the continent, had given the *ancien régime* blows from which, after a quarter of a century, it could not wholly recover.

But the natural tendency, especially after a long and arduous conflict, is to equate the restoration of peace with that of "normalcy," interpreted in turn as synonymous with the *status quo ante*. The whole nineteenth century is filled with the struggle between the old (absolutism, reaction) and the new (liberalism, democracy, or progress), a contest in which, viewing the century as a whole, the old will appear to be fighting a retreating action. The battle was fought out in France as elsewhere, but it was only natural that in France should be found the greatest strength of the new and that France should be its standard bearer and the weather vane of change. Especially during the first half of the century, until 1870, this state of affairs is adequately expressed in the quip, "When Paris sneezes, Europe catches cold."

A. France and the Coalition

Napoleon had been defeated in 1814, and peace with France had been promptly made by the first Treaty of Paris (March,

1814). 'Napoleon had abdicated (Treaty of Fontainebleau) and the Bourbons had returned to France, in the person of Louis XVIII, brother of the executed king. France was not punished for the misdeeds of Napoleon; she was confined to the frontiers of 1792 and no indemnity was imposed upon her.

Obviously, however, the danger stemming from France could not be considered destroyed for all time, and the successful coalition had cemented its bonds by the Treaty of Chaumont (March, 1814). Also, while it was relatively simple to deal with France alone, the map and the status of much of Europe had to be re-examined. This the allies proposed to do at a subsequent meeting which took place in Vienna from the autumn of 1814 to June, 1815.

1. The Hundred Days. From March to June, 1815, Napoleon made a sensational, but short-lived, reappearance upon the scene. Waterloo definitely marked his exit from history. Peace had to be made again with France (second Treaty of Paris, November, 1815), setting her frontiers at those of 1790, imposing upon her an indemnity of 750,000,000 francs, and occupation for a time by foreign troops.

B.   The Settlement of Vienna

The arrangements made at Vienna were not affected by the Hundred Days. The task of the Congress of Vienna had not proved easy. All Europe, the rulers and their delegates that is, was at Vienna, but decisions were largely in the hands of the four chief allies (Russia, Prussia, Austria, and England) in whose discussions, taking advantage of their differences, the wily Talleyrand soon managed to insert himself. France had an important voice in Vienna. With the addition of Sweden, Portugal, and Spain, the five became the eight.

1. The Leaders, the Issues, and the Guiding Principles. Metternich was host and guide to the Congress. He sincerely held the Jacobin ideal to be a dangerous fallacy, under whose guidance no society or state could hope to function; restoration of the old regime was not only necessary, but the preservation of the "ideology," as we should call it now, was the proper concern of all, not the purely domestic task of individual states and rulers. In addition to this, the European community as a whole could best function under the aegis of the principle of the balance of power. In this last view, he found support from Castlereagh, the British representative; Tsar Alexander was more responsive to the former. Well-meaning, but impressionable and unstable, the Tsar was easily swayed by the contradictory influences that attracted his shifting fancy. Talleyrand, biding his time, made a telling point with his concept of legitimacy; in defeat, this was the best defense of French interest. Prussia, under the guidance of the timorous Frederick William, was not an initiator of ideas or policies.

Legitimacy, however, could be restored only up to a point. The outmoded structure of the defunct Holy Roman Empire, for example, could not be resurrected; Napoleon's job of simplification was in large measure allowed to stand. Also, the balance of power did not necessarily preclude the effort on the part of its participants to secure individual benefits. Tsar Alexander was desirous of securing all Poland for himself; he would assuage his liberal leanings of the moment by making it a separate kingdom and giving it a constitution. For a price (cession of Saxony), Prussia was willing to acquiesce in this. But neither Metternich nor Castlereagh could see the virtue of having destroyed excessive French power merely to replace it by Russian. The Polish-Saxon issue proved the most difficult problem that faced the Congress; for a time it threatened its continuance, and it was the wedge through which Talleyrand reinserted France in the councils of the powers. [1]

The outcome of these circumstances was ultimately compromise. The settlement of Vienna was made under the aegis of the principles of legitimacy and restoration, qualified by compensation.

2. The Results. The principal results were these:

Britain—since 1801 the United Kingdom of Great Britain and Ireland—had no direct territorial interests on the continent. She wished, however, to retain some of the overseas territories conquered during the recent wars. This was facilitated[2] by the

---

[1] In January, 1815 a treaty of alliance was made between Britain, France, and Austria oppose, by force of arms if necessary, the Russo-Prussian coalition.

[2] Britain acquired, as a result of the Napoleonic wars, some Caribbean islands, Mauritius, Guiana, and South Africa. In the Mediterranean, she took from temporary French control and retained Malta and the Ionian islands. These last she relinquished to Greece in 1863.

fact that her continental allies had generally little appreciation of or interest in colonies.

Holland was the chief sufferer from British acquisitions, but she was compensated by the incorporation of the former Austrian Netherlands. This had the additional advantage of creating a stronger barrier against France in the north, and specifically of keeping Antwerp and the mouth of the Scheldt out of French hands.

The same purpose of blocking French expansion was served by consolidating the conglomeration of minute states in the Rhineland, now a solid block of territory turned over to Prussia.

This arrangement, in turn, served to compensate Prussia for her failure to incorporate Saxony, only three-fifths of which she acquired. There was no compensation for Saxony, faithful until too late to the Napoleonic cause.

Austria was willing to relinquish the awkwardly distant Netherlands in exchange for nearer possessions in Italy; Venice was not restored, but instead, with Lombardy, became Austrian. This served to confirm the predominant Austrian influence in the Italian peninsula (members of the Habsburg house also ruled in the Duchies) where otherwise restoration was the order of the day, save that, like Venice, Genoa was not revived, being instead incorporated into the Kingdom of Sardinia. [3]

In place of the old Holy Roman Empire, a comparable German Confederation was set up within roughly the same boundaries. Austria, by right, was to have its presidency, and paramount Habsburg influence was thus presumably insured from the Baltic to Sicily.

Tsar Alexander of Russia did not get all, but only the major part, of Poland, substantially more than in the last partition of 1795. Russia also retained Bessarabia, acquired in 1812 from the Turks, but the Congress did not otherwise concern itself with the Ottoman Empire. In the north also, Finland, acquired in 1809, was retained by Russia.

---

[3] In 1814, Murat, King of Naples, had thought to save his throne by abandoning Napoleon. Metternich accepted Murat's assistance, and the Neapolitan question might have been an awkward one at Vienna had not Murat conveniently eliminated himself by throwing his lot with Napoleon during the Hundred Days.

There was no reason, however, · to punish Bernadotte's Sweden for this loss. It was made up by the adjunction of Norway, detached from her hitherto Danish allegiance. Denmark, like Saxony, had not deserted Napoleon early enough.

Spain and Portugal were restored, but the problem of their revolting American colonies was not dealt with.

3. Appraisal of the Settlement. The settlement of Vienna[4] was essentially a political one. It is a measure of the changed conditions that a century was to bring that, by contrast with modern treaties, those of Vienna were virtually unconcerned with matters economic.

The peoples had no voice at Vienna. Nationalism was ignored, and this has often been considered a valid criticism of these arrangements. There is no question that nationalism, like democracy, was to prove one of the guiding currents of the nineteenth century, much of the history of which can be written in terms of ultimately successful efforts to undo the charter of 1815. To the rulers of the day, nationalism meant little; and nationalism at the beginning of the century was not the sort of thing that we have come to know. In the context of its own time, the settlement of Vienna was a reasonable and moderate compromise. It proved rather more lasting than attempts of comparable scope in our own century.

4. The Holy and Quadruple Alliances. More important than nationalism in the eyes of the rulers was the matter of preserving the social and political structure of the various European states. Tsar Alexander, combining in his own inimitable fashion the various tendencies at work in him, contrived the Holy Alliance (November, 1815). This was a vague and pious declaration, of elusive content, entered into by the rulers under the aegis of the Holy Trinity, for mutual assistance and protection. What significance it would have, if any, would depend upon whether and how it was implemented when suitable circumstances arose.

The British monarch, on the plea of his constitutional status, declined to join in this "nonsense." Britain was more interested in a more concrete instrument, the Quadruple Alliance, which provided specific guarantees against a recurrence of French aggression, and also for further meetings of the powers.

---

[4] The final Act was signed in June, 1815, a few days before Waterloo.

II.   THE RESTORATION, 1815-1830

The period following the Congress of Vienna has sometimes been labeled the Era of Metternich. If Metternich is regarded as the most consistent and staunchest advocate of the old order, hence of reaction, the label for a time is suitable.

A.   The United Kingdom

The constitutional structure of Britain had been unaffected by events of the past quarter of a century. Victory over Napoleon redounded to the credit of the Tory administration, and the general revulsion toward the "excesses" of revolutionary France hampered the influence of the able but small band of "radicals" in and out of Parliament. Economic problems, those deriving from an already well-developed industry, and fiscal ones arising from the debts incurred in financing the war, loomed large. England was still devoted to protection of her still important agriculture and to an increasingly outmoded system of political representation. Unrest growing out of the economic crisis of 1819 was met by the repressive Six Acts, curtailing the traditional British liberties.

The private affairs, or scandals, of the Regent, who became George IV upon the death of George III in 1820, did not enhance the prestige of the Crown. If Britain had not joined in the Holy Alliance, the policies of her government were satisfactory to Metternich.

B.   The Germanies

In the German Confederation, the enthusiasm of the war of liberation had much abated. In Prussia, the reforming zeal of Stein had yielded to conservative rule, and the king had conveniently forgotten his promise of a constitution. The ferment of a romantic liberalism was still at work, especially in the universities; student societies, the *Tugendbund* and the *Burschenschaft*, were its chief expressions. The murder of the writer Kotzebue, an agent of the Tsar, by an exalted fanatic, provided Metternich with a suitable pretext for calling together the representatives of the various states. The Carlsbad Decrees, in 1819, inspired by the same spirit as the British Six Acts, were the result.

C. France

In France, Louis XVIII, anxious not to set out on further travels and realizing the irreversible imprint of the past twenty-five years, had granted a charter, or constitution, that provided representative institutions, albeit with a very limited franchise. The reactionary party was strong, and the episode of the Hundred Days was followed by a White Terror and the election of the so-called *Chambre introuvable*, more royalist than the king, by whom it was dissolved in 1816. The new chamber had a majority of the center in favor, like the king, of the charter and constitutional monarchy.

1. The Congress of Aix-la-Chapelle. France was under enemy occupation. The seeming restoration of stable government, the fulfillment of her financial obligations to the allies, and the fear of these lest their troops become "infected" with revolutionary ideas, induced a reconsideration of France's status at the Congress of Aix-la-Chapelle in 1818. The result of this meeting was to reinstate France to the status of a member in good standing of the Concert of Europe. She joined the Holy Alliance, but the Quadruple Alliance was also secretly renewed.

This apparent stabilization was interrupted by the assassination of the Duc de Berry, the king's nephew. This was the signal for a new instalment of reaction, endorsed by the elections of the same year. The split between right and left was thus accentuated, and the latter, under persecution, tended to resort to the conspiratorial activity of secret societies.

D. The Concert of Europe; The Issue of Intervention

1. The Revolutions of 1820 in Italy. Activity of this nature was particularly flourishing in the Italian peninsula where the *Carbonari* and other similar groups had their main strength. The slogan of liberals at this time was "Constitution," a word which seemed to carry an aura of magic attributes. In Naples, King Ferdinand I of the Two Sicilies, was setting an example of thoroughgoing and blind reaction. In July, 1820, a virtually unopposed rising extorted from him the grant of a constitution, modeled after the Spanish one of 1812. The Neapolitan situation had echoes throughout Italy, and particularly in Piedmont.

2. The Congresses of Troppau and Laibach. Intervention in Italy. Here was a potentially dangerous situation, in Metternich's view, a proper subject for consideration by the Concert of Europe. A meeting was held at Troppau in Silesia, in November, 1820 and reconvened at Laibach the next month. It was about this time that Tsar Alexander, frightened away from his uncertain liberalism by the spectacle of plots, conspiracies, and assassinations, yielded to Metternich's guidance and gave his support to a policy of armed intervention. Britain assumed an ambiguous position of formal opposition, while Castlereagh privately reassured Metternich. France also hedged, refusing to associate herself formally with the decisions of Troppau and Laibach.

In these circumstances, the appearance of Austrian troops in Naples restored the situation with ease. The triumph of reaction was assured throughout Italy. Its manifestations were particularly brutal in Naples, but suppression was also severe in the Papal States, in the Austrian territory of Lombardo-Venetia, and in Piedmont. In that state, the abortive rising of 1821 had resulted in the abdication of Victor Emmanuel, and its success had been hampered by the gyrations of the temporary regent, Charles Albert. Many liberals were imprisoned, while others sought the safety of exile, pursued where possible by the long arm of Metternich acting through the Concert of Europe.

3. The Congress of Verona. Intervention in Spain. Spain had been the scene of rebellion even earlier than Italy, to whom she set an example. The trouble began in January, 1820 among the troops gathered at Cadiz for embarkation to South America, where the colonies were fighting for independence. King Ferdinand had been forced to grant a constitution which operated after a fashion between the pressures of the extremes of the left (*exaltados*) and right (*apostolicos*). After the Italian situation, nearer the center of Europe, had been dealt with, Spanish affairs came up for consideration at the Congress of Verona (October, 1822). No one was anxious to entertain the Tsar's offer of his armies for service in Spain. If Europe were to intervene in that peninsula, the logical agent of its mandate was France. After some hesitation on the part of the French government, somewhat uncertain of the spirit of its armies, French forces entered Spain in 1823. They met with little resistance, and King Ferdinand was restored to full and arbitrary power, of which he made the same abusively repressive use as his Neapolitan namesake.

4. The Monroe Doctrine and England. The Spanish affair had other repercussions. England eyed with suspicion the French intervention. When it came to the possibility of Europe assisting Spain in the recovery of her American possessions, not only would she not join, but she actually opposed such intervention. It was useful, for British purposes, that the support of the desire for independence in South America should fit with her commercial interests. The United States found itself in essentially the same position. But sufficient suspicion on the American side still tinged Anglo-American relations to prevent overt concerted action. In December, 1823, President Monroe sent to Congress the famous message containing the declaration associated with his name since then. The Monroe Doctrine was an American statement; its effectiveness would inevitably depend for a considerable time to come upon British maritime supremacy, and Canning, who had meantime succeeded Castlereagh after the latter's suicide, claimed ample credit for the successful birth to independence of the South American republics.

E.   The Decembrist Rising in Russia

At the other extremity of Europe from Spain, the liberal ferment had made some impression, especially among army and educated circles. There was no sufficient basis for revolution in Russian society, however, and the Tsar, though wedded by now to reaction, did not seriously interfere with the impotent talk and scheming of secret societies. His death, in 1825, followed by an interval of uncertainty over his succession, was the occasion for an ill-planned and hopeless rising in December. Tsar Nicholas, once on the throne, dealt severely with the "Decembrists" and their following.

By the mid-twenties, Metternich could contemplate with satisfaction the state of Europe, largely under the rule of reliable conservative governments.

II.   THE EASTERN QUESTION

A.   Nature of the Problem

1. Ottoman Decline.   The story of the Ottoman Empire during the eighteenth century had been one of gradual territorial recession, mainly under the joint pressure of Austria and Russia. In addition, France had long-standing interests, economic and cultural, in the empire of the sultans, and the imperial and commercial growth of Britain caused her to take increasing interest in its affairs. The Turks had lost their former expanding vigor, and instead of keeping up with the modern world, their state, beset by maladministration, was in a condition of advanced decay.

Although the Congress of Vienna, partly in deference to Russian wishes, had not dealt with Ottoman affairs, it was clear that the fate of the still vast Ottoman domain would be of concern to the powers, particularly the four just mentioned. This is the essence of the eastern question.

2. The Straits.   More narrowly, in the purely European sphere, the traditional Russian push toward warm and open waters, had become clearly focused on some form of control of the straits (the Bosporus and the Dardanelles), a desire generally opposed by the other powers and by the Turks themselves. In their weakness, the sultans consistently pursued the policy of seeking to prevent agreement among the powers, not too difficult a task.

3. The Balkans.   The problem was further complicated by local considerations. The bulk of the European possessions of the Turks—roughly the Balkan peninsula—was inhabited by Christians, mainly of the Greek Orthodox persuasion. Religion playing the central role that it did among Moslems, by contrast with the secular West—the Sultan was also Caliph of Islam—the fact of Christianity had been the chief agency in preserving the distinct identity of the Balkan peoples. The Greek Patriarch of Constantinople, head of this Christian community and regarded by the sultans as its representative, was in effect an important official of the Ottoman state.

B.   The Independence of Greece

1. The Greeks. This personage was normally drawn from the Greek community of Constantinople (Phanariotes). This community was important because of its wealth, largely drawn from commerce, an activity in which the Turks took little share. To a considerable extent also, Greeks, always a seafaring people, manned the fleets. This contributed to give the Greek element, as distinct from Bulgarian, Serb or other, a special position in the Ottoman Empire. The Greeks, moreover, however low and sad their current estate, especially in Greece proper, had the memory and example of "the glory that was Greece" to look back to. For some time there had been a revival of the Greek national spirit, in great part literary in its manifestations, as is normally the case with nationalities awakening after a long eclipse. The echoes of the French Revolution, though muffled, had reached distant Greece, and the revival began to take on political overtones, a desire for independence. [5]

2. The Greek Revolt. Active trouble began in 1821 with simultaneous action in the Danubian Principalities and in Greece proper (Morea). The Tsar, despite his sympathies (Ypsilanti had been allowed to prepare his filibustering expedition in Russia), refused to give the hoped-for support, and even disavowed Ypsilanti. Metternich's view that this was a rebellion against legitimate authority, the Sultan, a revolt moreover taking place "beyond the pale of civilization," prevailed, and the attempt in the Principalities was a failure. It went otherwise in Morea where the movement initiated a ten-year period of brutal and ferocious warfare.

3. The Powers Intervene. In western Europe there was much sympathy, largely romantic, for the revolting Greeks, but little concrete aid at first, despite such individual instances as that of Lord Byron. But as the war dragged on, European chancelleries began to concern themselves with the problem. The Sultan·had appealed for help to his vassal, Mehemet Ali of Egypt. The new Tsar, Nicholas I, abandoning in 1826 the restraint of his predecessor, began to interfere more actively.

---

[5] As early as 1804, there had emerged a principality of Serbia, endowed with a degree of autonomy, but still under Turkish suzerainty.

By the Treaty of London (July, 1827), Russia, Britain, and France agreed to put an end to hostilities, and an Anglo-French fleet sailed for Greece.

By accident rather than design, this fleet became involved in action which resulted in the destruction of the Turco-Egyptian fleet in Navarino Bay in October, 1827. Greece, hard pressed, had been saved, but the issue was more than ever an international one. In April, 1828, losing patience with the tergiversations of the Sultan and of diplomacy, Russia declared war on Turkey.

The campaign proved more difficult than expected in Russia, but in the spring of 1829 Turkish resistance was broken, and the frightened Sultan signed the Treaty of Adrianople (September, 1829) which, in addition to providing for Greek independence, secured advantages for Russia in the Principalities.

This independence of Greece was formally sanctioned by the powers meeting in London (February, 1830). It was a very small Greece, leaving out much Greek-inhabited territory, but its sovereignty was unfettered by any limitations. All that remained was to give the new state a ruler, whom the three powers finally agreed should be Otto, the second son of the King of Bavaria, who thus became the first king of modern Greece.

IV.   LIBERAL SUCCESSES AND FAILURES

The successful emancipation of Greece was as much a triumph of nationalism as of liberal forces, sympathetic to it. Despite the seemingly secure hold of reaction in the twenties, there were other instances of liberal successes at this time.

A.   The Revolution of 1830 in France

In France, Charles X had succeeded his brother Louis XVIII in 1824. He was a thoroughgoing reactionary and acted accordingly, creating much discontent and opposition among a people whose wishes he willfully ignored. The climax came when he dismissed an uncongenial and relatively liberal ministry in 1829, arousing strong protests in the Chamber and in the press. Elections merely confirmed the strength of the opposition. The king's answer, in the form of four ordinances that dissolved the Chamber, curbed the press, and further restricted the franchise, produced an explosion at the end of July, 1830.

Three days of barricades and street fighting in Paris were sufficient to overthrow the government. Charles X took the road to exile, and the Chamber invited Louis Philippe, of the Orléans branch, to mount the throne. When the smoke of battle had cleared, the French revolution of 1830 proved to be a success of political economic liberalism. The Charter of 1814 was essentially maintained, but the fact is important that, instead of that document deriving its validity from the will of the ruler, it was he who derived his power from the will of the nation. This was given expression in his title, Louis Philippe I, King of the French—no longer of France.

A lowering of the property qualification widened the franchise, but the electorate was still not much above 200,000. The influence of the old aristocracy was weakened in the upper house through the abolition of the hereditary peerage. The year 1830 was definitely a triumph of the commercial, moneyed bourgeoisie, and Louis Philippe has been properly dubbed the bourgeois king, a role which he himself emphasized.

B. The Reform Bill of 1832 in England

The same forces that had won the day in France were clamoring for greater recognition in England. They were even stronger in the latter country, where industry was more advanced. The hold of reaction had been weakening in England despite the continued tenure of the conservatives. Legislation, economic and social, began to be enacted: partial repeal of navigation acts; freedom of association (1824). Catholic emancipation took place in 1829.

The advent of Louis Philippe in France was well received in England, especially when it became apparent that the orientation of the new government was moderate in its domestic as well as in its foreign policy. In the same year 1830, the accession of George IV to the throne weakened the support that the Tories had received from the Crown, and an election returned them to power with a much diminished majority. All this combined to give a fillip to the agitation for reform which had been going on for many years.

The issue was essentially, as in France, confined to the dominant layers of society; the rising, and by now powerful, industrial bourgeoisie wanted a recognition that the antiquated system of representation granted in disproportionate measure to the landowning aristocracy. The "rotten boroughs" were the clearest expression, most easily attacked, of the inadequacy of the representation. The Whigs, led by Grey, espoused the cause of electoral reform, to which the Prime Minister, Wellington, opposed an uncompromising refusal. Grey formed a ministry of Whigs and Canningites, and the defeat of a Reform Bill led to a dissolution of Parliament. The new House of Commons (1831) was favorable to reform, which was blocked by the Lords. Feeling ran high in the country, where agitation, enlisting the working class, reached impressive proportions. But in contrast with France, Britain's revolutions were too far in the past and had given way to an evolutionary tradition of political change.

The crisis was ultimately resolved through the device of threatening to create a sufficient number of new peers to procure an amenable majority. On this, as on other comparable occasions, when faced with inevitable defeat, the Lords yielded rather than destroy the exclusiveness of their order. In 1832, the great Reform Bill became law. It redistributed representation and increased the electorate from some 500,000 to about 800,000. The election of December, 1832 overwhelmingly endorsed the reform. Henceforth Whigs and Tories became known as Liberals and Conservatives. The British tradition of peaceful change had been further entrenched, and when the king sought to impose a Tory ministry in 1834, Robert Peel, calling an election, declared that the Reform Bill was accepted by the Tories. The Liberals were returned in the majority and in 1835 regained the prime-ministership.

C. Repercussions of 1830 Elsewhere in Europe

The liberal ferment which had achieved success in France and in Britain was not confined to those countries.

1. The Independence of Belgium. The former Austrian Netherlands, modern Belgium, which had in 1815 been incorporated with Holland, was largely different from that country. King William I showed little wisdom in imposing an essentially

Dutch administration in Belgium instead of allowing some scope for autonomy in a territory that was economically advanced and politically conscious of its diversity. The difficulties of the Dutch administration might have come to a head even earlier had it not been for the Belgian division between Catholics and Liberals.

These tendencies managed to come together in 1830. Encouraged by the example of events in Paris and confronted with the stubborn intransigeance of the Dutch ruler, they made revolution in Brussels in August 1830, and the movement culminated in a Belgian proclamation of independence. Not until 1839 did Holland recognize the irreversible fact, but Belgium was in effect independent from 1830.

This result was made possible by the action of the powers. The Belgian issue was an important one in the eyes of Europe. France, for reasons of ideology as well as of national interest, looked upon Belgian freedom with a kindly eye. Britain was not averse, with one proviso, that it be not a prelude to renewed French expansion. Metternich would have been inclined to respond to King William's appeal to the powers against this breach of the settlement of 1815, but Prussia would move only in the event that France threatened the Rhine. The Tsar was prepared to send armies which, however, found more pressing tasks nearer home, in Poland.

In these circumstances, the powers responded to an invitation to meet in London, where the Belgian problem was essentially solved at the beginning of 1831 through their recognition of the new state. An important part of their agreement was the declaration that they would henceforth respect Belgian neutrality, an engagement which held good until the German aggression of 1914. As in the case of Greece, there remained the question of finding a king for the new country. Peacefully inclined Louis Philippe made the solution easier by withdrawing the candidacy of his second son to whom the crown had been offered. Eventually, Prince Leopold of Saxe-Coburg, uncle of the future Queen Victoria, became King of the Belgians, a constitutional ruler, founding the reigning dynasty of Belgium.

2. Revolution Fails in Poland. The Greek and Belgian successes had no counterpart in central Europe. Poland, redivided since 1815, was under three different rules of varying quality and liberality. In the largest portion, the Russian Tsar Alexander had allowed considerable autonomy, constitutional practice, a separate administration and army. Nevertheless, opposition to the Russian connection, or a simple desire for moderate reform, persisted and came to a head in 1830 with the proclamation of a completely separate government. The revolution was inadequately led, it nourished illusions devoid of foundation on the likelihood of British and French assistance, and Russian armies put down the rebellion. The disillusioned Poles were subjected to brutal repression, lost their constitution, and, worst of all, became the objects of a deliberate policy of Russification. Many sought refuge in exile. With greater mildness, the Russian example was emulated in the Austrian and Prussian parts of the nation.

3. Revolution Fails in Italy. The hope of foreign assistance, specifically French in this case, likewise disappointed Italians whose risings achieved some initial and misleading successes in 1831. The bourgeois government of Louis Philippe was bent on reassuring Europe of its peaceful intentions. [6] Soon reaction was seemingly secure in the saddle again in Italy.

D. Europe, East and West

By 1830, or 1832, the ideological cleavage had been accentuated between western Europe and the rest of the continent. With the advent of Louis Philippe in France and the passage of the Reform Bill in England, these two countries had taken further steps along the democratic path, far though they still were from the ultimate goal of full political democracy.

As against this, in Prussia, in Austria, and in Russia, the agitation for reform had been a failure. Whether among their own peoples, or among alien populations whom they ruled, as in Poland and Italy, those governments had been able to withstand any concession to liberal demands, or had in some cases retrogressed. Metternich and the Tsar could take heart again and feel that the spirit of the Holy Alliance, albeit deprived of British and French cooperation, was still dominant over much

---

[6] The Italian situation became one of rivalry between France and Austria. The latter country sent forces into Italy, which France matched by landing troops in Ancona. Both countries withdrew their armies in 1838.

of Europe. It was destined to remain such until the signal came again from France for a renewal of revolutionary outbursts.

V.   EUROPE IN MID-CENTURY

The revolutionary fever of 1830 abated, Europe remained undisturbed until the outbreaks of 1848. This was due in considerable measure to the fact that domestic change and growth absorbed the energies of its peoples. This economic growth and the thought that accompanied it will shortly be surveyed. We may briefly look first, however, at the relations and controversies among the powers, for these disputes, though subdued, remained important.

A.   International Rivalries and Conflicts

1. The Eastern Question. The successful independence of Greece had left unsolved an issue between the Sultan and his vassal Mehemet Ali of Egypt. The rivalry of the powers over the Near East made this internecine Ottoman quarrel a European question.

a. THE RISE OF EGYPT. Mehemet Ali was an able and successful adventurer, whom the backward semifeudal condition of the Ottoman Empire had furnished with an opportunity to establish personal power in Egypt. No liberal, Mehemet Ali was progressive in that he understood the elements of power in a changing world. He provided Egypt with a more efficient administration, developed her economy, and modernized her armed land and naval forces. The technicians to whom he appealed for assistance were in large numbers French. Egypt for a half century was to become a Franco-British problem, for Britain, if she had no designs of her own on Egypt, did not wish her to fall under predominantly French influence.

Mehemet Ali wanted to consolidate and extend his power from the Sudan to Syria, and possibly into Arabia. Had it not been for outside interference, he would have been able to subdue for the Sultan the rebellious Greeks. From the fact that he wanted his price for assistance, regardless of the outcome in Greece, there developed a quarrel which degenerated into war. By the end of 1832, the Egyptian forces had conclusively shown their superiority over the Turkish.

At this juncture, the Sultan's appeal to the powers was eagerly answered by the Tsar. The appearance of Russian forces in Constantinople for his protection overshadowed Anglo-French differences. A compromise was effected with Mehemet Ali, and the Russians withdrew, but not until they had extorted from the Sultan an ostensible alliance (Treaty of Unkiar Iskelessi, July, 1833), whose secret terms made it tantamount to a Russian protectorate. There matters rested for a time, until Sultan Mahmud II, eager for revenge against his vassal, and thinking that he had adequately reorganized his forces, took the initiative of renewing hostilities. The military outcome in 1839 was the same as in 1832. This time Constantinople became the scene of rival British and French intrigues.

b. ANGLO-FRENCH RIVALRY. The French Prime Minister, Thiers, thought to effect a compromise favorable to his protégé, Mehemet Ali, and then to confront the powers with a *fait accompli*. Before this could be done, he was himself confronted with another *fait accompli*, the work of his nemesis, Palmerston, the British Foreign Minister, in the form of a four-power agreement, excluding France, for concerted action in the East (Treaty of London, July, 1840). Feeling ran high in France over the prospect of the revival of the 1814 alliance, and there was talk of war. Bellicose Thiers was dismissed by the more peacefully inclined Louis-Philippe; Guizot, an anglophile, succeeded him, a compromise was arranged for the Near East, and the crisis blew over. In the process, Britain had scored a definite diplomatic victory over France, and incidentally over Russia, for a revised international Convention of the Straits (July, 1841) went far to undo the unilateral Russian advantage of Unkiar Iskelessi.

Anglo-French rivalry cropped up in many quarters. There had been virtually no British opposition to the French occupation of Algiers in 1830, just before the fall of Charles X, an occupation which, after some hesitation, the government of Louis-Philippe decided to make permanent and extend, thus laying the basis of the future vast African holdings of France. But in Spain the two powers eyed each other with suspicion.

2. *The Spanish Marriages.* Spain was troubled by civil war during the thirties between the partisans of the claimant

Don Carlos, brother of Ferdinand, who had died without male issue, and those of Ferdinand's daughter Isabella. By 1839, the Carlist forces were defeated. A similar situation had developed in Portugal, and there also, Maria Christina won out against her uncle Don Miguel. These results were, in a measure, successes for liberalism, and served to emphasize the cleavage between East and West in Europe. There was made in 1834 a quadruple alliance [7] involving Britain, France, Isabella, and Maria Christina, against which agreement the three eastern powers manifested their displeasure by simultaneously withdrawing their representatives from Madrid. The presence in office of Aberdeen in England and of Guizot in France made for superficially better relations between the two countries. The expression "first Entente Cordiale" has even been used, but it is premature. Differences between them over Isabella's prospective spouse were complicated by the intrigues of their respective ambassadors in Madrid and the return of Palmerston with his highhandedness to the Foreign Office in 1846. The affair of the Spanish marriages restored Anglo-French relations to their normal state of suspicious acrimony.

3. Imperial Expansion and Conflicts. These two powers began to meet as well on the opposite side of the planet. The quarrel of rival missionaries in Tahiti ended with French control of that Pacific island, but not until much feeling had been aroused, feeling which incidentally, forecast of more recent occasions, ran higher among peoples than governments. British Far Eastern interests, through India, were of long standing and growing. They led to the Opium War with China, as a result of which the Treaty of Nanking in 1842 opened certain Chinese ports to foreign trade. China was soon compelled to extend similar privileges to France and to the United States.

The shadow of Russia's expansion in the Far East, and more especially in central Asia, was also beginning to enter British imperial calculations.

The pressure of imperial conflict was, however, a relatively minor factor during the first half of the century, mainly because there were still vast unpre-empted areas in the world and because economic developments nearer home absorbed the bulk of the nations' energy.

---

[7] Palmerston had initially sought to exclude France from the alliance.

B.   Changes in Economic Practice and Thought

1. The Industrial Revolution. This phase, of relatively
recent coinage, constitutes an apt recognition of the importance
of the new phenomenon, industry, in shaping the course of
mankind during the last century and a half.

Clearly, no specific date can be assigned to an obviously
gradual change, but it may be said that the last third of the
eighteenth century is the period in which the new development
assumed recognizable shape. This it did first in England owing
to the simultaneous existence of a suitable set of circumstances.
The presence in close proximity of deposits of coal and iron,
basic materials to this day, is one. But of equal importance are
the prior economic growth of England, the progressiveness of
her commercial class, the accumulation of capital, the fiscal
policies of the state, and last but not least, a number of specific
inventions and technical developments such as those associated
with the name of James Watt.

By the time Napoleon was overthrown, English industry
had assumed substantial proportions. Britain was launched on
the path that was to make her the most highly industrialized
nation in the world and had achieved a primacy that she was
to retain throughout the century.

a. THE SECOND PHASE. The period from 1830 to 1870, sometimes described as the second phase of the industrial revolution,
is that during which Britain effected the transformation to a
virtually exclusively industrial economy. It is the period during
which the application of steam to transportation, in the form
of the railway engine, for the first time enabled man to overcome the limitations of his traditional modes of transportation
depending upon animal power. Steam also began to displace
sail on the seas. By mid-century, Europe was well launched
on the building of its extensive railway system.

This growth of industry was uneven in space and time.
Launched in England, it may be said to have gradually spread
on an eastward course. Across the Channel, in Belgium and
northern France, industry was next to be developed, and thence
to the Rhineland and into Germany, whose level of development, by 1870, was roughly comparable with that of France.
In the Habsburg domain proper (Bohemia) and in progressive

Piedmont, some industry began to grow, but the rest of Europe was still an overwhelmingly agrarian society by the middle of the century.

The growth and spread of industry went hand in hand with the expansion of financial activity. Industry created much wealth and in turn drew upon accumulated capital for its expansion. The importance of banking paralleled that of industry.

2. Economic Thought. Laissez Faire and Free Trade.
These developments were accompanied by a changing outlook in economic thought. Already in the preceding century, Adam Smith and the Physiocrats had expounded the *laissez faire* philosophy. The new class in society, whose activity centered in industry, tended to be in favor of economic liberalism. Finding irksome the fetters of the mercantilist system, it thought it could best prosper under a system of free competition and enterprise. This tendency was particularly marked in England where it meant, in addition, the advocacy of free trade. The battle was fought out during the thirties and forties, led by such men as Richard Cobden and his Anti-Corn Law League. The repeal of the Corn Laws in 1846 [8] and of the last of the Navigation Acts in 1849 marked the definite victory of free trade, to which England remained long devoted thereafter. One consequence of this was the virtual destruction of English agriculture.

The continent did not enjoy the English advantage of earlier beginnings and, on the whole, remained devoted to protectionism. After a time, it became clear that the dream of a free-trade world was not to be realized. But the domestic aspects of economic liberalism flourished on the continent as well.

3. The Impact of Industry upon Society.
The effects of the industrial phenomenon upon the structure of society were gradual and uneven, but deep. More and more the old putting-out system gave way to factories where the machines were

---

[8] The failure of the potato crop in Ireland in 1845 and the ensuing famine gave a fillip to the agitation for the repeal of the Corn Laws. It is worth noting that the population of Ireland was 8,500,000 in 1845. It had declined to 6,500,000 in 1851 and continued to decrease thereafter as a result of large and sustained emigration.

gathered, although it must be stressed that the farther back in time one goes, the more one finds of industry in the form of small undertakings, organized and directed by an individual owner-manager.

The labor force that tended the machines and manned the factories, small and large, naturally was in large part recruited from the fields. This labor force congregated in urban centers, with the result that the ratio of urban to rural population steadily increased. The growth of cities, especially in England first, was such as to warrant the expression "mushroom cities." With it went the customary problems of early urbanization.

But industry also introduced a new element of instability in the economy of nations. No longer were famines and the vagaries of the forces of nature to be feared so much as the fluctuation of prices and the operation of the market. The industrial worker, unlike the peasant growing part at least of his own prime necessities, was wholly dependent for his livelihood on money wages. Industry could not but accentuate the alternating cycle of boom and depression resulting from the ever-shifting balance between production and consumption.

An important aspect of the doctrine of economic liberalism was the belief in freedom of contract applied to labor. This meant that labor was to be regarded as a commodity, the value of which would be determined by the operation of the law of supply and demand, not interfered with by extraneous controls and regulations so familiar to our day. Such views may seem inhuman to a later age, and the conditions of British labor were truly miserable. Dickens and Marx have both, with different motives, depicted them.

The free-contract view was bolstered by analyses like that of Malthus at the beginning of the century, which stressed what they believed to be the inescapable effects of the constant pressure of population upon available resources. And it is indeed true that the enormous and unprecedented growth of Europe's population—roughly trebled during the nineteenth century—was in large part made possible by Europe's drawing on the food and raw material resources of the whole world, for which it paid with manufactures.

a. POLITICAL REPERCUSSIONS. The gloomy Malthusian outlook could hardly be expected to be supinely accepted by the victims of its operation. From the growing working class of England, to whom the Reform Bill of 1832 had brought no benefits, emerged the Chartist agitation. The core of the People's Charter was political: universal suffrage would provide the means to institute reforms. The small, but articulate, band of radicals espoused the extension of democratic practice. This agitation failed, and by 1848 the movement had virtually collapsed. This failure had much to do with the subsequent and long-adhered-to tendency of British labor to stress trade unionism rather than politics.

The Reform Bill of 1832, and the repeal of the Corn Laws in 1846, were triumphs of political and economic liberalism, manifestations of the growing power of the new capitalist industrial bourgeoisie in competition with the older land-owning aristocracy. It was essentially the same group that reaped the benefits of the July days in Paris in 1830. Despite the devotion of this class to the ideal of noninterference by the state in matters economic and social, there began to be enacted in England a modicum of factory legislation. [9] But this was likely to be at first Tory rather than Liberal legislation.

The liberal outlook prevailed in matters imperial as well, and this is one reason why imperial rivalry was at a relatively low ebb prior to 1870. The view was held by many that colonies, like children, were eventually destined to abandon the family fold when they would reach maturity, and that coercion was therefore futile. To this view the example of American independence gave strength. Lord Durham's Report of 1839 laid the bases for self-government in the Canadian colonies.

4. The Victorian Compromise. In the case of England, the battles between Conservatives and Liberals were fought within the bounds of a wide area of agreement, sometimes described as the Victorian Compromise: [10] neither party questioned either the fundamentals of the British constitution or the fact that it was the proper appanage of an élite to govern society.

The greater strength of reaction and the precedent of the

---

[9] The first of these acts, dealing with children's employment and hours of labor, dates from 1819. This was extended and strengthened in 1833. There was a Mines Act in 1842 and another Factory Act in 1844.

[10] Queen Victoria came to the throne in 1837 and reigned until 1901.

French Revolution made for sharper divisions on the continent. In France especially, there flourished certain movements that are called socialistic. This socialism was of the utopian variety, in part derived from the Rousseau approach, and was concerned with broad schemes of social reorganization with a large humanitarian content. It produced some interesting experiments, but had little effect in practice. [11]

Of greater moment was the influence of the "utilitarian" approach associated with Jeremy Bentham (1748-1832). Such "radicals" as he, James Mill, and Richard Cobden were the standard-bearers of the early agitation for reform in England.

Later in the century, James Stuart Mill (1806-1873), influenced by both Bentham and Comte, carried on the tradition under the banner of the "new liberalism," stressing the need for social reform along with the devotion to individual liberty. Mill's *Essay on Liberty* remains a classic to this day.

VI.   THE INTELLECTUAL CLIMATE OF THE PERIOD

The concern with economic growth and political change did not monopolize the thought of Europe, whose activity flourished in many directions. Scientific development was not at this time, as it was to become later, closely connected with the industrial, but science was well launched on its astounding career of expansion, which the twenty-five years of warfare at the turn of the century did not interrupt. Perhaps the most significant aspect of this phenomenon is the rapid accumulation of a vast store of knowledge, an accumulation the rate of which was destined to increase with time. The very quantity of information, as well as its diversity, made for enforced specialization. More and more, the scientist and the scholar were compelled to devote their efforts to the study of a particular field of knowledge, and often to some branch of a particular field.

One consequence of this scientific growth was the progressive encroachment of science into the domain that traditionally had belonged to philosophy. Science is not philosophy, but the latter had to take increasing notice of the contributions,

---

[11] Saint-Simon and Fourier in France, Robert Owen in England belong in this development. Utopian socialism also flourished in the United States.

presumably less speculative, of the former. Fact tended to be worshipped. The positivism of Auguste Comte (1798-1857) is an apt expression of this state of affairs.

The brilliant eighteenth-century contribution to mathematics was continued, especially in France and Germany, though by no means confined to those countries. In astronomy, physics, and chemistry important new discoveries were made and theories propounded. Most significant of all was the new organization of scientific inquiry which came to center in the universities. Mainly under state sponsorship, except in England, these ancient institutions became the modern centers of learning that we know, and new ones came into existence. The victory of the eighteenth century enlightenment was made manifest in their secularization.

The natural sciences, hitherto less advanced than the exact and physical, also made progress preparatory to the great blossoming later in the century.

The so-called social sciences, disciplines with a large literary content, sought to emulate the qualities of precision usually associated with scientific disciplines. The desire for accurate knowledge of man's past led to the search into the extant records of that past. German scholarship led the field, emulated by others. The vast collection *Monumenta Germaniae Historica* is a typical product of the activity of the new historical school whose aim was best expressed by Ranke's ideal of writing history *wie es eigentlich gewesen* (as it actually occurred). Beyond the written record of man, archeology, prehistory, and anthropology undertook a great task of reconstruction and analysis. The work of Champollion in Egypt, that of Schliemann at Troy, are instances of this activity in its most spectacular form.

Such discoveries have a romantic quality. And the early part of the century was the romantic age. From its original eighteenth-century home in Germany and England, the movement penetrated in France and elsewhere on the continent. It was a reaction against eighteenth-century rationalism, and its manifestations were outstanding in the pictorial arts, in music, and in literature. Along with scholarship, it rehabilitated the Middle Ages, considered dark since the Renaissance.

There was also a revival of interest in religion after the great revolutionary upheaval. But in this case the part of scholarship worked in a contrary direction, for the new Higher Criticism, where again German scholarship took the lead, tended to weaken the hold of holy books and of tradition. Such an approach could logically best prosper in the Protestant atmosphere of free inquiry or in the hands of free thinkers; the Church of Rome had little part in it.

The economic and political changes brought ever larger masses of men in contact with the forces that molded a changing world. Education and the demand for it at the lower levels were spreading, a phenomenon that gave sharpness to the long-term issue of the control of education. The church, traditional dispenser of education, fought to retain this privilege. The issue is not settled to our day, but, allowing for many vicissitudes in the contest, the tendency was to increase the area of control of the secular state.

All these developments went on apace. Literary, artistic, and scientific production flowed on uninterrupted, reflecting and in turn acting upon the intellectual climate of the time. The direction of thought gradually altered. In the political realm a major upheaval was to shake most of Europe at the exact middle of the century.

ADDITIONAL READINGS

Alison, J. M. S., *Thiers and the French Monarchy* (1926); Artz, Frederick B., *Reaction and Revolution, 1814-1832* (1934); Ashton T. S., *The Industrial Revolution, 1760-1830* (1948); Bury, John P. T., *France, 1814-1840: A History* (1940); Halévy, Élie, *History of ¹·² English People, 1815-1841* (3 vols., 1924-1928); Halévy, Élie, *The Growth of Philosophic Radicalism* (1950); Laski, Harold J., *The Communist Manifesto, a Socialist Landmark* (1948); Marriott, J. A. R., *The Eastern Question* (1940); Marx, Karl and Engels, Friedrich, *Revolution and Counter-Revolution, or Germany in 1848* (1919); May, Arthur, *The Age of Metternich, 1814-1848* (1933); Namier, Lewis B., *1848: the Revolution of the Intellectuals* (1946); Ruggiero, Guido de, *The History of European Liberalism* (1927); Schenk, H. G., *The Aftermath of the Napoleonic Wars: the Concert of Europe—an Experiment* (1947); Seton-Watson, R. W., *Britain in Europe, 1789-1914: a Survey of Foreign Policy* (1937); Soltau, R. H., *French Political Thought in the Nineteenth Century* (1931); Valentin, Veit, *1848: Chapters in German History* (1940); Webster, Charles, *The Congress of Vienna, 1814-1815* (1920); Whitridge, Arnold, *Men in Crisis: the Revolutions of 1848* (1949); Woodward, E. L., *The Age of Reform, 1815-1870* (1931).

INDEX

Aberdeen, George, 285
Abjuration, Act of, 80
Absolutism, 36-37, 124, 134, 135, 203, 205, 267
Adrianople, Treaty of, 278
Africa, claimed by Portugal, 43
Agricultural revolution, 184-185
Agriculture, in 17th century, 88, 89
Aix-la-Chapelle, Congress of, 273
  Treaty of, 126, 151, 181
Alais, Edict of, 91
Aldine press, 25
Alexander, Tsar I, 244-246, 248, 249, 260, 269-271, 274, 282
Alexander VI, Pope, 26, 27, 43, 52
Alsace, 99
Alva, Duke of, 80
American Revolution, 199, 200
Amiens, Treaty of, 237, 238
Ancien Régime, 206, 212-213, 240, 242, 253, 267
Andrussovo, Treaty of, 158
Anglicanism, 60-61, 68, 136
Anglo-Dutch Wars, 175-176
Anne, of England, 138, 139
Antwerp, 80
Aquinas, St. Thomas, 9, 25
Armada, Spanish, 83, 84, 174
Arras, Treaty of, 80
Art, in 16th century, 22-24
Artois, Count of, 214
Asiento, 134
Assignats, 212
Astronomy, 189
Augsburg, confession of, 55, 56, 85; peace of, 57, 59, 67-68, 94; War of the League of, 129-130, 176, 178
"August Days," 209
August, Insurrection of, 217

Augustus II, Saxony and Poland, 165-166
Augustus III, Saxony and Poland, 163, 166
Austerlitz, battle of, 245, 247
Austria, 73, 231, 233, 236-238, 243-246; and Napoleon, 249, 252, 259; (1815-1848), 268-270, 276; transformation of, 142-154
Austrian Succession, War of, 150-151, 181
Authoritarianism, 122-123, 160
Azov, 160, 171

Bacon, Francis, 31, 33
Balance of power, 129, 131
Balboa, 42
Balkans, 276
Baptists, 66
Barebone's Parliament, 117
Bastille, fall of, 209
Bavaria, 95-96, 99, 144, 145, 153, 245
Beccaria, 198
Belgium, independence of, 280-281
Bentham, Jeremy, 290
Berlin Decree, 247
Berry, Duke of, 273
Bernadotte, General, 252
Bill of Rights, of 1689, 137
Boccaccio, 27
Bodin, Jean, 78
Bohemia, 16, 73, 95, 96
Boleyn, Anne, 60, 62, 82
Bonaparte, Joseph, 248, 251, 256; Louis, 251; Napoleon, *see* Napoleon I
Book of Common Prayer, 61, 62
Borodino, battle of, 260
Bosporus, strait, 276

Bossuet, Bishop, 123, 124, 135
Bourbon, family, 78
Bourgeoisie, 92, 121, 204, 206, 213, 224, 225, 279
Brahe, Tycho, 30
Brandenburg, 134; Elector of, 145, 146; peace of Westphalia, 99, 146
Brazil, claimed by Portugal, 43
Brumaire, coup of, 233-234, 238
Bruno, Giordano, 31, 35
Brunswick, Duke of, 217
Burke, Edmund, 211, 214
Burschenschaft, 272
Byron, Lord, 277

Cabinet system, in England, 139-140
Cabot, John, 42, 45
Cahiers, 207
Calmar, union of, 15, 84
Calvin, John, 28, 58-60, 65-66
Calvinism, 59, 60, 69
Cambrai, peace of, 74
Campo Formio, Treaty of, 231, 238, 243
Canning, George, 275
Capitalism, rise of, 46-48
Carbonari, 273
Carlowitz, Treaty of, 143, 170
Carlsbad Decrees, 272
Carnot, 225, 230
Cartier, Jacques, 42, 45
Casas, Bartolomé de las, 44
Castiglione, Baldassare, 24
Castlereagh, Robert Stewart, 262, 269, 274-275
Cateau-Cambrésis, Treaty of, 77
Catherine, of Aragon and England, 60
Catherine II (the Great), of Russia, 152, 167-171, 218
Catholic Church, anglicanism and, 60-61; and French Revolution, 212; and Napoleon, 240; at beginning of 16th century, 8, 9, 50-52; in 16th century, 25-27, 61-62, 64; in 17th and 18th centuries, 123, 124

Catholic League of German Princes, 96
"Cavaliers," 114
Censorship, 123, 242
Cervantes, 28
Chambers of Reunion, 129
Champollion, Jean Francois, 291
Charlemagne, 9, 10
Charles Albert, of Sardinia, 274
Charles V, Emperor (Charles I of Spain), 57, 61, 71-76
Charles VI, Emperor (Archduke Charles of Austria), 143, 144
Charles I, of England, 36, 112, 113
Charles II, of England, 116-117, 128, 130, 135-136
Charles VIII, of France, 71
Charles IX, of France, 77
Charles X, of France, 278-279, 284
Charles I, of Spain, 71, 72
Charles II, of Spain, 126, 131
Charles IV, of Spain, 248
Charles IX, of Sweden, 85
Charles XI, of Sweden, 161
Charles XII, of Sweden, 161, 163, 166
Charles XIII, of Sweden, 252
Chartists, 289
Chaumont, Treaty of, 262, 268
Christian II, of Denmark, 57
Christian III, of Denmark, 57
Christian IV, of Denmark, 96
Christianity, 19-20, 50-52, 64, 65, 223, 240
Church of England, *see* Anglicanism
City States, in Italy, 16, 18
Civil Constitution of the Clergy, 212
Clement VII, Pope, 60
Clergy, 13, 14; in France, 89, 207; *see* First Estate
Cleves, Duchy of, 146
Clive, Robert, 182, 183
Coalition, first, 219, 227; second, 232-233, 236, 237; third, 244-247

Colbert, Jean Baptiste, 48, 120-122, 126, 176
Colombo, Cristoforo, 41
Commercial Revolution, 39-48
Committee of Public Safety, 221, 225
Commonwealth, English, 115, 116, 135
Comte, Auguste, 290, 291
Concert of Europe, 273-274
Concordats, of 1516, 68; of 1801, 240
Condé, Prince of, 93, 104, 126
Condorcet, 198
Confederation of the Rhine, 245-246, 251, 252, 259
Congregationalism, 66
Conservative Party, England, 289
Consulate, France, 236-243
Constantinople, fall of, 19, 24
Constituent Assembly, French 210-212, 215
Constitution, American, 200; English, 107, 117, 139; French, of 1791, 210-211; French of Year I, 224; French of Year III, 224, 225, 227; French of Year VIII, 239
Continental system, 247-248, 254, 255
Conventicle Act, 136
Convention, National (French), 218, 220, 222
Cook, Captain, 184, 189, 198
Copernican Revolution, 29, 30
Copernicus, Nicolaus, 29, 30
Corn Laws, 287, 289
Cornwallis, Lord, 183
Corporation Act, 136
Cortez, Hernando, 42
Cossacks, 158
"Council of Blood," 80
Counter Reformation, Catholic, 32, 33, 62-64
Cranmer, Thomas, 61, 62
Cromwell, Oliver, 115-117
Cromwell, Richard, 37, 117
Culture, in 16th century, 22-28

Dante, 27
Danton, 223
Darnley, Henry, 82
"Decembrists," 275
Declaration of Independence, 184, 200
Declaration of Rights of Man, 209-210
Deism, 191, 192
"Democratic Revolution," 216-223
Denmark, 85, 163, 252, 271
Descartes, René, 33-35, 186; Cartesian influence, 187, 191, 194
Devolution, War of, 126
De Witt, John, 128
Diaz, Bartholomew, 41
Dickens, Charles, 288
Diderot, Denis, 167
"Diplomatic Revolution," 151, 152
Directory, 225, 227-234
Dissenters, English, 111, 112, 176
Divine Right, theory of, 124
Dover, Treaty of, 128, 136
Drake, Francis, 45
Dumouriez, Charles Francois, 219
Dupleix, Joseph Francois, 181, 182
Duquesne, Fort, 181
Dürer, Albrecht, 24
Durham, Lord John, 289
Dutch, 45, 173-175, 178, 232
Dutch War, 128

East India Company, Dutch, 175; English, 174
Eck, John, 54
Economic liberalism, 287-288
Edward VI, of England, 61
Egypt, 232, 283
Elba, 262
El Greco, 24
Elizabeth, Queen of England, 62, 68, 107
Elizabeth, of Russia, 151, 152
Émigrés, 214, 219
Encyclopedia, The Great, 191, 192
England, see Great Britain
Enlightened despotism, 153, 193, 194

Enlightenment, 34, 153-154, 169, 186-200, 204, 256, 257
Entente Cordiale, 285
Episcopal Church, *see* Anglicanism
Erasmus, 25, 32, 63
Erfurt Congress, 248, 249, 260
Estates-General, 89, 109, 206, 208, 211, 263
Estonia (Livonia), 85, 161
Eugene, Prince of Savoy, 132
Evangelicalism, 66
Exclusion Act, 136, 137
Eylau, battle of, 246

Factory Act, 289
Family Compact, 152
Farnese, Alexander, Duke of Parma, 80
Ferdinand, of Aragon, 15, 70-73
Ferdinand I, Emperor, 41, 95
Ferdinand II, Emperor, 95, 96
Ferdinand I, King of Italy, 273-275
Ferdinand VII, of Spain, 248, 285
Feudalism, 11, 209
Fichte, Johann, 258, 259
Finland, 270
Five-Mile Act, 136
Fontainebleau, Treaty of, 262, 268
Fouché, 242
Fourier, Charles, 290
Four Year Diet, 169
France, absolutism in, 36; colonization, 177; explorations by, 42; imperialism, 45, 174; in 16th century, 24, 73, 74, 77-79, 87, 88; in 17th century, 175-178; in 18th century, 178, 181, 193-195; in early 19th century, 267-273, 278-279, 284; reconstruction of, 87-94; revolution, 202-234; rise of, 102-103; under Louis XIV, 120-140; under Napoleon, 236-264
Francis I, of Austria, 151
Francis I, of France, 24, 68, 72-74, 77
Francis II, of France, 77, 82
Franklin, Benjamin, 200

Frederick, Elector Palatine of the Rhine, 95
Frederick II, of Denmark, 57
Frederick II (the Great), of Prussia, 144, 148-154, 166, 253
Frederick William (the Great Elector), 146, 148
Frederick William I, of Prussia, 149
Frederick William II, of Prussia, 218, 226
Frederick William III, of Prussia, 246, 259, 269
Free trade, 184, 287
French and Indian War, 181
French Revolution, 202-234, 253-255, 258, 259, 278-279, 290
Friedland, battle of, 246
Fronde, 93, 94, 120
Frontenac, Count, 178
Fugger Family, 47

Galileo, 30, 32-33, 35, 186, 187
Gama, Vasco da, 41, 46
George I, of England, 139
George II, of England, 139
George III, of England, 140, 152, 272
George IV, of England, 272, 279
German Confederation, 270, 272
Germany, 87-88, 94-102, 243, 251, 256, 258, 261, 272
Ghent, pacification of, 80
Ghiberti, Lorenzo, 23
Gibbon, Edward, 190
Girondins, 215, 220-221
"Glorious Revolution," 130, 137-140, 194
Granada, fall of, 44
Grand Alliance, 132
Grand Army, 260
"Grand Design," 89
Great Britain, absolutism in, 36; and French Revolution, 202-203, 205, 214, 218-219, 230; and Napoleon, 243-245, 247, 248, 252-255, 259, 260; colonization, 177; explorations by, 42; Glorious Revolution in, 134-140; im-

perialism, 45, 174; in Asia, 183; in 16th century, 75-76; in 17th century, 108-118, 175-176; in 18th century, 178, 181, 194-195; in early 19th century, 269-272, 275, 279-290, 288-289; protestantism in, 61, 62; under Elizabeth, 81-83

Great Northern War, 161, 162, 166

Greece, 270, 283; independence of, 277-278

Greek Revolt, 277

Gregorian Calendar, 30, 157

Gregory XIII, Pope, 30

Grey, Charles, 280

Grotius, Hugo, 37

Guilds, abolished, 213

Guise Family, 78

Guizot, Francois, 284-285

Gustavus I (Vasa), of Sweden, 57, 84-85

Gustavus II (Adolphus), of Sweden, 97-98, 101, 103, 161

Gutenberg, John, 25

Habeas Corpus Act, 138

Habsburg Empire, 10, 16, 18, 71, 75, 102, 132, 134, 141-145, 270

Hampton Court, debate at, 111

Hanover, 145

Hanoverian Dynasty, 137, 139

Hanseatic League, 84, 142

Hardenberg, Chancellor, 259

Harvey, William, 31, 32

Hastings, Warren, 183

Hawkins, John, 45

Henrietta, Maria, 112

Henry VII, of England, 42, 45, 70, 82

Henry VIII, of England, 60, 61, 68, 72, 76

Henry II, of France, 77, 78

Henry III, of France, 77, 78

Henry IV, of France, 68, 79, 88-91, 102, 110

Henry, Duke of Guise, 78

Henry, the Navigator, 41

Herder, Johann, 256-258

"Higher Criticism," 292

Hobbes, Thomas, 37

Hohenzollern Family, 145, 146

Holbein, Hans, 24

Holland, 35, 37, 79-81, 116, 128, 226, 227, 251, 269; independence of, 80-81

Holy Alliance, 271, 273

Holy Roman Empire, 9-12, 16, 75, 141, 269-270; and Napoleonic Era, 243; and the reformation, 54-57, 60, 61; Charles V of, 71-86; end of, 245

Hubertusburg, Treaty of, 152

Hudson Bay Company, 177

Huguenots, 68, 89-91, 124, 148, 176

Humanism, 24-27, 192

Hundred Days, 262, 268, 270, 273

Hungary, 73, 74

Huss, John, 54

Imperialism, 285

Independents, 35, 135

India, 177, 178, 183, 285

Index, 64

Indulgences, 53, 54

Industrial Revolution, 185, 195, 286-288

Intellectual Climate, 188, 290-292

Intendants, 92

Isabella of Castile, 15, 41, 70-71

Islamism, 8, 19, 20

Italy, at beginning of 1500, 16, 18, 70, 71; in 16th century, 22-27, 46; in 17th century, 35, 233; in early 19th century, 251-252, 256, 270, 273-274, 282

Ivan III (the Great), of Russia, 18, 157

Ivan IV (the Terrible), of Russia, 18, 84, 157

Jacobins, 215, 220, 225

Jagello, House of, 85, 165

James I, of England (James VI, of Scotland), 36, 95, 109-112

James II, of England (James VII, of Scotland), 130, 137

Jansenists, 35, 36
Jassy, Treaty of, 171
Jefferson, Thomas, 200
Jena, battle of, 247, 258
Jenkins' Ear, War of, 150, 181
Jesuits, 44, 45, 63, 64
John, Don, of Austria, 79
John III (Sobieski), of Poland, 165
Joseph II, Emperor, 154, 171
Josephine, of France, 230
Julius II, Pope, 52
July Days, Paris, 289
Junkers, 259

Kalisch, Treaty of, 261
Kappel, battle of, 58
Kaunitz, Count, 151, 249
Kepler, Johann, 30
King George's War, 181
King William's War, 178
Knights' War, 75
Knox, John, 59, 82
Kotzebue, August F. F. von, 272
Kutchuk Kainarji, Treaty of, 171

Lafayette, 210
Laibach, Congress of, 274
Laissez faire, 184, 195, 213, 287
La Rochelle, siege of, 91
Laud, William, 113, 114
Legislative Assembly, 212-215
"Legitimacy," 269
Leibnitz, 187
Leipzig, battle of, 98
Leopold I, of Belgium, 281
Leopold I, Emperor, 129, 131
Leopold II, Emperor, 214, 215
Lepanto, battle of, 79, 86
Leszczinski, Stanislas, 165, 166
Le Tellier, 120
Leuthen, battle of, 152
Levellers, 117
Liberalism, 287-290
Liberation, War of, 261
Limited Monarchy, 138
Linnaeus, 189
Literature, in 16th century, 24-25, 27, 28

Lithuania, 18, 158
Locke, John, 138, 140, 189, 190, 194, 200
London, Treaty of 1827, 278; of 1840, 284
"Long War," 143
Louis XI, of France, 70-71, 88
Louis XIII, of France, 89-90, 112
Louis XIV, of France, 92, 94, 104, 120-136
Louis XV, of France, 193, 205
Louis XVI, of France, 214, 218
Louis XVIII, of France, 262, 268, 273, 278
Louis Philippe, of France, 279, 281-282, 284
Louisburg, capture of, 181
Louvois, Francois Michel, 126
Loyola, Ignatius, 63, 64
Lübeck, peace of, 96, 98
Lublin, union of, 165
Lunéville, Treaty of, 237-238, 243
Luther, Martin, 53-54, 65-67
Lutheranism, 53-57
Lutter, battle of, 96
Lützen, battle of, 98

Machiavelli, Niccolò, 26-27, 36
Magellan, 42
Magna Carta, 107
Mahmoud II, of Turkey, 284
Malta, surrender of, 232, 237
Malthus, Thomas R., 288
Marengo, battle of, 238
Margaret of Parma, 80
Maria Cristina, of Spain, 285
Maria Theresa, of Austria, 144, 150, 154
Maria Theresa, of France, 104, 126
Marie Louise, 249
Marlborough, Duke of, 132
Marston Moor, battle of, 114
Marx, Karl, 288
Mary, of Burgundy, 16, 71
Mary I, of England, 61, 62, 76
Mary II, of England, 130
Mary Stuart, of Scotland, 59, 82, 83, 109

Matthias, Emperor, 95
Maximilian I, of Bavaria, 95, 96, 144
Maximilian I, Emperor, 16, 71
Maximilian II, Emperor, 95
Mazarin, Cardinal, 36, 92-94, 104, 120
Medici Family, 23, 24; Catherine de, 77; Florentine, 22; Lorenzo de (the Magnificent), 26; Marie de, 89, 90
Mehemet Ali, of Egypt, 277, 283, 284
Mercantilism, 48, 116, 121-122
Metternich, Era of, 272-275
Metternich, Prince Clemens, 249, 261, 262, 268-270, 272-275, 277, 281-282
Mexico, 42
Michelangelo, 23
Miguel, Don, of Portugal, 285
Milan, 70, 71
Mill, James Stewart, 290
Milton, John, 35
Missionaries, 44, 45
Mohacs, battle of, 19, 74
Mohammed, 8
Mohammed IV, Sultan, 143
Monasticism, 13, 14
Monroe, Doctrine, 275
Montaigne, 28
Montcalm, 181
Montesquieu, 194, 195, 197, 200
Montreal, fall of, 182
Monumenta Germaniae Historica, 291
Moors, 15, 44
More, Sir Thomas, 28
Moscow, retreat from, 260, 261
Mountainists, 220, 221
Münzer, Thomas, 66
Murat, Joachim, 251, 270
Muscovy Company, 85
Mutiny Act, 137

Nanking, Treaty of, 285
Nantes, Edict of, 67, 68, 78, 88; revocation of, 124

Napoleon I, of France, 229-234, 236-264, 267-272, 286
Napoleonic Codes, 241, 242
Napoleonic Wars, 270
National Assembly, in France, 208-212, 217
National Guard, 210
Nationalism, 256, 257, 271
Nations, battle of the, 261
Navarino, battle of, 278
Navarre, 78; Henry of, 77
Navigation Acts, 48; of 1651, 116, 174, 175
Necker, Jacques, 206
Nelson, Lord, 232, 247
Netherlands, 45, 72, 73, 80, 81, 128, 173-175, 178, 232, 269-270
Newton, Sir Isaac, 30, 186-190, 194
Nicholas I, of Russia, 275, 277
Nimwegen, Treaty of, 128
Ninety-Five Theses, 54
Nobility, 12, 89; in France, 91, 94, 120, 121, 206, 208; in Poland, 165
North, Lord, 140
Northern War, First, 146
Northern War, Great, 149
Nystadt, Treaty of, 164

Opium War, 285
Orders in Council, British, 254
Orleans, Duke of, 134
Orthodox Church, 19, 20
Otto I, of Greece, 278
Ottoman Empire, 19-20, 86, 142, 143, 160, 170, 171, 270, 276, 283
Oxenstierna, Chancellor, 98, 103, 104

Painting, in 16th century, 22-23
Palatinate, 95, 96, 99, 129, 130
Palestrina, 24
Palmerston, Henry, 284-285
Papacy, 51, 52, 62, 63
Paris, Treaty of 1763, 182; of 1814, 267; of 1815, 268
Parlement, 92-94, 109, 206

Parliament, 107, 108, 112, 113, 138, 139; short, 114; long, 114, 115
Pascal, Blaise, 34
Paul I, of Russia, 237
Paul III, Pope, 63
Peasantry, 14, 89, 204, 206, 213, *see* Third Estate
Peasants' Revolt, 55, 75
Peel, Robert, 280
Peninsular War, 248
Peru, 42
Peter I (the Great), of Russia, 159-161, 163, 164
Peter III, of Russia, 152, 167
Petition of Rights, 113
Petrarch, Francesco, 24, 25, 27
Philip I, of Spain, 71
Philip II, of Spain, 36, 61, 76-84, 103
Philip IV, of Spain, 103, 104, 126
Philip V, of Spain (Philip of Anjou), 131, 132
Philosophes, 191, 192, 194
Physiocrats, 184, 195
Pillnitz, Declaration of, 214, 215
Pitt, William (Earl of Chatham), 139, 181
Pizarro, Francisco, 42
Poland, 18, 85, 158, 164-166, 214, 269-270, 281-282; partition of, 153, 167-171, 218, 226
Polish Succession, War of, 166
Politiques, 68
Poltava, battle of, 163, 166
Pompadour, Madame de, 151
Poniatowski, Stanislas, 166, 169
Port Royal, 178
Portugal, 15, 41, 43, 173, 248, 271
Pragmatic Sanction, 144
Prague, defenestration of, 95; treaty of, 98
Pressburg, Treaty of, 245
Printing, invention of, 25
Protectorate, 116, 117
Protestant Revolt, 53-64
Protestantism, 53-69, 111, 142

Prussia, 161, 269-270, 272; and French Revolution, 218, 226, 227; and Napoleon, 245, 246, 251, 258-260; rise of, 145-154
Ptolemy, 29, 30
Puritanism, 35, 111, 115
Pyrenees, Treaty of the, 104

Quadruple Alliance, 271, 273
Quebec, fall of, 181, 182
Queen Anne's War, 178

Rabelais, Francois, 28
Ranke, Leopold von, 291
Rationalism, 190-197
Reformation, 33, 34, 50-69
Reform Bill (1832), 279-280, 282, 289
Reformed Church, 59
Regulating Act, 183
Reichsdeputationshauptschluss, 243
Reign of Terror, 221-222, 224
Renaissance, 21-37; art in, 22, 23
Requesens, 80
Restitution, Edict of, 96
Restoration, 117, 118, 135
Richelieu, Cardinal, 36, 90-94, 98, 99, 101-104
Robespierre, 215, 222-224
Romanov Family, 158
Romanticism, 196, 197, 256, 257, 263-264
Rossbach, battle of, 152
"Roundheads," 115
Rousseau, 195-197
Rudolph II, Emperor, 95
Rump Parliament, 115-117, 221
Russia, 18, 163, 164, 166; and Napoleon, 232, 233, 244-249, 252, 259-262; in early 19th century, 270, 275-276, 278; partition of Poland and, 167, 169-170; to 1689, 84, 85, 156-159; under Catherine II, 167-171; under Peter the Great, 159-160
Russo-Turkish War, 171, 278
Ryswick, Treaty of, 130, 178

Sacramental system, 51, 55
St. Bartholomew's Day, Massacre of, 78
St. Helena, 262
St. Petersburg, 164
Saint-Simon, 290
Sardinia, 15, 270, 274
Savoy, 134
Saxony, 145; Elector of, 54, 145
Schliemann, Heinrich, 291
Schmalkaldic League, 55-56, 75
Schönbrunn, battle of, 249
Science, 187-190; beginnings of modern, 28-34; development in 17th century, 35, 36
Scotland, 15; revolt, 113-114
"Sea Beggars," 81
Second Estate, see Nobility
September Massacres, 217
Serfdom, 154, 259
Settlement Act, 137
Seven Years' War, 151, 152, 181, 182
"Ship-money," 113
Siéyès, Abbé, 207, 233, 234
Sigismund II, of Poland, 85, 165
Silesia, 151, 274
"Six Acts," 272
Slave trade, 44, 134, 178
Slavs, in Russia, 157
Smith, Adam, 184, 195, 287
Soleiman, the Magnificent, 74, 86
South America, 275
Spain, 43, 44, 125; absolutism in, 36; and Napoleon, 248; decline of, 103-104; division of, 132; explorations by, 41, 42; imperialism, 43, 44, 173; in 1500, 15-17; in 16th century, 71-88; in 17th century, 130-134; in 18th century, 182, 226-227; in early 19th century, 271, 274-275, 284-285
"Spanish Fury," 80
Spanish Inquisition, 79
Spanish Succession, 130, 131, 143, 144; War of the, 132, 144, 145, 180
Spenser, Edmund, 28

Speyer, Diet of, 55
Spinoza, 35
Stein, Heinrich, 259, 272
Stockholm, Treaties of, 164
Straits question, 276, 284
Streltsi, meeting of, 159, 160
Suarez, 37
Sully, Duke of, 88, 89
"Swamp," 220, 221, 224
Sweden, 84, 85, 160-163, 252, 271
Switzerland, 251

Taille, 122
Talleyrand, 240, 248, 249, 262, 268, 269
"Tennis Court Oath," 208
Thermidorian Reaction, 223-225, 228
Thiers, Adolphe, 284
Third Coalition, War of, 244-246
Third Estate, 114, 203, 206-208, 234; in 16th century, 89; in France, 91
Thirty-nine Articles, 62
Thirty Years' War, 37, 143, 146; and Franco-Spanish Conflict, 103, 104; background, 94-95; Bohemian phase, 95, 96; Danish phase, 96-97; French phase, 98-99; settlement of Westphalia, 99, 101-102; significance of, 101-102; Swedish phase, 97-98
Tilsit, Treaty of, 246-248, 260
Toleration, religious, 67, 68
Tordesillas, Treaty of, 43
Tories, 137, 280
Towns, early, 14
Townshend, Charles, 185
Trafalgar, battle of, 247
Trent, Council of, 32, 64
Triennial Act, 114
Troppau, Congress of, 274
Tudor, House of, 15, 37, 70, 108, 110
Tugendbund, 272
Tull, Jethro, 185
Turenne, 93, 104, 126
Turgot, 206

Turkey, 40, 74, 75, 79, 171, 276, 278

Ulm, battle of, 245
Uniformity, Act of, 136
Unitarianism, 66, 67
United States of America, 243, 275; and Seven Years' War, 181, 182; discovery of, 41, 42; in 17th century, 174, 176-178; in 18th century, 178, 181, 205; independence of, 182; Indians, 44; revolution, 199-200
Unkiar Iskelessi, Treaty of, 284
Utopian Socialism, 290
Utrecht, Treaty of, 132, 134, 143, 178; union of, 80

Valla, Lorenzo, 25
Valmy, 217, 218
Vauban, 126
Vendée, revolt of, 219
Venice, 16, 18, 39-41
Verona, Congress of, 274
Versailles, 125; march on, 209-210; Treaty of, 183
Vesalius, 31
Vespucci, Amerigo, 41, 42
Victor Emmanuel I, of Sardinia, 274
Victorian Compromise, 289
Vienna, 74, 143; Congress of, 268-272, 276
Vinci, Leonardo da, 23, 24
Volksgeist, 257, 259

Voltaire, Francois, 153, 167, 190, 192-195
Vulgate, 64

Wagram, battle of, 249
Wallenstein, 96, 98
Walpole, Robert, 139
Warsaw Decree, 249
Waterloo, battle of, 262, 268
Watt, James, 286
Wellesley, Marquis of, 183
Wellington, Arthur W., 261, 280
Westminster, Treaty of, 175
Westphalia, 81, 129, 143; peace of, 99, 101, 161
Whigs, 137, 280
White Hill, battle of the, 96
White Terror, 225, 273
William III, of England (Orange), 128, 130, 137, 139, 175
William I, of Netherlands, 280, 281
William I (the Silent), of Orange, 80
Williams, Roger, 35
Winter, General, 260
Wolsey, Cardinal, 76
Worms, Diet of, 54

Xavier, St. Francis, 44

Ypsilanti, 277

Zeitgeist, 186, 197
Zwingli, 58